COLDWALTHAM

A STORY OF
THREE HAMLETS

COLDWALTHAM

a story of three hamlets

Sandra Saer

Copyright © 1987   Sandra M. Saer

ISBN 0 9512619 0 8   *hard cover*
ISBN 0 9512619 1 6   *paperback*

Published by SMH ENTERPRISES
Pear Tree Cottage, River Lane, Watersfield,
PULBOROUGH,   West Sussex.   RH20 1NG

First published   August 1987

British Library Cataloguing in Publication Data

Saer, Sandra
    Coldwaltham: a story of three hamlets
    1. Coldwaltham (West Sussex) —
    Social life and customs
    I. Title
    942.2'64   DA 690.C 70/

Typeset in 11 on 13pt and 9 on 10pt Baskerville

by David J. Ellis

Fernwood, Nightingales, West Chiltington,
PULBOROUGH, West Sussex. RH20 2QT

Maps on end-papers drawn by Laurence Greenwood
Jacket/Cover photograph   Richard Leathers
Jacket/Cover design   Sandra Saer

Printed and Bound in Great Britain by
Billing & Sons Limited
Worcester

for the Ruff family
especially in loving memory of Peggy Ruff
whose peaceful way and quiet encouragement
inspired, without her knowing it,
much of my writing

CONTENTS

ix

INTRODUCTION

Anyone descending the slope from Pulborough station, turning left towards Storrington, then right on to the A29 Bognor Road at Swan Corner—as I frequently did with four small children on bicycles over a decade ago—might easily pass through the parish of Coldwaltham without knowing it existed.

I well remember our first bicycling foray into that unknown. We pedalled up over Pulborough Bridge, along the easy flat of the causeway and, after a mile or so, a sign for HARDHAM at least told us where we were. We glimpsed a very old, very small church,[1] tucked away behind trees in a slip road to our left, with some pretty cottages alongside, and, further on, I noticed athe fine façade of a Georgian house on the right.[2]

Then we came to a railway bridge: a tortuous-shaped affair which even foolhardy road-users would have to slow down to cross safely. But there was a footbridge to the left. I steered children and bicycles down on to the footbridge, just as a train chuffed under the bridge—"Trai-ain!" sang out two of the children (the echo is with me still). Then, back up on the road again, with another sign proclaiming COLDWALTHAM. A farm and some pretty, old houses on the right, a road to the left, apparently going into the blue although a sign showed that at least the Labouring Man pub was in that 'blue'), and then we whizzed (delighted screams from the children; concern for dangerous speed momentarily stopping mother's heartbeat) down a very steep short hill. Now there were close houses to left and right, and we all saw a lovely stone church with a belfry that was alluring (*they* called it something else), on the right. We got off our bikes, then, and walked up another hill, past an enticing house set

1 St. Botolph's
2 Hardham House

back from the road on the left called Barn Owls Restaurant, and a lovely brick-and-pebble cottage opposite. Alas for mother, yet another steep short hill, but briefer; cries of delight, as another bicycle whizz-down took place . . . woods on the right, council houses on the left (was that a crossroads that we left behind us? . . .), then a glimpse, across open fields, of the lovely South Downs— "nice blue hills", to the children—more trees and a hidden driveway on the left; a sign LODGE HILL on the left and, down yet another steep hill (mother now immune), and suddenly, on the left also, a sign: WATERSFIELD, houses either side, a well-lit shop on the left, soon another on the right, a pub on the left — our cue for turn-off.

Had we been motorists onward-bound for Bury or Arundel or Chichester, we would have passed the pub, lanes to left and right, brightly illuminated Watersfield Garage, and gone up a steep hill (Beacon Hill) and on.

Our journey ended in Watersfield, where we pedalled down with relief between pub and garage into River Lane, screeching to a halt with the front wheel of the first bike touching the side gate of Pear Tree Cottage: bliss for a weekend's escape—with crackling open fire, warming Rayburn and soundless nights—from our usual London life.

But drivers on four wheels (or more), many of whom anyway ignore the 40-mile-per-hour speed-limit signs through Coldwaltham (becoming a 30-mile limit through Watersfield) take much less time and are scarcely aware—unless they know otherwise—that they are travelling through a most interesting parish, made up of three hamlets, and they must be forgiven, for the busy A29 cuts ruthlessly and noisily right through the place, and the Bognor and Portsmouth to London railway line also passes right through a corner of Coldwaltham's heart. It is a wonder it has any heart left, but it has.

It is because of the Coldwaltham heart —beating strong through its residents, despite concrete and railroad dissection, that I have decided to write this 'story'.

Alone, I certainly could not have done it. The Rev. Roger Hodgson springs especially to mind, because it was he who 'got me going' on the project. But I must thank all those in the parish, and they are numbered in hundreds, who have helped by (to paraphrase Lady Mary Maxse's introduction to *her* book, *The Story of Fittleworth*[3]) ransacking their memories to give me information on the past, or by lending me precious old photographs, postcards and other illustrative material for the book.

I want also to thank the Rev. Desmond Bending, for assistance over the history of Watersfield Chapel; Mr. D. R. Holt, whose *Study of the Parish of Coldwaltham, 1958-1959* inspired my research, and contributed to the actual text of this book; the Rev. Canon Kerr-Dineen, for his assistance with information on Hardham Church; Mr. John Boxford and Miss Frances Carder, for generous support; Miss Heather Page, for lending me especially precious documents and photographs relating to her mother and to Coldwaltham and Watersfield Women's Institute; Mrs. Marjorie Hessell Tiltman, for allowing me to draw from her book, *Cottage Pie*[4]; Mr. and Mrs. Chris Harris, for long hours of meetings about the Youth Club; Mr. Gerald Clark, for much help with documentation on Watersfield Cricket Club, Watersfield Football Club, and the Alban Head Playing Field; and all those who contributed generously and enthusiastically to Chapter 9, with their memoirs.

Finally, I gratefully acknowledge permission by Robert Hale Limited, to quote from Esther Meynell's book, *Sussex;* by John Murray (Publishers) Ltd. to reproduce four drawings (Fig. 2 in Chapter 2, and Figs. 1, 3 & 4 in Chapter 3) from *Old Farms: An Illustrated Guide*[5] by John Vince; and by *Antique Collector* magazine and the *West Sussex Gazette*, to reprint articles I wrote for both these publications.

Watersfield
July 1987

3   The National Review, 1935
4   published by Hodder & Stoughton, 1940
5   copyright John Vince 1982

Chapter 1

SETTING THE SCENE

*"Of this parish there is little to be said. It is small,
and, as its name imports, in a bleak situation."*

This description[1] of Coldwaltham did not provide much encouragement[2] to one who was determined to write a warm and vital account, as well as a true one, of the parish in which she lives. Still, I consoled myself, the lines were written and published in 1835, and much has changed since then.

The recorded etymology tells us that in 683 it was called Uualdham, in 997 Waltham (it is one of two Walthams; the other—Upper Waltham—is mentioned in the Domesday Book) and it first became Cold Waltham in 1340. In 1419 it is recorded as Est Waltham, in 1430 it was Caldwaltham, and by 1539 it was Waltham on the Hethe.

Root information shows that we(e)ald-ham signifies ham (or hamlet) at a wood, and 'cold' was added presumably because of the bleak aspect of the place. *That,* we admit, hasn't changed much since 1835, nor even since 1340!

Bartholomew's *Gazetteer* deals summarily with Coldwaltham: "2 miles/3 km sw of Pulborough", with a map reference. But I have more space, and can spend time putting Coldwaltham on the map.

The parish consists of three hamlets: Coldwaltham itself, with Watersfield to the south-west of it and Hardham to the north-east. Watersfield in 1226 was Watresfeld, and Wateres-

---

1 from *The History, Antiquities and Topography of the County of Sussex*, Vol. 2, by T. W. Horsfield (Kohler & Coombes)
2 I received some encouragement from the late John B. Paddon, of Watersfield (whose family once lived at Lodge Hill when it was a private residence). In his book, *Sequestered Vales of Sussex*, Mr. Paddon records graphically the position of the village, which "stands high and dry above the water level, extended in a long line — quite like a seaside town."

feld from 1256 to 1418. The meaning is 'open land (feld) of
or by the water or stream'.

Hardham gets its first mention in the Domesday Book,
however, in 1086 as Heriedeham. This became Herham
(1203), Herietham (1300), Herietheham and Erytham
(1380). All these meant the ham, or hamlet, of a woman
called Heregyd. There is another, alternative origin: Eringeham
(1283), becoming Heringham and Heryngham (1189, 1279,
1298), Heryngeham (1279, 1356), Herrynggeham (1314),
Heryngham (1316, 1338, 1349), Herringham (1724), with
the forms, Helingham (1189) and Helingeham (1130), also
cropping up. The two forms of the name were both accepted,
as shown by both occurring in the same document, in various
forms. The first form of the name, Heriedeham, translates
into 'the ham, or hamlet, of a woman called Heregyd'. The
other form, Eringeham, means 'the home of Here or Here's
people'. Historians have continued to quote both origins. For
instance, in *A Description of the High Stream of Arundel*[3], it
is referred to as "Herdham, alias Herringham".

The parish's boundary to the east is formed by the River
Arun, and to the north partly by the River Rother. About
three-quarters, if not more, of the parish boundaries are
dictated by the confluence at Coldwaltham of these two
rivers, which run into the English Channel at Littlehampton,
ten miles away.

The A29 London to Bognor Regis road runs through the
centre of the parish, as does the main London to Portsmouth
and Bognor Regis railway route. Pulborough railway station
is the nearest for the parish, which—putting it literally on the
map—is seven miles north of Arundel, fifteen miles north-east
of Chichester, and also fifteen north-west of Worthing,
twenty miles north-west of Brighton, eight miles south-west
of Billingshurst and fifteen south-west of Horsham. It is
fifty-two miles from London.

Coldwaltham is a wealden parish and, in geological notes
on the formation of the Weald, Mr. D. R. Holt describes the

---

3 edited by Fowler

Weald[4] as "an anticlinorium rather than a simple anticline, containing within its general arch of strata numerous small subsidiary arches. The parish of Coldwaltham is situated on one of such 'wavelets', where the summit of a miniature anticline in the Lower Greensand escarpment is exposed as an

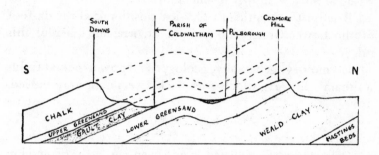

Fig. 1 A minor syncline and anticline within the main anticlinorium of the Weald, showing Coldwaltham (from D. R. Holt's study)

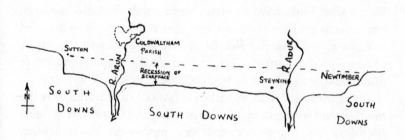

Fig. 2 Sketch map to show two changes of direction of scarp face of the South Downs (Holt)

---

4 *A Study of the Parish of Coldwaltham, 1958 - 1959* by D. R. Holt (unpublished)

inlier, flanked on either side by Gault Clay. The Gault Clay in the northern part of the parish is a small portion, in a small syncline which has not yet eroded away.

" . . . this miniature anticline extended from near Sutton (West Sussex), where the scarp of the Downs clearly faces eastwards for two or three miles, to near Newtimber, north of Brighton. Here the scarp slope, having receded from the Weald at Sutton, now readvances into it."[4]

Briefly: Coldwaltham's physical position is at the dipfoot of the Lower Greensand escarpment, near an inlier of this ridge.

Etymology, geography, geology—and now a look at Coldwaltham's history, which goes back a very long way indeed.

*   *   *   *   *

Coldwaltham seems to have been an area of human habitation since the dawn of prehistoric times. Crude flint implements used by Paleolithic man, who lived in the area between 10,000 and 20,000 years ago, have been found in Wiggonholt and Greatham, just across the River Arun. Similar discoveries were made in Coates, about two miles from the parish but on the same side of the Arun; not separated by it. No similar finds have actually been made in Coldwaltham, but there is no reason to suppose that these people, who lived in Coates, did not also live in nearby Coldwaltham: the type of terrain, the sandy ridge in which the inplements were discovered, is common to both places.

It is more than likely that Celts lived in the area, but the next period of history of which ample remains have been found is that of the Roman occupation of Britain (from 55 B.C.). At this time the Weald was densely forested by what the Romans called 'the Forest of Anderida', and most of the native population lived south of the scarpface of the South Downs. They were known as the Regni, and when the Romans built a city in their region it became their capital and the Romans therefore named it after them: Regnum. We now know Regnum, or Noviomagnus, as Chichester.

Blessed, as we all know, with brilliant engineering talents, the Romans soon set to work to build what was to become the best-known road in the whole of the Weald region. Some fifty-eight miles in length, the road ran from Regnum to Londinium (London), on the River Thames, being completed around 70 A.D. It was named Stanstret—or that was how it was spelt when first recorded in the documents known as the 'Feet of Fines', in 1270. Coldwaltham's gravel pit (now closed) provided some of the material used in the construction of this road.

Stane Street, as we now call it, did not follow a straight course for the whole of its journey, but a series of alignments. The first of these alignments, or stages, was from the east gate of Regnum to Hardham *mansio*, or military station. On the way, it passed within a mile of the Roman villa at Bignor, crossed the Bury and Fittleworth Road and entered Coldwaltham parish at Watersfield, crossing within a quarter of a mile of Ridge Farm (now a private house called The Ridge) in the extreme south-west stretch of the parish. Stane Street then descended Windmill Hill, along the edge of what is now the Alban Head Playing Field, almost coinciding with Stane Street Lane, south of the playing field. From there, it began to climb again, passing two hundred yards to the east of Ashurst House, where the common was so steep that a cutting had to be made. Sadly, as a result of quarrying for building on the site, all traces of this cutting have been lost, but it had been proved to be in a direct line with the last visible piece of Stane Street, at Grevatt's Wood, more than a mile and a half to the south-west. Thus, although traces of the road between these points have long since disappeared, this must have been the direction it took.

The next evidence of Stane Street is at Hardham, at the entrance to the former Roman *mansio*, or military station there. This cutting is easily spotted, and looks like a miniature railway cutting. It lies east of the gravel pit at Coldwaltham, which provided material for the building of the road itself.

The Romans usually planned their roads in straight lines, regardless as far as possible of gradients, so they would have no doubt disliked the way this steep ridge on the top of a little hill caused a tilt in the road!

Along Stane Street, at convenient invervals of around 13 miles[5], *mansiones* were built to provide convenient stop-over points on the journey between Chichester and London. Stane Street was used mainly by small forces, such as the police, but large bodies of troops also used the road. *Mansiones* were established at Alfoldean, in the parish of Slinfold, and in what is now the centre of Dorking town. But Hardham *mansio* was the first on Stane Street, from Chichester, and the best-preserved until comparatively recently, although the north-western part of the camp was cut through and destroyed by the single-track railway which was built in 1859 to connect Pulborough with Petworth.

The *mansio* at Hardham was built in the narrow 'neck' of Coldwaltham parish, close to the River Rother. It was sited on dry, gravelly soil, at a level just high enough to avoid the threat of winter floods, yet low enough for a water supply to be available, in a shallow well. Materials for building the *mansio* were probably brought by boat along the Arun. Stone would have come from nearby Pulborough, and timber (oak) would have been transported from the clay areas to the north and south.

In Roman times, the Rivers Rother and Arun both flowed closer to the *mansio* than they now do to its ruins. In fact, the former course of a large 'meander' of the Arun still exists as a line of drainage ditches. This line forms the parish boundary here, while the main river cuts off the bend nearly half a mile away, in Parham parish.

Hardham station was just rectangular, measuring 420 feet by 435 feet: about four acres. This was the usual size of such small stations, which acted as posting houses where remounts, stores and other supplies could be obtained. Most stations

---

5　This does not seem much, but it was the rough distance between stations on Stane Street, and marked the average length of a day's march. It must be remembered that thirteen miles is a good distance for armies on the march, and that the Roman legionary's equipment far outweighed the route-march packs our troops carry today.

were planned with two principal crossways and, when furnished with buildings, could shelter 7,000 to 8,000 men. When very large numbers of troops were on the road, they would be accommodated in tents in the open. Stane Street skirted two main gateways right through the centre of Hardham camp, which was surrounded by defensive earthwork. Sleeping accommodation and stables were in a stone building presumably incorporating an arch to allow the road through.

Also within the enclosure was a pottery factory, where tiles and crockery were made. Remains of these have been unearthed at various Roman sites, including that of Bignor Villa, about four miles away. The villa was discovered by a farmer in 1811, and excavated by the archaeologist Samuel Lysons.

According to archaeological evidence, Hardham *mansio* itself was occupied within ten years of the Roman invasion, in 43 B.C. The latest time it was known to have been occupied was 150 A.D. The *mansio* is thought to have transferred to a site just east of Pulborough parish church, where there was much Roman settlement at that time. No conclusive evidence, however, has yet been found.

On leaving Hardham *mansio*, Stane Street ran straight across the gravel river terrace, to where Winter's Farm now stands, on the road just outside Pulborough. From this point, knowing that the land there was liable to flood, the Romans built their road on a causeway, making a sharp angle at Winter's Farm towards where Pulborough's bridges, old and new, now stand. This was probably the Romans' first bridging point on the Arun, although they bridged again at Alfoldean.

In addition to Stane Street, there was another main Roman road in Sussex, between London and Lewes, and the two roads were connected by a secondary road which ran from Hardham *mansio* to Barcombe Mills. The existence of this road was suspected for many years, and was eventually proved by trial cuttings. Its eastward course from the *mansio* is lost on the ground, and can only be followed within this parish by a farm track. It crossed the river at a point where, in Medieval times, there was a weir known as Caldecote Weir,

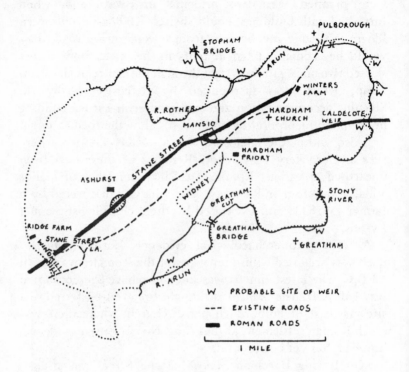

Fig. 3   Roads, rivers and weirs of Coldwaltham

and proceeded across the marshes to Wiggonholt on a causeway. It is likely that the Roman ford here was used as a
foundation for the weir.

The area is still rich in Roman remains, ranging from
the country villa at Bignor (seen to be a roomy one, on the
evidence of its reconstructed foundations and beautiful mosaic
pavements) to the more humble finds of local gardeners, who
still dig up pieces of pottery, tiles or glass—and often, if they
have sandy soil, put the unknown treasures back into the
earth again to help to weigh it down! One digger struck it rich
in Watersfield in 1811. He was a local farmworker, who, when
he broke a pottery vessel he found buried in the soil, watched,
no doubt mesmerised, as 1,700 Roman coins came spilling
out of it. Treasure trove indeed.

The Roman occupation of Sussex, continually under threat, was finally broken up by the Saxons, who settled down in strength at the end of the fifth century. The Saxons, as the short history of St. Giles[6] eloquently puts it, "suffered ... the civilising impact of Christianity". So widespread,

Fig. 4 A section of the exterior wall of St. Botolph's, Hardham, showing Roman materials taken from buildings at the nearby mansio

6 *A Short History of the Parish and Church of St. Giles, Coldwaltham* (out of print)

indeed, was its hold that the region became known as 'selig', or 'blessed' (an epithet often misinterpreted as 'silly' Sussex).

The Saxons lacked the engineering skills and building expertise of the Romans, but some of their churches, still standing in this country, demonstrate that they were capable of vision in this field. Of specific interest is the small church at Hardham, built in the eleventh century just a few years before the Norman Conquest, and dedicated to the Saxon Saint Botolph. Much of the material used in the church's construction was second-hand Roman tiles and bricks, but the church itself is very much a Saxon one.

Also in Hardham, and connected with Stane Street, is Hardham Priory. This monastic establishment indubitably owes its position to the Roman highway. It was built of local sandstone, along with material from the ruined *mansio*. (Later builders were not slow to make use of such precious debris, which was embodied in many buildings of that time. No doubt the ruined material of the Priory was carried off in its turn for later building.) All that remains now is the Chapter House and the refectory. The Chapter House is a mere shell, showing traces of Early English work, but the cellarage, with the refectory above it, is now a house (reconstructed after a disastrous fire in 1912).

In 1234, the Priory of St. Cross, or of The Exaltation of the Holy Cross, was founded, during the reign of Henry III, by Sir William Dawtrey, who held Hardham Manor and a great deal of other land in the neighbourhood. As a Priory of the 'Black Canons of St. Augustine', it seems to have had few inmates — in 1380 and 1521, only five! One Prior, Richard, was the anchorite for whom a squint was pierced in Hardham Church. In 1272, the Prior had an action brought against him by Milane, the anchorite of Steyning, on the plea that she was owed 5,600 loaves of bread, 5,600 cooked messes and 6,800 gallons of ale! In 1299, the Prior, Robert Bedeketon, was deposed for misrule. Another Prior, in 1542, was concerned in a poaching affray in Bignor Park. The Priory was not involved in the Dissolution of smaller Monasteries in 1536, although its history does not appear to have been at all

salubrious. There was some suggestion in 1532 that it might
be suppressed, but "by Cromwell's prudent counsel and
charitable words", not to mention the grant by the Canons
of an annuity to Cromwell, it continued to stand until 1545,
when it was dissolved by "agreement" between the Prior and
Sir William Goring, the patron. It was then that the buildings
were converted into a house, remaining in the possession of
the Goring family until the nineteenth century.

In Saxon times Waltham, as it was then called, was already
a larger village than Hardham. It had two manors, one held
by Godwin, a freeman, and also a small chapel on the site of
the present church of St. Giles. The Domesday Book (1086)
lists Waltham as having 900 acres, and describes its two
manors—one of six hides[7].

Little is known about Watersfield. A Roman battle is said
to have been fought there, and it is mentioned on several
occasions in records between 1256 and 1418. In 1316, a
charter for a market and fair to be held in Watersfield was
obtained by John de Langton, Bishop of Chichester. The
market had to be held on a Wednesday, and the fair "on the
vigil and morrow of St. Giles, Abbott" (could that be where
St. Giles' Church gets its name from?); that is, on August 31st
and September 11th.

Looking in more detail, and in an historical context, at
the *boundaries* of Coldwaltham parish, it can be seen that,
where the River Arun bounds the parish, river and boundary
do not coincide all the way. There are several small loops,
where the boundary crosses either on the right bank, or on
the left. Almost without exception, this is due to the cutting
of an alternative channel for the river. *A Description of the
High Stream of Arundel* makes a list of the various weirs
along this part of the river. There were no less than thirteen
of them below Stopham and above Bury: —

---

7 In one sense, a hide meant an actual area of land, often 1.2 acres, or
the amount on which a single family could support itself. But in the
Domesday Book hides were a means of tax assessment more than a
description of the cultivatable land of a manor.

Langley Weir
Mr. Olney's Weir
Pulborough Passage Weir
The Ferry Weir
Cawkett Weir
Humphry's Weir
Stedman's Weir
Wiggonholt Weir
Washington Weir
Mr. Mills' Weir
Juttons Weir
Widney Weir
Deep Weir

These were all in existence in 1937, either being used or in a decaying condition. Pulborough Passage Weir dates from the days when there was no bridge at Pulborough; only a ferry (in Medieval Latin, *passagium*). Widney Weir was on the Widney meander, which was out of common use by 1863.

In 1400, Prior John of Hardham took out a lawsuit in which he sought redress from the cutting of a ditch which had damaged one of his fisheries. He had a weir which had been owned by the Priors of Hardham "from time out of mind", traversing the river from bank to bank. The defendants had dug a ditch on the Wiggonholt side of the river, by-passing the weir and diverting most of the stream from it, so ruining the fishery. The ditch in question has since become the main course of the Arun, and all that remains of the original course is a narrow ditch running along the Coldwaltham-Parham boundary on the Coldwaltham side of the river.

It was clearly stated that the weir crossed the channel from bank to bank, and that from time immemorial the main stream had flowed "through the middle of the said weir itself". Probably the weir was a bar of stones, similar to that built at North Stoke to carry a Roman road across the stream. There is no reason why the weir at Wiggonholt should not have been constructed for the same purpose, as it lies in line with the Roman road running eastwards from the *mansio* at Hardham.

For administrative purposes Coldwaltham was placed, and still lies, within the area of the Rape of Arundel and the Hundred of Bury. What do 'rape' and 'hundred' mean in this context?

The Hon. Lady Mary Maxse, in her *Petworth in Ancient Times*[8], writes:—

> "The very name, 'Rape', which we use so glibly, is lost as to its origin in obscurity. 'Rapes' are peculiar to Sussex as are Ridings to Yorkshire and Lincolnshire. It was formerly held that the county was divided into Rapes at the Norman Conquest, but it has now been fairly conclusively proved that the Normans adopted administrative areas already in existence, and that Rapes date from the Saxons. The word itself is derived from 'rope'. There was an open-air court of justice and administration for each Rape, whose site was railed off with stakes and ropes—and the court gave its name to the whole area."

A 'Hundred' originally designated a hundred households. Lady Maxse writes:—

> "When we gaze at a map of the sixty-eight Hundreds of Sussex, varying in size from the Hundred of Butling Hill, containing a dozen or so parishes, to the tiny Hundred of Patching, it is hard to conceive that they were governed by uniform obligations. In general, however, the Hundreds are smaller in extent along the sea coast, the most thickly populated part in the early days, and grow larger to the north of the county in the thinly peopled forest tract known as the Weald."

From the fourteenth century on, Coldwaltham parish is comprehensively 'on record'. By 1340, as we have seen, 'Cold' had been added to 'Waltham', and 'ham' on the heath had acquired the much more desolate ring of 'ham on the black heath'! Being prone to floods during certain months of the year no doubt contributed to its re-naming. It was part of the possessions of the See of Chichester, and the *Short History of St. Giles* tells us that, in one of the volumes issued to members of the Sussex Record Society in 1925, there are several pages dealing with the Rents of Assize, Custom and Services of Waltham.

---

8 Articles by the Hon. Lady Mary Maxse, reprinted from Petworth Parish Magazine (published by Petworth Parochial Church Council, revised edition 1972)

These documents were originally written in Middle English. Bishop Rede had them transcribed into monkish Latin in 1369, for Diocesan convenience. The *Short History* quotes some fascinating details translated from these records and should be read. It includes a typical example of the obligations of Cold Waltham freeholders, pertaining to one of their number:—

> "Emma de Parc' holds 1 cottage and renders 18d. at St. Thomas' Day and 1 porting penny, 1 hen at Xmas and 10 eggs at Easter . . . She shall drive the lord's pigs from Waltham to pannage and when they come back from pannage she shall drive them to Amberle or Aldingbourne . . . And if the lord [of the manor!] wishes to have a pigstye she and the others of the same holding shall make it and have the timber on the lord's land."

In 1538, Thomas Cromwell ordered the keeping of parish registers, but it was not until 1547, when Edward VI was forced to renew the order, that such records — which were to become a valuable source of local history as well as of genealogical investigation—were properly kept.

Coldwaltham Church's parish registers date from 1561. From that time, we can look back and read of the marriages, burials (from 1572) and baptisms (1594) of parishioners, and piece together from this information whatever we will.

Chapter 2

SETTLEMENT

Although it is believed that there was a Celtic settlement in Coldwaltham, the first recorded date relating to population is 683 A.D., when Coldwaltham was referred to as Uualdham. Hardham was first mentioned, as we have seen, in 1086, in the Domesday Book; and we first see Watersfield written about in 1226.

The Hardham settlement was established on a low spur in open, unsheltered country, with the River Arun and its flood plain on three sides. The original settlers would have found that the meadows near the river provided grazing land to balance the amount of good ploughland, and that they could effectively construct shallow wells for water. River transport was conveniently placed, and dwellings were built along the London-Chichester line of communication originally marked by the Romans with the construction of Stane Street. The old Roman road, however, was abandoned and replaced by an almost parallel one close by.

Abundant material for building was there for the taking—timber, a mile or two away; on-the-spot wattle-and-daub; stone, when needed, from the Pulborough ridge across the river.

During Saxon times, the settlement formed part of the Manor of Heriedeham. Although it never grew larger than a hamlet, the Manor gained importance from Heringham Priory, which was founded during the reign of Henry III as a small establishment for Black Canons of the Order of St. Augustine.

As a unit, Hardham has been called a 'street village', because almost all the buildings in the hamlet are on, or near, the road—that is, the old main road which, when the A29 was constructed in the 1930s, was transformed into a quiet lane. It contains the Saxon church of St. Botolph and three good examples of timber-framed buildings, although these have tiled roofs instead of the original thatch. Some less ancient structures in the hamlet are of sandstone, but little modern development has taken place. The group of buildings in the lane, including Hardham Church, led to Hardham being designated a Conservation Area[1] on April 3rd, 1973.

Illustrated on the next page is an old house typical in construction of those near Hardham Church. It has only one unique feature: the thatch is set on top of a normal tiled roof. The lower four feet of the outside wall are of local sandstone, as is the low garden wall. The remaining walls are timber-framed, filled with wattle-and-daub and, at the rear, the upper storey is 'weather-boarded' with galvanised iron.

The (happily) stunted development of Hardham is very different from that of Coldwaltham and Watersfield. In both, the element of shelter was obviously foremost in the minds of those who settled there. Coldwaltham is really only protected from the east, by Lodge Hill and the high heath nearby, whereas Watersfield nestles cosily in the valley between Lodge Hill and Beacon Hill, sheltered on all sides except perhaps from the east.

---

1 "Many of the centres of our old towns, villages and hamlets are in danger of losing their former character, mainly through the increase in pressures for development, and the intrusion of the motor vehicle. It is necessary to recognise and plan to meet these changing requirements, for such settlements should acknowledge the spirit of our age while retaining their basic historic character. It is very easy for this character, which has been built up by so many generations, to be thoughtlessly neglected and destroyed.

"In order, therefore, to retain this important aspect of our heritage, Local Planning Authorities are required, under Section 277 of the Town and Country Planning Act, 1971, to determine those areas of special architectural or historic interest which should be preserved or enhanced, and to designate them as Conservation Areas. Designation is not an award of merit—its purpose is to draw the attention of public bodies and private individuals to the necessity of maintaining and improving the character of the locality. Historic buildings and features of special merit should be retained; every opportunity should be taken to improve the appearance of buildings and spaces which at present conflict with the historic character of their setting, and any new development necessary to meet changing needs should be sensitively integrated into the environment." *(West Sussex County Council leaflet)*

Fig. 1 Roadside cottages at Hardham (now one house, 'Marchwood')

Coldwaltham has a variety of land types: good ploughland in the medium soil to the north; permanent grass—especially near the river in the south, and pannage land in the woods for pigs. A spring in the centre of the village was there to provide water, and building materials, particularly timber, were readily available on the spot. When this site was first settled, the River Arun flowed within two hundred yards of it, which was convenient for transport.

Watersfield, too, was close to woodland, and accordingly reaped its benefits. It was also (and still is, of course) within easy reach of permanent pasture by the river, although the soil in the immediate vicinity has always been a little light for good ploughland.

Like Hardham, Coldwaltham began as a street village, partly along the narrow lane (once the main road and now called the loop road) which now contains the Labouring Man pub and some interesting old houses. Another part of the

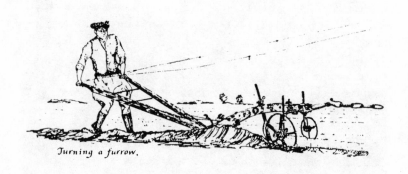

Turning a furrow.

Fig. 2　Hand ploughing

village street, on the northern extremity of Coldwaltham, is
also called 'loop road'. Both stretches of loop road, on either
side of the main road, show how winding and narrow the
original street was.

Watersfield, by contrast, is not a street village. In the
centre of its cluster of houses is the meeting-point of five
ways. A minor road from the river (River Lane) crosses the
main road at Watersfield and continues up into a little valley.
It is joined at the same focal point by another lane, known as
Stane Street Lane. Houses have been built on all five 'radii',
and more spacious houses were constructed in Colebrook
Lane, a turning off the main road near Lodge Hill.

The tiny group of cottages and farm buildings on the
northern side of the old loop road, in King's Lane, have
changed little. They are thought to be timber-framed, although
some have been stuccoed and others fronted with Pulborough
stone. Unlike the northern section of the old village street,
the greater part of the southern section is not readily visible
from the A29. Topography causes it to bend and cut across a
slope, with the result that the buildings lining each side are

set above, at and below the level of the road. The buildings are irregularly spaced, but most have been built close to the highway. Although predominantly nineteenth-century, they have been constructed in a range of materials and in various architectural styles. Stone is the building material mostly used here, and it has gone into the houses and into the retaining boundary walls. On December 3rd, 1973, both these sections of Coldwaltham were designated Conservation Areas.

In recent years, the face of the parish has been changed dramatically by residential development, of which there has been a prodigious amount. In the 1930s, a council-house estate, Brookview, was built. In the early 1960s, two private housing estates went up: Arun Vale in 1963 and Silverdale in 1965. This spate of building alarmed many local inhabitants, and in 1963 the then vicar, Rev. Eric Newcombe, apparently expressed the general concern in a letter to Chanctonbury Rural District Council, for he received the following reply from the Council's Surveyor, Mr. C. A. Brace:—

1st May 1963

Dear Sir,

Possible future development, Coldwaltham

I refer to your letter of the 20th April, and apologise for the delay in replying. I will endeavour to give briefly information pertaining to the parish of Coldwaltham, i.e. Hardham, Watersfield and Coldwaltham village.

I do not envisage any large scale development taking place within the foreseeable future and I would add that compensation for loss of development has already been paid on appreciable areas of land, particularly in the Watersfield area. It must be assumed, therefore, that Watersfield is likely to remain more or less as we know it today. Likewise, I feel there will be little or no change in the present position at Hardham.

With regard to Coldwaltham, i.e. approximately between the area of the Labouring Man and Brookview council houses, the position is somewhat different. The Arun Vale Estate is now approaching completion and immediately to the east adjacent to the Old Priest House development has been approved and is now commencing for the erection of approximately 30 dwellinghouses.

I would add also that an outline application has been received in respect of several acres of land immediately to the south of Arun Vale. This proposed development was refused by my Council but the final outcome is in the balance until the result of an appeal to the Minister has been made known.

Apart from these specific cases it is quite possible that a small amount of infilling, i.e. approval being given to the odd individual dwelling here and there may arise . . .

Houses did go up on the 'several acres' of land to the south of Arun Vale, annoying and upsetting residents at the lower end of the estate, whose hitherto marvellous view of the South Downs became restricted. Building of new houses seems currently to be at a standstill, but it is encouraging to see several *old* houses being improved in the most sympathetic way, and old thatch being replaced by new on roofs here and there, in spite of the very high cost of this work.

Fig. 3 A timber-framed cottage at Watersfield (now called 'Quintins')

The use of building materials throughout the parish is varied. Until the eighteenth century, generally speaking, transport was not normally good enough to allow much in the way of building materials to be transported from areas any great distance away. Local resources had to be tapped as far as possible. The wealth of local timber, clay and loam made it easy to build timber-frame houses, like those in the northern part of the old village street, the framework being filled with wattle-and-daub. Roofs were always thatched, with either reeds or straw. Many of these timber-frame houses still grace the parish, thatched or re-thatched, although the framework of the walls has been filled in with materials more durable that wattle-and-daub, such as brick, stone or modern plaster. Examples of this kind of house are 'Applegarth' in Watersfield and 'Widneys' in Coldwaltham.

A fascinating insight into the use of natural materials in building a typical Sussex house in days long gone by is given by Esther Meynell in her book, *Sussex*[2]:—

> "The timber skeleton of a typical old Sussex farmhouse or cottage is an almost perfect example of the natural use of natural materials. Upon the low foundation wall of brick or stone or flint a massive oak sill was placed. Into this, upright posts were tenoned —in early building usually set close, in later times, wider spaced. There were two reasons for this: the closer set uprights were stronger against attack, and as times grew safer the timber was also growing scarcer, as the forests dwindled, and was used more thriftily. The corner posts of ancient houses were often whole tree trunks, usually root end at the top, for the broader base served to support the upper storey, and it was found that when the sap could run out by this reversal the timber had a much longer life. On this simple principle the whole oaken cage, with its diagonal 'dragon beam' and its rafters for the roof, was constructed. In the old days they talked of 'rearing' a house. There then remained the filling of the spaces between the timbers, which was very commonly done by springing wooden laths between the uprights and plastering them on both sides—'wattle-and-daub'. Sometimes in early examples the filling was like sheep hurdles are made today — a very ancient craft with the plaster laid on. In some of the prettiest old houses, the filling between the timbers is brick-nogging, either plain or herringbone brickwork. Sometimes this is the original filling, sometimes it has been added later, because the old wattle-and-daub has shrunk and let in the rain."

Although Coldwaltham parish sprawls over a sandstone area, most of its own stone is unsuitable for building purposes. In the past, much has been brought in from the Pulborough, Petworth and West Chiltington areas.

A different type of building stone is quarried from each of the three stone divisions of the Lower Greensand group.

---

2   published by Robert Hale in their County Book series

The Hythe beds produce a grey sandstone, quite weather-resistant, and this has been used in the walls of Hardham Church and in the tower of Coldwaltham Church. Evidently, it is not markedly jointed, as it is frequently found to be in walls not laid in courses, but as a 'ragstone' bond. A small portion of the stone walling shown below is of this type of stone.

Pulborough Stone   hard, dark Sandstone of Folkestone Beds

Grey 'Ragstone' from Hythe Beds

Fig. 4   Three types of building stone of the Lower Greensand

Most stone buildings in the parish, especially later ones, are built of Pulborough stone: a yellow-ish brown, distinctly sandy stone from the Sandstone Beds. It is unique among the Lower Greensand stones: strongly bedded, it squares off nicely as masonry. Waltham Farmhouse is built of this stone (again look at Fig. 4), as are the entire structures of nearby Greatham Bridge and the old Pulborough Bridge.

The Folkestone Beds consist mainly of a very friable sandstone of low resistance to weathering and little use as masonry. However, there is a narrow band—in Coldwaltham,

hung tiles

Figs. 5 & 6 'Applegarth', front and back views

where formerly stood a wing,
similar to the one at the other end

at any rate – of highly resistant, dark brown sandstone containing, and stained by, iron. On weathering this turns almost black, and it is frequently seen in buildings all over the parish.

Another feature of some Coldwaltham houses, although it is more typical of parts of the Weald Clay and Hastings Beds, is a tile-hung upper storey, as in the medieval cottage called 'Applegarth' (Figs. 5 & 6). The cottage is largely timber-framed, as the view of the back of the house shows. It appears that structural alterations were carried out in Tudor times, and these involved the re-building of the wall at the northern end and part of the front wall, in large blocks of 'ragstone' from the Hythe Beds. The recess in the front wall at ground-floor level is quite common among cottages built in the fourteenth and fifteenth centuries. This particular building was divided into four separate cottages, although it is now one house[3].

Among other building materials which are in use in the parish, brick is of course the most common. As the Georgian style caused a great vogue in their use, bricks began to be made in large numbers. And as methods of communication and transport improved, bricks came to be used to build less splendid houses. By the time Queen Victoria was on the throne, labourers' cottages were being built predominantly of brick.

Flint pebble – a material to be found on the Downs and the coastal plain – is not common in Coldwaltham houses, but it does occur, along with the use of knapped flints. The frequency of occurrence seems to decrease with distance away from the Downs; several examples are found in Watersfield, but they are rare in Coldwaltham and non-existent in Hardham. Figure 7 (page 25) shows a house in Coldwaltham which, until the mid-1950s, was two semi-detached cottages. The lower three feet of the front wall are of Pulborough stone, and the corners, windows and doors are all dressed with brick.

3　See also Chapter 6, *Landmarks and Features*

lower walls of Pulborough Stone

Fig. 7   Flint pebble used as a building material at Coldwaltham
('Church Cottage')

Hardly any examples of weather-boarded cottages are to be found in the parish—this style is more common in the Weald Clay area—but the pre-war-built council houses on the Brookview estate maintain this upper-storey tradition with their pantile roofs.

Residential development in the area has naturally increased the parish's population. In 1801, as can be seen from the graph overleaf, just over three hundred people lived in the parish, but in 1831, only thirty years later, there were almost six hundred—a doubling in size. During the Second World War, the population dropped to about 450, but dramatically increased after it to over 700, by which time the council houses were nearly completed. By 1961, the population had dropped to 661 (due to the nationally-recorded fall in birth-rate), only to rise substantially to 871 in 1971. It had dropped to 820 by 1981. The official projections for 1986 show a

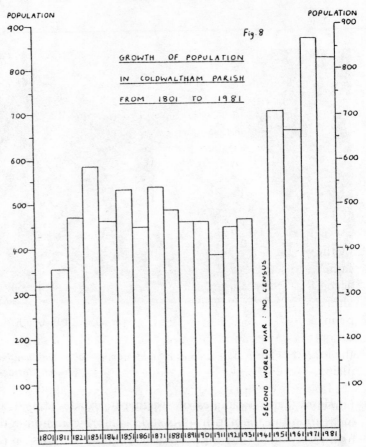

Fig. 8 Population changes: Coldwaltham parish

population of 830, and the predictions are that this figure will remain fairly constant until 1996.

I was tempted to continue this chapter with a pictorial look at more old houses and other landmarks whose existence is due to settlement throughout the parish. However, the settlements would not have grown and developed without first farming and secondly the creation and growth of communications in the area, and it to these aspects of Coldwaltham's story that I turn next.

Some of the loveliest and most interesting houses are, however, included in Chapter 6, *Landmarks and Features*.

Chapter 3

FARMING

"I have lawns, I have bowers,
I have fields, I have flowers,
And the lark is my morning alarmer.
So, jolly boys now, here's God speed the plough;
Here's a health and success to the Farmer."

This 'Farmer's Toast'[1] conveys in a few words the pluses
of the farmer's lot, but at the end of the eighteenth century
farming in Sussex was not very productive. According to one
account (1798), almost all the land was under arable crops—
although much of this could have been put to better use as
permanent pasture. In addition, the rotation system had
become outdated, and unhealthy for the land. On the whole,
the intelligent and wealthier farmers were those on the coastal
plain, and those between Pulborough and Midhurst.

In the early part of the nineteenth century, however,
farmers — in common with most working people—were very
badly off. The quantity of poverty and distress resulted in
high rates, which in turn made even more people suffer, and
gave Wealden farmers a burden they could not bear.

With the end of the Napoleonic Wars came a depression
which made farming a very poor business to be involved in,
and many left it, especially when a widespread outbreak of
sheep-rot struck it a further blow in 1820. It was difficult to
find tenants to take the land, which as a result fell in value.

---

1 sung by Frank Gamblin, when an inmate of Portsmouth Workhouse,
to H. Gardner, who subsequently included it in his *Marrowbones: workhouse songs*, published by the English Folk Song and Dance Society.
(An even more local, remembered folk song, "Ship in Distress", was
recalled in 1907 by a Mr. Harwood, of Watersfield, for George Butter-
worth, and included in *The Penguin Book of English Folk Songs*. Mr.
Harwood is duly credited in the book.)

Fig. 1   Sussex plough

Some land even lay untenanted, particularly round the East Grinstead area. In places, the poorer type of land fell back into heath, marsh or wasteland.

The fifty years following the 1820s saw a concerted movement towards the conversion of arable land into permanent pasture. The increase in cattle-farming in the Weald was noticeable, and the development of the south-coastal resorts at this time created a rapidly extending market for agricultural and garden produce.

At the same time, the complaints of a serious depression continued. Rentals stayed low, but in spite of this many tenant-farmers were dropping into arrears with their rents.

During the 1870s, most Wealden farmers were held to be insolvent, even though they lived and worked harder than the average labourer—while their children, ironically, were in the main less well-educated.

Yet, on the Downs, farmers were working on a larger scale, and making their businesses pay better, having bought out the smaller farmers around the middle of that century. There, and in the Pulborough district, good cottage accommodation was available to labourers for a weekly rental of from one shilling to half-a-crown. There were fewer allotments then than before, but the labourer's general lot had definitely improved.

From 1875 to 1890, the increasing popularity of poultry-farming and dairy-farming was the result of a fall in the price of both corn and sheep, and a further decrease in the arable acreage took place.

In the Weald, farms were small and thus readily acceptable to the requirements of poultry-farming; tenants were easily found, and farms could now be let at higher rentals. On the Downs, however, the large farms could not be sub-divided easily, and were difficult to adapt to new trends. Rents had to come down in order to secure tenants, and good labourers, too, were hard to find. In the Weald this did not matter so much: for the most part, farms here were small enough for the family to work without employing outside help.

Schools and instruction centres were being set up by the county council to help farmers and market gardeners, who were facing stiffening foreign competition, and therefore needed to learn more efficient methods of production and distribution. But in the first few years of the twentieth century fewer young men were enrolling for these beneficial courses. They simply could not afford the fees.

Eighty-five years ago, the average wage of a labourer in Great Britain was 16s. 10d. The corresponding average for Sussex was 17s. 10d., although this figure was boosted by piece-work payments. In West Sussex, the average time-rate weekly wage was not more than 14s. 2d. and, on the whole, allowances 'in kind' were small and infrequent. The highest wages were earned by shepherds and men in charge of horses. They got just about 19s. a week.

Going back to the mid-1850s, there was great domination of arable land over permanent pasture. Every field capable of being cultivated *was* cultivated, irrespective of the character of its soil.

The woodland area, on Lodge Hill and covering quite a large stretch of the west and north-west side of the parish, coincides roughly with the Folkestone Beds—although much of the large wooded area is on Hill Gravel, characterised usually by its *lack* of woodland.

A more visible pattern is to be found in the permanent pasture, confined largely to the low-lying alluvial brookland near the river, and liable to flood. A line of pasture land

followed the lowest part of the valley between Lodge Hill
and Windmill Hill, especially on the side of the main road
nearer to the river. Here and there, small fields of pasture lay
scattered among the vast mass of arable land in the centre of
Coldwaltham.

In those days, very few cottage gardens seem to have
contained orchards.

Land use more recently showed a fairly distinct pattern,
based on a closer relationship to geological divisions in the
area.

The Valley Gravel is a medium soil, eminently suitable
for ploughing, and in the late 1950s very little of this was
used for permanent grass. A map of land use in 1958 shows
that the arm of valley gravel in the northern part of Hardham
is given over to arable, while that in the southern part, which
is sandier, and therefore a much lighter soil, was almost
untouched by the plough. Then, from the narrow 'neck' of
the parish, westwards along the south side of the disused
Midhurst railway line, a strip of arable fields corresponds
with one of valley gravel.

Hill Gravel has rather more clay in it and, as a heavier soil,
is understandably given over to an even distribution of arable
and grass. On the arable land, cereal crops predominated.

The Gault Clay on the whole tends to leave land as
permanent pasture, and this was found (still in 1958) in some
large fields just south of Hardham, where the clay is gravelly
in places, and green fodder crops, such as kale, were grown.

The higher parts of the Folkestone Beds—drier, because
further away from the water-table—are marked by pine and
birch woodland, and by gorse and bracken heath. But the
lower parts, where the water-table is nearer the surface and
the soil is less light and porous, make reasonably good arable
land, and these parts were more or less equally divided
between arable and grassland. Near The Ridge (in 1958 still
called Ridge Farm), on the top of Windmill Hill, there is a
patch of plateau gravel, and the plough took advantage of it.
No one crop was grown more significantly than another on
the arable parts of the Folkestone Beds.

The Alluvium is of course level and low-lying. As such, it is almost everywhere liable to flood. This is not conducive to crop-growing, and almost all of it was used as permanent pasture. In most parts, the grass was quite good and lush. It was mainly used for fattening cattle and lambs, and for hay, particularly on the stretch by the River Rother.

The extensive woodland areas, west and north-west of the parish, have not changed in size since 1841, although there must have been some felling and replanting, and indeed in some places, confirming this, there were in 1958 plantations of conifers not more than twenty or thirty years old.

Cattle, then, on the parish's farms, were partly dairy and partly beef. Sheep-farming was confined mainly to the north and west of the old parish of Hardham: Hardham Gate Farm had flocks feeding on the alluvial meadows north of the old Midhurst railway line, and between the electrified line and the main road. Few, if any, sheep were folded on the arable land.

In general terms, land in the 1840s appears to have been forced to produce a large acreage of crops — either because it was necessary, or profitable, or both — whereas, in the 1950s, the use of each field was governed much more by the character of the soil, and by what it is naturally capable of producing.

Much of this information on the farming scene up to 1958 has been gleaned from Mr. Holt's study, which covers the years 1958-1959. At this time, one of the dozen or so farms around was Waltham Farm. Of this, Mr. Holt compiled a short but detailed account, and I reproduce some of it here:—

"Waltham Farm occupies land to the north and north-west of Coldwaltham . . . , and the farm buildings are in the sleepy remnant of the village street to the north of the village. It is a small, mixed farm. The stock is entirely cattle: no sheep, pigs, or even poultry.

"The farmer sold his dairy herd a few months ago, but still has thirty head of cattle: eighteen cross-breeds, patterned for beef, and twelve Ayrshire store heifers. He will probably buy another dairy herd of twenty-five cows in the near future, but is so far undecided on breed. They may be Ayrshires, but he is becoming interested in Channel Islands breeds and might try them.

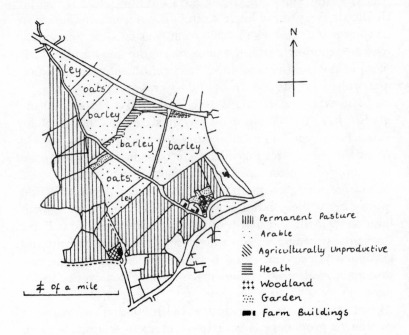

Ley
oats
barley
barley   barley
oats
Ley

N

‖‖ Permanent Pasture
∴ Arable
⦚ Agriculturally Unproductive
☰ Heath
⁂ Woodland
⦂ Garden
◼▮ Farm Buildings

¼ of a mile

Fig. 2 Plan of Waltham Farm

"The farm land is portioned out in the following way:—
    17 acres barley
     7 acres oats
    23 acres hay and silage
    36 acres grazing land.

"Of the thirty-six acres of grazing, eight acres are to be ploughed and re-seeded to grass in 1959.

"When milk is being produced, it is collected by Express Dairies, and taken to the depot at Billingshurst. None is supplied to the immediate locality.

"All meat stock goes via Pulborough Market[2] to the Fatstock Marketing Board[3].

"Recent improvements on the farm are a new Dutch barn and a new silo."

Long ago, the Harwoods lived at Waltham Farm, but from the 1730s it was the residence of the Neale family. Before he married, around 1847, John Neale (then the recorded owner of the property) extended the tiny farmhouse. The Neales sold the farm back to Stopham Estate, who sold it to the Henly sisters. They owned it until just before World War I, and had cows and poultry on the farm, but lived down the road at Oxford House, Coldwaltham[4]. In their day at Waltham Farm, there was a pond in the middle of the yard, and the present owner, Mr. Roy Cooper, remembers hearing that it took 100 tons of chalk to fill it in.

In 1911, Mr. Henry Gordon Poland moved to Waltham Farm. He had it as a private house, with 20 acres of land. When Mr. Poland went to live in Liphook, Hampshire, he sold the farm to his stepson, Mr. Frank Cooper, who, during World War II, added sixty-odd acres to the holding. From the age of fourteen, his son, Roy, helped to run the farm and he has continued to run it since his father's death in 1951. Mr. Cooper sold the dairy herd in 1960, and went in for store cattle and arable farming. For five years, he grew a sizeable potato crop but in 1984, with the staff-shortage problems experienced by all farmers in the area, he returned the land to cereals.

In the days when staff were easy to come by, staff cottages were also available. Pear Tree Cottage was once a farmworker's cottage, and Mr. Roy Cooper remembers that, at his end of the parish, there were two very old cottages on the road, just before Hardham Gate. Originally called Priory Cottage and attached to what was then Priory Farm, they were bought by the Dallyns, but Mr. Cooper sometimes housed his workers there. (The cottages were demolished in 1939, when the A29 by-pass was constructed.)

Waltham Farm was *not* one of the local farms sold in 1957, when the Leconfield Petworth Estate disposed of some

---

2 Pulborough Market closed in 1974, through lack of trade, and local farmers now transact stock business at the markets in Chichester, Guildford and Haywards Heath. From 1974 to 1979, however, a Christmas Fatstock Show and dinner were held annually at different venues, including Park Farm, Pulborough, and — the last — at Kithurst Farm, on the Parham Estate.

3 The Fatstock Marketing Board, re-named the Fatstock Marketing Corporation (F.M.C.), is now no more.

4 see Chapter 7, *Amenities*

7,466 acres of its "outlying portions". All the land, farms, cottages and other properties—including a sandpit (at Coates) and a cornmill — lay within a ten-mile radius of Petworth, where the beautiful Petworth House, with its fine walled park to the west, has been the seat of the Leconfield family for many generations.

The sale was so extensive that it took two whole days, with two sessions on each day, for Messrs. Strutt & Parker, Lofts & Warner, to auction off all the 170 lots involved.

Of these, Lots 74 to 144 were the "Coates, Fittleworth and Coldwaltham Portion", which, the sale catalogue read, was "a compact area . . . largely bounded in the north by the River Rother, [extending] through the picturesque village of Fittleworth through Coates, Watersfield and Coldwaltham to the edge of Amberley Brooks and a frontage to the River Arun."

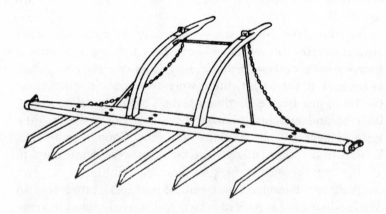

Fig.3   Hay collector

Much of the Coldwaltham portion was bought by Miss Joan Campbell[5]. Several farms and much farmland changed ownership at this time, and Lord Leconfield's long-standing connection as Lord of the Manor in this area was severed for ever.

Coldwaltham Farm, the tenants of which were "Mr. C. Secomb and Son", was—with over 137 acres of farmland and 1½ acres of woodland—one of the major farms in the sale.

Along with the already modernised farmhouse of brick and stone, went a timber and slated barn with a granary over half of it; a slated four-stall stable used as calf boxes with wooden hayracks; loosebox with concrete floor; concreted stockyard; three cowhouses for twenty-six with concrete standings, mangers and partitions; boiler house and dairy with sliding door; range of three looseboxes and engine bay, and range of brick and asbestos pigsties. The outlying farm-buildings comprised a three-bay Dutch barn, a six-bay open cattle shed, and a timber, brick and iron barn. In the same lot was the brick and timbered Frylands Cottage.

The land itself, according to the catalogue, "forms a compact block and lies to the north of the homestead. It has a south frontage to a public road. The brook meadows in the north are bounded by the River Rother. There is a small wood containing oak and elm trees and some useful hedgerow timber". The lot also included "36 Bullock Leazes giving the right to graze in Coldwaltham Brooks one bullock or two sheep in respect of each leaze or one horse in respect of each two leazes".

It was in 1903 that John Secomb left Gweek, Cornwall, with his family and came to farm Ratford Farm, on the Leconfield Estate at Balls Cross. He had three sons, Hugh, Edward (Ned) and Charles, who was the youngest. In 1923, a year after his marriage, Charles Secomb moved to Cold-waltham Farm and in 1925 his son, James Charles (Jim) Secomb, was born. At that time, the farm was a mixed one. Edward (Ned) worked the horses and Charles Secomb did the rest. In 1940, on leaving school, Jim Secomb joined his father on the farm and in 1956, a year before the elder's death, they became partners. In 1956, too, Jim Secomb was married.

---

5 Upon her death in 1960, Miss Campbell left this portion to her nephew, Mr. Ian Anstruther, who added it to his Barlavington Estate near Sutton, where he lives.

In 1957, when the Leconfield Estate sold Coldwaltham Farm, Jim Secomb was already a tenant (although only just) and he was able to stay on at the farm, which he has run ever since, first alone and then with his son, Piers, on his leaving school in 1978.

The farm is still predominantly a dairy farm but, since 1969, when Mr. Secomb, Senior, took over the tenancy of Waltham Park Farm as well, from Mr. Arthur John Sams, most of the work has been done from there, using the modern dairy unit erected by Mr. Anstruther to this end. Piers Secomb now lives in the cottage adjoining this farm.

The 1957 sale catalogue places Waltham Park Farm "not far from Coldwaltham Farm, three-quarters of a mile north of Watersfield, and reached by a public track". That description still stands today; in fact this little farm has remained the most rural holding of all those in the parish.

The flint, brick and stone farmhouse was described as having three bedrooms, two with fireplaces (nostalgically recalling the days when people went to bed by the light of flickering, golden fires). The farm buildings, grouped near the farmhouse, comprised a timber and iron range of four stalls used as calf pens; fertilizer store, workshop, three looseboxes with wooden mangers; brick and tiled cowhouse for eight, with concrete standings and mangers and wooden hayracks; grain store and timber; iron and thatched barn partly adapted as cattle pens.

The land—some 72 acres of it—was "well placed round the homestead . . . with . . . good frontage to public or other roads. Much of it slopes southwards. There are some oak, elm and Scots pine hedgerow and other trees." With this lot also came "10 Bullock Leazes giving the right to graze in Coldwaltham Brooks one bullock or two sheep in respect of each leaze, or one horse in respect of each two leazes."

Other parts of Waltham Park Farm, sold in separate lots, were a "parcel of land" (16-odd acres of it) "to the north of Hook Wood and Waltham Park and . . . bounded on the north

---

6   where the author lives

by a railway", and another eleven acres to the north of the railway line with a north frontage to the River Rother, and including brooks.

Before Mr. Arthur Sams retired in 1969, he had run Waltham Park Farm for forty-five years. His farm was a mixed as well as a poultry farm, and he kept quite a number of pigs in the early days. Until World War II, he reared mainly poultry but, when the war came, he ploughed most of the land for arable crops. After the war, he reared pullets for sale, although he continued to sell eggs and cream locally. For many years, his horse and cart were a familiar sight, as he took his produce to Pulborough market, held near the station, and to Lodge Hill, when it was a hotel, and the Swan Hotel, at Fittleworth.

Fig. 4 Sussex barn with hayloft and cart hovel

Similar in importance, although with a slightly higher acreage than Coldwaltham Farm, was Torepsoes and Besleys Farm, which, with its 177 acres, was described in the Leconfield sale catalogue as a "T.T. and Attested Dairy Farm, situated to the south and east of Watersfield", with the farmhouse (Watersfield House), a cottage (Pear Tree Cottage[6], but in the catalogue just plain Cottage 30R), and Coldwaltham Allotments (1.130 acres), rented at that time by Coldwaltham Parish Council.

The tenant-farmer was Mr. George William Ruff, and the

farmhouse he lived in had (and still has) four bedrooms, three
with fireplaces, and two attic bedrooms, one with a fireplace.

The farm buildings, close to the farmhouse, are mainly of
stone and brick with tiled roofs, and comprise a loosebox;
brick and asbestos dairy and sterilising room; two looseboxes;
an asbestos-roofed, modernised cowhouse for twenty-one,
with concrete standings and mangers; tubular fittings and
concrete forecourt; two cattle yards; fodder and fertiliser
store; stone and tile barn; four-bay open cattle shed; two
looseboxes, three pigsties and foodstore; a two-stall stable,
and timber and iron two-bay tractor and implement shed.
A second range of buildings, round a cattle yard, include a
brick, stone and slated five-bay open cattle shed, loose box,
timber and slated barn, and store.

The "detached cottage" at the bottom of the farm drive
was, like the farmhouse, built of brick and stone, but with a
slated roof. Two of the bedrooms had fireplaces (now only
one has) and outside, in the large garden, was the "bucket
closet"—still in use even then.

Much of the land that was sold with Torepsoes and
Besleys Farm, lying to the south and east of the house in
two main blocks, slopes south-eastwards as far as the "Brook
meadows fronting the River Arun", with the railway inter-
secting the eastern part. Again, Bullock Leazes—forty this
time—were included in the lot, conveying the right to graze in
Coldwaltham Brooks one bullock or two sheep in respect of
each leaze, or one horse in respect of each two leazes.

Linked with Besleys Farm because it was also run by the
Ruffs, Watersfield Farm was sold by the Leconfield Estate in
1957 as well. It was a small stock and mixed farm on the east
side of Watersfield, with ten acres of land, a comprehensive
group of farm buildings, and a three-bedroomed farmhouse.

Mr. George William Ruff had taken over Watersfield Farm
from his father, George, in 1927 and he farmed and lived
there with his wife, Ivy[7]. His daughter, Peggy, was born there,
too. In 1945, Mr. Bill Dowick retired from Besleys Farm to
Baisley House and, a year later, 'G.W.' moved to Besleys. He
took the present tenant, Mr. Stanley Ruff, into partnership in

the early 1950s, the younger Mr. Ruff (no relation) having married Peggy Ruff. Thus Ruff married Ruff and it is hardly any wonder that the farm has been known as Ruff's farm ever since. When George William died in 1955, 'Stan' Ruff became the sole tenant of both farms, and for more than eleven years has been helped by his son, Mr. Charles (Charlie) Ruff, whom he took into partnership in 1979.

Another Leconfield property to come under that 1957 hammer—although I have taken it out of its sequence in the sales catalogue—was Watersfield Poultry Farm. This used to be run by a Mrs. Blake, helped by Mr. Les Goble, who then lived at 'Applegarth', Watersfield. Mrs. Blake's daughter continued to run the small poultry farm at 'Windmill Brow'.[8] She bred, reared and sold good birds, such as Rhode Island Reds. Apart from pullets, there were chickens sold for the table, and eggs. When she married Mr. Jack Murray, a BBC broadcaster, they went to live at 'The Pines', Coldwaltham, and Mr. Greenwood took on the tenancy of the poultry farm, running it for a few years until it was sold and, like so many of the country's smaller holdings, turned into a dwelling.

Coldwaltham came to have its own fruit farm when, in 1921, John and Dorothy Colwell moved to Ashurst Farm, through which the Roman Stane Street used to run. Converting it from a mixed farm, Mr. Colwell planted acres of apple trees, including strains no longer grown but still well remembered by many of us, such as Early Victorian and Keswick cooking apples, and Beauty of Bath eaters. John Colwell also planted pear trees and damson trees, but his only soft-fruit crop was gooseberries. The fruit was sold commercially, along with the jams made on the premises. To help him run the place and business, he was blessed with a wife and four daughters. One of the daughters, Mrs. Nina Weston, who now lives with her family in Brookview,

---

7 Mrs. Ivy Ruff, who became the 'Grannie of the village', died in March 1986, at the grand age of 93. One of her own oldest memories was that of delivering milk to local residents in pails—one in either hand. They used to raise "merry hell" if she was late!

8 now called 'Windmill Hill'

remembers learning to milk cows (they also had a small dairy herd), make cream, and churn butter.

In olden days, Nina Weston believes, the house was two cottages, with "diamond-paned windows", and there used to be a trap-door in each, to reach the first floor, before staircases were put in—which would have made the original cottages very old indeed[9].

In 1958, following the deaths of Mr. and Mrs. Colwell, the farm was sold to the Bowermans and, sadly, the orchards were ripped up and the land returned to pasture. Mrs. Weston especially remembers the pulling-up of the pear trees, which were in full blossom at the time.

Fig. 5 Pear trees in blossom at Ashurst Farm

9 There was also a small poultry farm and market garden at 'Fruit-fields', now Penn House, not far from Waltham Farm. It was run for the owner, Dr. Janet Aitken, for several years from 1938.

There was a market garden near Waltham Brooks, where Mr. Jim Jupp (who recently moved away) grew mushrooms, lettuce and strawberries[10].

The largest farm in the parish is Hardham Church Farm, which used to be called Priory Farm. As Priory Farm, it belonged to only two families after the dissolution of the priory in 1545. The Challen family came first, but when Mr. Challen died mysteriously from, it is said, "drinking water from the Brooks" (!), his widow stayed on and became housekeeper to John Dunning Aysh, when he bought the farm. The Aysh family, which can be traced back to Edward the Confessor, have lived in Hardham Priory House since about 1840, with the 600-acre mixed and arable farm. In 1932, the second John Dunning Aysh married Doris May Metters, who came from Stoneleigh Manor, Warwickshire, very near the site of the annual Royal Show. They had five daughters, all of whom were fine, prizewinning horsewomen. In those days Crawley and Horsham Hunt and the Cowdray Hunt both had their meets at Hardham Priory.

John Dunning Aysh, Junior, took over the farm from his father at 18, because the latter was ill, and became a pillar of the local community. He served on what was then Chanctonbury Rural District Council, and on the North-West Sussex Water Board, and he was a churchwarden of Hardham Church for sixty years!

Mrs. Aysh still lives at Hardham Priory House, but for the past 26 years Mr. John Gillingham has had the farm (for the last 13, with his wife and two daughters), which is mixed, dairy and arable.

Some years ago, Mr. Gillingham drained his own land, and was thus able to make use of every acre. He did not know when he reclaimed the land that Hardham Water Treatment Works would have a borehole sunk on it in 1965. Now, ironically, the land is sometimes even too dry. The water level, which used to be 4-5 feet, is now on average down

10 This is now run by Mr. Graham Barker, who is also Honorary Warden of Waltham Brooks nature reserve. See Chapter 6.

to 20 feet, but in the winter of 1985-1986 it went down to 22-23 feet.

Towards the end of the nineteenth century, with corn and meat coming into the country from the New World, farming declined and farmers were allowed to use the farms rent-free. It was at this time, during the 1880s and 1890s, that many farming families moved to Sussex to settle. Among them are the locally familiar names of Aysh, Batchelor, Dallyn, Heard, Lerwill, Langmead (perhaps the best-known Sussex farming family), Retallack, Secomb, Smallridge and Vinnicombe. Most of these are West Country names, and Secomb and Retallack are Cornish. 'Retallack' is just about as Cornish as you can get, and there must be many who have wondered how we came to have a Retallack family in our midst. The Retallacks farmed Lea Farm, between Fittleworth and Stopham — a fine old dairy farm. The farmhouse itself, which is extremely old, was once, it is said, a monastery. Ivor and Hugh Retallack, brothers and the two remaining members of the family, retired to Baisley House, River Lane, in 1968, where Hugh died a few years later.

A very familiar name in these parts is 'Dallyn'. . . . In 1887, Richard Dallyn, with his wife Susan (née Gibbs) and a young family (including John, born in 1879), moved from South Molton, North Devon, to Blackdown Farm, Haslemere. He hired a whole train to transport his stock. The family moved to Barlavington Farm and, from there, in 1896, to Hardham Gate Farm. First they were tenants, then they bought the property. It was there that Richard (Dickie) Dallyn (whose eccentric ways had made him something of a legend in his lifetime) died, and his son John moved for a time to Greatham Manor Farm. At Greatham, he met and married Viola, the daughter-writer of a distinguished but under-treasured poet, critic and writer, Alice Meynell[11], but things did not quite work out, and John Dallyn moved back to Hardham Gate.

Mr. Jake Dallyn, John's son, who had been born at Greatham. continued, after his father's death in 1947, to farm at Hardham Gate. The farm is mixed and, until 1970,

Fig.6   Richard Dallyn outside Hardham Gate Farm

included a dairy herd, sheep and corn. The animals were grazed on the 'brooklands', where Jake Dallyn used to hold four Leazes[12]. Jake and his middle son, Mark, now farm over

---

11   The Meynells came from London to live at Humphrey's Homestead, Greatham.

12   This is the last of various references in Chapter 3 to Grazing Leazes, so perhaps a word should be said here about them. All the leazes were related to rights of common land, and an Act of Parliament passed in 1965 — the Commons Registration Act — required such rights to be registered. The first registration period, 2nd January 1967 to 13th June 1968, involved no charges, but those registering during the second period, 1st July 1968 to 2nd January 1970, had to pay £5 per application. Once the Registers were officially closed in 1970, unregistered rights ceased to exist. Many leazes in the parish were left unregistered; among them, those that went with Besleys Farm, Coldwaltham Farm, and Waltham Park Farm. Most of the remaining leazes are now in the name of a Mr. Marten.

Under the same Act, the village green at Hardham was registered as a green in 1967. Officially, it can be used by residents as "a place of recreation", so the present tenants of Hardham Green (as the house behind part of the green is called) were 'reported' when it was noted that they had planted trees in front of their house and, apparently, on the green itself. Subsequently, the owners revealed that they had bought the land in front of their house from the district council. But was the council in a position to sell it? The saga continues . . .

250 acres, of which eleven acres, surrounded by Stopham Estate land, were bought several years ago from Mr. Ian Anstruther. On about 115 of the remaining acres which belong to the Stopham Estate, Mark Dallyn grows maize, sweet corn and forage crops for their sheep.

In the mid-1950s, Jake Dallyn acquired most of the land between the causeway and the railway line, which used to belong to Winter's Farm. This has not been a working farm in living memory and, before Mr. Dallyn bought the land, five owners shared it. It now forms part of Ingrams Farm, which was bought by the Dallyns in 1957 and, in its turn, added to Hardham Gate Farm. The Ingrams Farm sale took place one summer afternoon at Pulborough Village Hall. The Dallyns had to attend it en route to a Glyndebourne performance that evening, and they were dressed ready for the occasion. Mr. Dallyn reckons their appearance must have cost him a few thousand!

Chapter 4

COMMUNICATIONS

In Medieval times, Roman roads in the district mostly fell out of use, having 'submerged' into the Wealden mud, and no bridges had yet been built across the Arun round Pulborough. Travellers between the Storrington and Petworth areas had to cross the river by means of a ford, probably made originally by the Romans, between Hardham and Wiggonholt. This was converted into a weir – Caldecote Weir – in the fourteenth century, or possibly even before, and the crossing was then moved downstream to Stony River, where there was probably another ford.

Greatham Bridge, built between 1307 and 1327, was the first to span the Arun. Next came Stopham Bridge, in 1329. Houghton Bridge was constructed about a hundred years later. All three, along with the old Pulborough Bridge, were placed at points on the river where previously there had been a ferry. The building of the bridges led to the remaining ferries and fords falling out of use.

Whatever roads existed, following the decay of the Roman roads, took on certain forms according to the kind of country they passed through. On Hardham's clay, roads were green lanes; wide strips of grass and cleared land winding through the forest. They were wide because each cart that came along tried to pick out a less muddy track than the one that had gone before it, and the metalled carriageways that run along these lanes today are seen to go between wide grass verges of common wasteland, with cottages still squatting here and there behind them. On the other hand, in the sandstone country round Coldwaltham and Watersfield, the lanes were sunken. The soft sandstones have been ground down to sand through centuries of treading by men, animals and wagons. Heavy rains and the wind have gradually swept the loose sand away, so that many lanes are now gullies shut in by sandstone

cliffs, some as much as forty feet high. Gypsy Lane and upper
Sandy Lane, in Watersfield, are good examples of this.

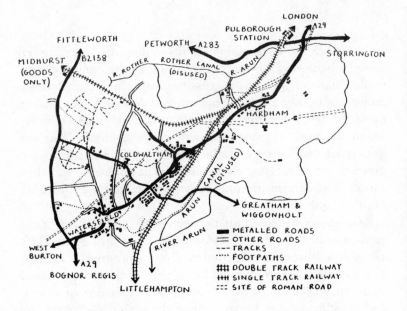

Fig. 1   Coldwaltham: communications

It was largely because of the poor, muddy condition of
the roads that water transport developed. In 1813, the Wey
and Arun Junction Canal Company was formed and it built
the Wey and Arun Junction Canal. The canal was part of
an ambitious scheme to link London and Chatham with
Portsmouth. Of the five stages necessary to achieve such a
goal, three had already been completed by the beginning of
the nineteenth century: the Navigations of the Rivers Thames,
Wey and Arun. With the joining of the two latter Navigations
and the linking of the Arun with Portsmouth via Langstone
Harbour, the waterway would be complete.

In 1785, improvements had been carried out to the Arun
Navigation. A cutting had been built from Hardham Mill,
through Coldwaltham to Greatham Bridge[1], to save three

miles on the old route along the Arun through Pulborough
(nearly four times as long). To make the cutting, £10,000
had been raised. The major obstacle to the works was not,
then, financial; it was physical. Right in the way of the
proposed Coldwaltham cut, rose the ridge with Hardham
Priory on it. To overcome the problem, a wide cutting was
dug, leading to a quarter-mile long tunnel. Barges were
propelled through the tunnel by poles or an endless chain,
or by 'legging'. The boatmen, or 'leggers', lay on boards
projecting from the barges, and pushed with their feet against
the sides or roof of the tunnel. It all sounds highly hazardous
— and it was! The men were advised to "strap themselves
to a short Cord affix'd to the Boat to prevent them being
drown'd" . . . The tunnel is still intact today, although it is
impassable because it is filled with water.

The route taken by the Wey and Arun Canal was up the
Thames to Weybridge, up the River Wey to Shalford, just
above Guildford, then across country by Cranleigh, Alfold
and Loxwood. There, it ran parallel with the Arun until
it joined that river at Pallingham. The canal's course then
coincided with that of the Arun as far as its confluence with
the River Rother, at which point it descended the Rother for
a quarter of a mile, and then cut across country once more.
The object was to save a five-mile journey, which is where
the canal cut across Coldwaltham came in. At the end of the
tunnel near Hardham Priory, the canal struck out across the
Widneys — the brooklands enclosed by the former broad Arun
meander, which has now dried up due to the construction of
the cut—and finally re-joined the mainstream of the Arun near
Watersfield. At Ford, the canal left the Arun again, as the
Chichester Canal, and headed across the plain for Chichester
Harbour, whence the barges proceeded to Portsmouth.

The main wharves on the canal, where 'wharfingers'
controlled the loading, unloading and storage of goods at the
principal distributing points along the Navigations, maintained

---

1 Coldwaltham Lock was the first lock on this stretch of the Arun
Navigation.

ledgers which detailed all the goods concerned, and rents for the use of lime kilns, or for coal, grain, timber and other goods stored on the quaysides. The main wharves south of Guildford were situated at Stonebridge and Godalming on the Wey; at Bramley, Run Common, Elm Bridge (for Cranleigh), Compasses Bridge (for Horsham), Tickners Heath (for Dunsfold) and Loxwood on the Wey and Arun; at Newbridge and Pallingham on the Arun Canal; at Coultershaw (for Petworth and Midhurst) on the Rother, and at Stopham, Coldwaltham, Pulborough, Greatham, Bury, Houghton and Arundel on the Arun.

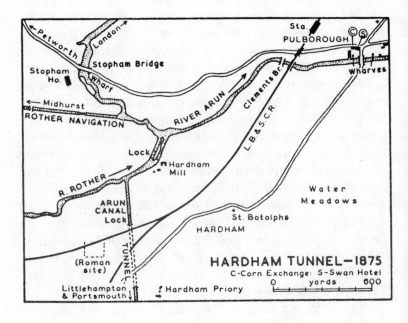

Fig. 2 The River Arun, showing local locks, including Coldwaltham

When the Napoleonic Wars ended in 1815, the main function of the Wey and Arun Canal was to transport coal,

household commodities and agricultural requisites to the
villages of the Western Weald. It was also used to convey,
from Tilbury Docks, the steel girders which in 1869 were
needed for the reconstruction of Greatham Bridge[2]. Canal
barges also brought steel girders up river from Littlehampton
in about 1858, for the construction of the railway viaduct
across the Arun at Pulborough.

Alas for the canal waterway, the Mid Sussex Railway
Line, between Horsham and Petworth, was opened in 1859.
This extended the London, Brighton and South Coast Line,
built from Three Bridges to Horsham in 1848, and, in doing
so, hailed the beginning of the end for the very real usefulness
of the Wey and Arun Canal. Undoubtedly, in its heyday it
was extremely prosperous, but it was impossible to compete
with the more rapid transport of the railway. From 1859,
Pulborough could be reached much more conveniently by rail
than by canal.

Today, the canal tunnel at Hardham, where the Midhurst
Line crosses it, is choked with a mini-mountain of clay
reaching to the very roof. No one seems to know when the
clay was put there, but it was not contemporary with the
construction of the railway, as the canal was still in use then.
An account exists of a barge pleasure cruise along the entire
length of the waterway from the Thames to Littlehampton in
1867 and, although the water in the tunnel was reported to be
shallow, no suggestion was made of a mound of earth within
it. The mound was probably put there at some later date in
order to strengthen the railway track. Certainly, the railway
authorities were worried that their line at that point cleared
the tunnel top by only eight feet.

The first blow to the canal's economic usefulness – the
construction of the Mid Sussex Line – was followed by a
second: the building of the Mid Sussex Junction. This ran

2   Greatham Bridge had previously been re-built in 1839. (The cheapest
estimate had been to re-build in wood.) In 1869, the existing iron span
was inserted by a Mr. Handyside, at a cost of £517. 12s. 6d. (*Sussex
Notes and Queries*, vol. 11; article in the *West Sussex Gazette*, March
1939)

from Hardham to join the existing railway along the south
coast near Ford, thus covering the entire course of the Arun
below Pulborough. In 1865, a branch line was opened from
Horsham to Guildford, coinciding with the course of the
canal between Cranleigh and Guildford. The canal was forced
to close in 1868 and finally became impassable in 1871. The
last barge passed through Hardham Tunnel in 1889, and Arun
Navigation officially closed down in 1896, by Board of Trade
consent.

Most of the line of the canal remains intact. It leaves the
River Wey at Stonebridge, climbing through Bramley and
Cranleigh to the five-mile summit level close to Dunsfold,
where it crosses the Surrey-Sussex watershed 163 feet above
sea level. Winding through Sidney Wood, it descends through
Alfold and Loxwood to Newbridge, then follows the Arun
valley to connect with the river at Pallingham Lock.

Some 23 miles in length, the canal averages a width of
25 feet and a depth of four feet. The locks are twelve feet
wide and about 70 feet long, with an average fall of about
six feet. Originally, there were twenty-six locks, together
with numerous bridges and three aqueducts.

Before the age of the train, the canal took not only goods
traffic but passengers. The toll for a passenger on the Wey and
Arun Canal was three shillings, and on the river Navigations it
cost much less.

It is people — passengers, if you like — who have come
to the aid of the Wey and Arun. In 1970, a few enthusiasts
formed the Wey and Arun Canal Society, and three years
later, with support steadily growing, the society was re-formed
as a Charitable Trust Company — the Wey and Arun Canal
Trust Limited.

The Trust's aim is "to restore as a public amenity . . . the
navigable link between the Rivers Wey and Arun, and so
to re-create the direct water link between London and the
south coast". The Trust believes that restoration is a feasible
proposition despite several difficulties, but, regardless of
whether full navigational status can be achieved, the remains
of the canal should (it believes) be preserved as a public

amenity and a monument to a unique industrial achievement.

The Trust is an entirely voluntary organisation, relying on the support of members and friends as well as on the goodwill of local businesses. It is fortunate in having available the services of volunteer professional engineers to design and supervise its restoration work. Somehow the Trust raises substantial funds for the work it feels committed to carry out. Between 1981 and 1984, for example, over £50,000 was raised for restoration work. The money was raised from activities which still go on—sponsored events, lotteries, and the recycling of waste paper and materials. In Coldwaltham, Miss Doris Cooper is one of the many who continue to house neighbours' great piles of newspapers (in her garage: they have to be tidily roped together!)—all part of the paper-recycling work.

As the loop saved by the Hardham Tunnel cut is navigable, the latter does not feature in the Trust's restoration plans, although the Trust recognises that Hardham Tunnel cut, the only one of its kind on a river navigation, should be preserved.

Moving from waterways to railways once more: the whole Rother Valley was given railway communications in the 1860s. The Petersfield Railway was opened in 1864 between Petersfield and Midhurst, and a rail link between Petworth and Midhurst was forged two years later. Hardham was connected with Ford, and Ford with Littlehampton, in 1863. At that point in time, another little canal—the Rother Canal, from Midhurst to a point just below Stopham—was usurped. Midhurst was connected to Chichester by railway in 1881.

The Mid Sussex Line enjoyed its greatest prosperity around the start of the twentieth century, when passenger services were good between Midhurst and London, and through trains between Victoria and Chichester ran along this route. The freight carried was largely milk and livestock, especially horses to and from the racing studs of the many large estates in the Rother Valley. But this little railway in turn suffered its own ever-tightening stranglehold when road transport was improved. Passenger services on the Chichester

to Midhurst line were withdrawn in 1935, and in 1953 freight
services were withdrawn from the Midhurst-Lavant section
of it, and the track was taken up. The remaining railway,
from Pulborough to Petersfield, was closed in 1955, and
the permanent way was taken up between Petersfield and
Midhurst, although one train a day still ran then between
Pulborough and Midhurst, carrying sugar beet, machinery and
sundry goods. Passenger services between Pulborough, Fittleworth, Petworth, Lodsworth, Midhurst, Elsted, Rogate and
Petersfield were replaced by an hourly Brighton-Petersfield
Southdown bus service — far more frequent than any single-
track railway service could hope to run. Southdown buses
also at that time took the passengers who would have been
carried on the Midhurst-Chichester railway line[3].

The old Mid Sussex Junction became the double-track
main line between London and Bognor Regis, with frequent
train services. The electrifying of the line in 1938 dramatically
reduced train-journey times. All express trains from Bognor,
and from Portsmouth, stopped at Pulborough (most still do)
and, at that time, Pulborough served the Rother Valley and
Storrington with auxiliary bus services.

In 1934, Gatwick Airport was opened to the public. The
enlarged airport was opened in 1958, in which year Gatwick
Airport Station was opened on the site of the old racecourse
station. In the late 1970s and early 1980s, the airport was
considerably developed and improvements, both to the airport
and to the station, have continued to be made non-stop
virtually ever since. From 1980, trains have gone the 23½
miles, 36 chains[4] from Pulborough to the new Gatwick
Airport station and thence as expresses to Victoria. The rail
journey from Gatwick Airport to Pulborough can now take
as little as thirty-five minutes. No wonder more people
working at Gatwick are coming out to rural Coldwaltham to
live! On a 'clear' day, it takes only 1¼ hours to travel from
Victoria to Pulborough — although I remember that, in the

---

3   See Appendix D for details of the old local bus services
4   One chain equals 22 yards

early 1970s, we used to take a 7.10 p.m. train from Victoria (complete with bikes, dog and provisions, as well as children) and arrive at Pulborough for an idyllic weekend away from it all just one hour later, at 8.10 p.m.

Nowadays, West Sussex has a good rail system, with a steady flow of passenger traffic—and Coldwaltham parish has its fair share of commuters *and* regular shoppers. The increase in passenger traffic noted in the late 1950s was a reflection of the county's population increase (11% in the 1970s, compared with a national population increase of only 1%). In fact, between 1976 and 1981, rail passenger traffic on West Sussex lines, excluding Gatwick, grew by more than 5%, compared with a national growth of 2.4%.

British Rail's recent work on the Brighton Line caused several years of engineering hold-ups and passenger aggravation but, since the Brighton works were completed, in 1985, those all seem to be a thing of the past.

Some eight and a half centuries after Stane Street was first recorded in the Domesday Book, the London-Bognor road was improved in the parish. In 1936, a modern by-pass road was built at Coldwaltham, cutting off the two loop roads on either side and diverting fast traffic from them. Another short stretch of road was constructed at Hardham in 1939, turning the loop road containing Hardham Church and some very old houses into the parish's third man-contrived backwater.

Before these improvements, the main road[5]—coinciding with the causeway of Stane Street across the brooklands—was not high enough to escape flooding and, when the river was actually in flood and the road impassable, main traffic had to go over Stopham Bridge to Fittleworth, joining the main road again in Watersfield. Part of the road improvement scheme was to raise the causeway above flood level (1934),

---

5 The main road between London and Bognor Regis, passing through Coldwaltham, became the A29 in 1923. This followed (not exactly swiftly) a comprehensive classification of, and report on, West Sussex roads by the County Surveyor. The roads covered were those which hitherto had been maintained by the parishes through which they ran.

Fig. 3 Pulborough Causeway in flood

and to straighten the bend between the causeway and the bridge by building a new bridge at Pulborough. This was completed in 1936 — so there are now two bridges, side by side, in Pulborough. The old one has been pushed out of use and into decay, and is now little more than a picnic spot (and, alas, a 'black spot' for petty thieves).

Of the other two bridges of relevance to Coldwaltham, Stopham Bridge is outside the parish. However, if there ever had to be a diversion away from this old bridge: for example, through pressure of traffic that might endanger it, traffic tended to be diverted through Coldwaltham. This will no longer be necessary. A new by-pass and bridge across the water meadows north of the old bridge were completed in June, 1986, and the lovely *old* bridge, which is a Scheduled Ancient Monument, will henceforth be preserved for posterity, safe from the constant overweight of cars and lorries.

Hardham Bridge — or, rather, the footbridge that runs beside it across the railway track—is also known as "Barber's Bridge". Mr. Tom Barber was a Coldwaltham Parish Councillor for ten years, and has been Coldwaltham's representative on Horsham District Council way back to the days when it was Chanctonbury Rural District Council. He has spent years waving banners and getting things put right, but at Hardham Bridge he was especially successful. He was worried for the safety of pedestrians crossing the bridge en route from Coldwaltham to Pulborough, or vice versa.[6] Mr. Barber recognised that people crossing that narrow, twisted bridge often did so in peril of their lives. Having persuaded the County Council to consider seriously the erection of a parallel footbridge, he organised a site meeting of parish councillors and county surveyors. Where did he hold the meeting? Bang in the middle of Hardham Bridge! By the time a couple of lorries had crossed the bridge, sending the participants at the meeting scampering in all directions, Mr. Barber had proved his point.

Although the County Council recognised that a footbridge was essential, they did not go overboard on rash expenditure. Having decided they could not afford to buy a new bridge, they located an old one for sale, in Kent, for some £16,000. At midnight one night, the A29 was duly closed, while the new — or, rather, the second-hand — footbridge was brought along by trailers and lowered over the road bridge, into place . . . Alas, it was found to be six feet short and, for a day or so, one end was secure but the other swung slightly into space, until an extension secured it to the other bank. It had been a brave, successful and ultimately complex exercise. The parishioners are unlikely to forget the saga, nor indeed, will the County Council — and both sectors, for their own reasons, will connect it with Tom Barber!

---

6 The fashion to walk that stretch is coming back: on morning (car) runs to Pulborough, I often spy a student with briefcase, a lady with shopping bag, wearing what my neighbour calls 'townie' shoes, and even the odd City-bound gent, twirling his furled umbrella against a background of willows on Pulborough Causeway.

Chapter 5

THE CHURCHES

Of the three churches in the parish, one in each hamlet, Hardham is the oldest, Coldwaltham the largest, with the most social and, perhaps, spiritual influence, and the unpretentious Watersfield Chapel is the smallest place of worship of all three. We will first look at Watersfield Chapel, if only to qualify my comments on its size and humble aspect.

The Toleration Act of 1689 allowed Nonconformists to meet legally for public worship, so long as the place of meeting had been registered with the ecclesiastical authorities or the local magistrates. Whether or not a congregation at Watersfield first met in someone's house, as was often the case in Sussex villages from c.1790 onwards, it is known (the brick above the chapel entrance confirms the date) that in 1823 the Rev. James Edwards, Minister of Petworth Congregational Church, received from the Chichester Archdeaconry the registration for "a certain building newly erected" in Watersfield. Mr. Edwards seems to have been the founding minister of Watersfield Chapel, and one reason for the formation of the chapel might well be gleaned from notes made in 1941 by the late Mr. Snashall, secretary of the Western District of the Sussex Congregational Union, who recorded: "In 1822, two ladies worshipping in Parish Church at Coldwaltham withdrew on ? doctrine, and Ch. in present building founded in 1823 ... The two ladies (Misses Ide) had it built & kept up. After a time, the Chapel closed, but for 1 service a year, to enable the Trustees to claim money left for upkeep."

The past history of the chapel is further outlined in a recent issue of the *Monthly Messenger,* the district magazine of the United Reformed Church. In it, the Rev. Desmond Bending, Pulborough-based minister of that church, and editor of the *Messenger,* printed an extract from *The Sussex and Congregational Magazine,* vol.1, no.8 (August 1894):—

"Petworth — Watersfield: A VILLAGE STATION[1].

"In 1823, long before the Sussex County Association and Home Missionary Society was formed, a little chapel was built at Watersfield by a few Christian friends residing in the place. It was used as a Sunday School during the day and for religious service in the evening. Apparently, the work was for some time carried out under the supervision of 'The Sussex Congregational Society for the Diffusion of Religious Knowledge', since in the fifteenth Annual Report of that Society, presented at the General Meeting, held on September 6th, 1837, in Hanover Chapel, Brighton, the Rev. F. Perkins, of Petworth, reported: 'I visit occasionally the village of Watersfield, and hold a week evening service in the Chapel. Tracts are distributed, and the children are regularly taught on the Lord's Day.' What the members of some of the Congregational Churches at the present time would have thought of the original Watersfield Chapel, it is difficult even to imagine. In 1843, the building was taken down, and a larger Chapel erected: 'Two Services were then held on the Sunday, also a service during the week'. That even this second structure was not luxuriously finished may be inferred from some notes supplied by the Evangelist, who says:— 'In 1890, £35 was spent on repairs and improvements. A boarded floor was put down in the room of bricks, match-boarding placed

---

1 Information on Sussex Churches in the *Congregational Magazine* and *Congregational Year Book* often links Watersfield with Petworth (shown as "Byworth" in the 1851 Year Book, being so known in Nonconformist circles in olden times, because the Congregational cause met at Byworth in the seventeenth century). Ministers named included: John Young (1826 or before to 1831 or 1832), Thomas Wallace (1832 to 1837), Frederick Perkins (1837 to ?), Richard Gould (? to 1851), Henry Rogers (1851 to 1878). Mr. Rogers also had preaching stations at Graffham, Selham, Lodsworth and Northchapel — Watersfield alone remains active today. Mr. J. J. Ingold assisted as Lay Pastor from 1862 to 1910. In the non-parochial Register for Petworth is a note by the Rev. F. Perkins: 'The word Revd. is not affixed to all the names yet it is justly applied to all as to some.' In 1837, he also mentions Lurgashall and Watersfield as village stations connected with Petworth but having no registers. (Mr. Snashall's notes, 1841).

round the walls, and new seats were added instead of the old rickety ones.'

"At the re-opening, the meeting was presided over by W. A. Hounsom, Esq., and the addresses delivered by the Rev. R. Jackson, Messrs. Ingold, Sherrell, and others. At the close, Mr. Jackson made the very gratifying announcement that the whole cost of the alterations had been met.

"The two services are still continued on Sunday. Sunday School is also held and a week evening service. It is evident that other forms of religious activity prevail at Watersfield, since the last report, received some little time ago, mentioned a 'Flower Service', an 'Open-Air Service', and a 'Band of Hope' meeting, at which two Oxford Teachers' Bibles, subscribed for by the Sunday School Children and Members of the Church and Congregation, were presented: one to E. Batty, Esq., 'as a mark of esteem for the kind interest he had taken in the place and service', and the other to the Evangelist, Mr. J. J. Ingold, 'as a mark of their appreciation of his many years of faithful service amongst them'."

Mr. Bending has added notes to this 'history' of the Chapel, which include identification of some of the people mentioned.

"The rebuilding of the Chapel in 1843 incorporated a brick bearing the date, '1823', which still remains above the entrance.

"The boarded floor (laid in 1890) was removed some years ago and the brick floor found underneath. It was taken up and replaced by a solid concrete floor, covered with the vinyl sheeting which is still in use.

"The Rev. F. Perkins and the Rev. R. Jackson were both among the Ministers of the Petworth Congregational Church (founded in 1740), the 'mother' church not only of the village station at Watersfield but also of others at Graffham, Lodsworth and Bedham—all evidently in use in 1894, according to the *Sussex Chronicle* 'intelligence'.

"Mr. J. J. Ingold was an Evangelist employed to serve this group of village stations, under the superintendence of the Minister. Mr. Sherrell was the Evangelist for Pulborough (Mare Hill) and Amberley Chapels, 'out-stations' of the Arundel Congregational Church, whose Minister in 1894 was the Rev. Edwin Legg, A.T.S. The Sussex Congregational Union and Home Missionary Society was formed in the 1830s, its first meetings being at Arundel, a newly-built church."

Structurally, little has happened this century to the chapel, or to its adjoining graveyard. As Mr. Bending admits: ". . . the peculiar roof-shape has not significantly changed in 25 years!" However, kitchen and toilet facilities were added in 1973, to mark the 'triple jubilee' of the first chapel being built.

Administratively, things have changed more. The United Reformed Church Act of 1972 led to the fusion of the Congregational and English Presbyterian Churches into the United Reformed Church. Watersfield Chapel, along with sister churches in the district forming the West Sussex Area Ministry, became part of this Church. The group now consists of congregations at Petworth, Watersfield, Pulborough and Billingshurst, under the care of two Ministers: the Rev. Desmond Bending, Pulborough, and the Rev. Derek Morill, Petworth.

Only one monthly service is now held at Watersfield for members, on the second Sunday, but in 1984 a request from the Rev. Roger Hodgson, Vicar of Coldwaltham Church, to use the chapel for church services, led to an interesting development, in terms of the use and usefulness of the simple little building, with its stark Communion table and *décor,* and hard wooden benches. The vicar asked to have the chapel on the third Sunday in the month, to hold a 'family service', organised, and usually taken, by himself. Now, in addition, on the first Sunday of every month, there is a Sunday Club for children. Both are morning functions.

The economic advantage of renting the chapel is augmented by the purely practical one of having the place 'lived-in' more regularly by people, combating the cold and damp, as well as lightening the chapel's atmosphere.

Mr. Bending's wife, Joan, expresses this need that buildings have for people with simple and charming eloquence in an article reproduced in the November 1985 issue of the *Monthly Messenger:*—

"We all do visiting some time or other to houses and different buildings, and I wonder what reaction you feel on entering a place? Do you feel warmth or a cold atmosphere, or do you feel as I did just recently when asked to pay a visit to a small building beside a very busy road (lots of cars going by but none stopping out of curiosity to see what this little building was all about)?

"When I opened the door, and stood and looked, I found not just an empty, cold building but a friend who was desperately needing help. (Sometimes in our own lives we have come across such a friend, in need of guidance and love, and we are able to help him.) So I just want you to imagine with me this little building, a chapel, as a person. The door was the face, very dirty-looking; the windows were the eyes, that were becoming misty with cobwebs; the organ was the voice, crying, 'If only I could sing again soon!' The floor, the body, looking very tired with the burden it had had put upon it; and the pews, the arms and legs of my imaginary friend whom I saw there.

"Soon we talked together in silent language and, before I knew it, I saw my building friend's face beginning to shine with happiness. The eyes were sparkling bright. The voice was saying, 'I've been reborn. I've come alive again! Oh, how happy my whole body will feel, now that it's freed from its tired-looking state . . .' And the arms and the legs were reaching out for joy.

"Then my building friend invited me to see the kitchen, but had to say, 'Sorry, I can't make you a cup of tea; we haven't any teabags'. (So I looked in my pocket, and had a barley sugar sweet!)

"The time came when I had to leave, and as I looked up I saw my building friend had a picture on the wall—a picture of the other Friend we know and very often need: Jesus, knocking at the door with a lighted lantern in his hand. My building friend and myself seemed to be transformed together as we stood gazing at the picture, with radiance and a glowing feeling inside us both; and on leaving my building friend, I whispered, 'Don't despair. We will come back and make you happy again, and soon to give you a hair-cut (meaning the grass!).

"The moral of this story is that Buildings are like people; they also cannot do without love and affection."

The Christian and, more especially, the ecumenical gain is that both church and chapel have publicly welcomed—in their magazines and elsewhere—mutual participation in all services. The monthly Sunday Club is for *all* children, and there is beginning to be a small, but perceptible, interchange of congregations.

This desire for mutual understanding between the churches is not a new one. At the annual meeting in 1949 (during the Rev. Ronald Chatwin's incumbency), Coldwaltham Parochial Church Council recorded:

"The Vicar was encouraged by the forward thinking of the P.C.C. There had been interesting debates on Liturgical Revision and Anglican/Methodist Unity . . .

"Many resisted change; they had an affection for the old ways, but our spirit, thought and purpose must be renewed, beginning at the heart of Christian worship—the Eucharist."

Fig. 1   Coldwaltham Church—a sketch by Doris Oliver

The Parish Church of Saint Giles, Coldwaltham, is about one mile from Watersfield Chapel — over Lodge Hill, then Church Hill—and in Church Lane, just off the main road.

There was probably a small chapel on the site of the present church in Saxon times, and there are two pieces of evidence to support this theory, both to be found in the leafy churchyard. One is the yew tree, some thirty feet in circumference, reputed to be over 1,000 years old, and one of the twelve oldest in the country. The other is an eleventh-century gravestone recovered from the churchyard, narrow in width but one foot thick, with a cross carved upon it. Thought to have been designed for a royal child, the stone is now in the belfry. The simple stone font in the church might also be Saxon (although its carved wooden cover, suspended from the ceiling above, is Victorian).

Domesday Book lists Waltham (as it was known then) as consisting of nine hundred acres, with one manor of six hides and another of four, but after that date there are no known records of the village until the fourteenth century.

However, there is fairly conclusive evidence that the parish church, then having only Nave, Chancel, South Aisle

Fig. 2 Measuring the girth of the yew tree in the churchyard

and Porch, was constructed in the early thirteenth century. Apart from the fashion of its architecture, this was the period of a great Norman building drive, and is when the main fabric of St. Mary's Parish Church, Pulborough, and the lower part of the Priest's House, opposite Coldwaltham Church, on the other side of the road, were both built.

Of the medieval church, only the original Early English tower remains more or less as it was, with a topmost portion in wood — although the tower's shingled turret is of a much later date. It is no doubt especially on account of the tower that the church is included in Chanctonbury Rural District's list of buildings of special architectural or historic interest. This list was compiled (countrywide) by the Minister of Housing and Local Government "in pursuance of Section 30 of the Town and Country Planning Act of 1947", which regarded the church — in this context — as being charitable property.[2]

In the booklet, *A Short History of the Parish and Church of St. Giles, Coldwaltham,* by Marjorie Hessell Tiltman, recently revised and shortened by the present vicar as *A Short History of St. Giles, Coldwaltham,*[3] there is a useful description of the part that St. Giles' Church, in common with every other country parish church, would have played as "the heart and hub of all the social life in the village—not from Sunday to Sunday, but from day to day.

> "Local business would have been discussed in the nave, laws and customs framed, disagreements thrashed out.
> "At proper times and seasons, there would be pageants or modest festivals, perhaps the performance of a miracle play or a morality by a travelling company. These could be enacted inside or outside, according to the exigencies of the weather, or of the play itself.
> "In the churchyard, the men might practise their archery

---

2 The effect of the church being included in this list is that, if the building ceased to be used for 'ecclesiastical purposes', it will be an offence to "demolish, alter or extend it in such a way as to seriously affect its character, without first giving two months' written notice to the local planning authority".
3 *A Short History of St. Giles, Coldwaltham,* 20p, from the church

without disrespect; the youths play Fives against the walls and buttresses; mothers put their children to play in safety.

"Somewhere conveniently to hand would be a yard for the brewing of ales to pay for the repairs to the [church] fabric, which were as annoying and common a necessity in those days as in our own. And standing as it did on a road that had been in constant use for a thousand years or more, the church would certainly have been forced to erect a modest lodging house for the pilgrims who were so frequent a feature of the Middle Ages."

It could be significant that the church's patron saint, Saint Giles, is the Patron Saint of the halt, the maimed and the blind—and that Saint Botolph, Patron Saint of Hardham Church, a mile along the road, is the Patron Saint of Travellers.

In 1349, the Black Death reached England, and its effects on the labour situation must have contributed to the drastic changes in social conditions and terms of employment. The text of the church booklet suggests, rightly, that "the role of a parish church and its priest in those hard and troublous times must have been a supremely difficult one, for the Middle Ages saw great changes of thought in theological matters, not only in the seats of the high but those of the lowly. Henry VIII could not have imposed his sweeping changes on a wholly unwilling or rebellious people: in many cases, inclination had preceded them."

It was Thomas Cromwell who ordered the keeping of parish registers: a sensible step but, couched in the language of officialdom, it was difficult for both priests and their congregations to understand. In 1547, Edward VI was forced to renew the order. Even then, it was not heeded properly, and the order was once again renewed by Elizabeth I.

Parish records form one of the most important classes of historical document in existence. As local records of a public nature, they are required as evidence in legal and administrative business and, containing as they do much information that is unique, they provide vital information for the writing of English history.[4]

Saint Giles' was as remiss as most small country churches, but at least its marriage registers go back as far as 1561, and those for burial go back to 1572, and for baptisms, to 1594.

All these records, except for the very latest, are deposited in the County Archives at Chichester, but anyone can inspect them on request.

Among the many old houses in Coldwaltham, there must be those whose sixteenth-century inhabitants would have contributed to the parish's first records.

Local wills, however, could not be treated with the same sort of casualness. The frequency with which St. Giles' is mentioned in them suggests its importance in the community.

"Usually the bequest is meticulously specified. For example, in 1534 Richard Brayly left:

" 'To every Lyght in the church of Waltham 1jd.' (viz., 2d., a sum equivalent to 10s. in our present currency).[5]

"And in January of the following year, Robert Downall of Eartham bequeathed:

" '. . . to the church of Waltham a kowe to be ordred yn lyke manner aforesayde, viz, hawlfe the reintte to the vycar, he to say dyrege and masse yerelye for my soule, and the other halffe to the bedrolle to be prayde for.'

" 'Reparacions' to altar, images and lights were often mentioned, but there were practical depostions to remind us of the primitive country roads of those days, such as the will of Richard Bacheler on August 1st, 1550:

" 'I will to have x lodes of gravyll to be layed in Waltham Street.' "

The following century's religious and political dissensions caused damage and neglect to all ecclesiastical institutions. Thus, there are numerous omissions in the history of most churches at that period, and Saint Giles' is no exception. One custom did, however, persist, and the documents relating to it bring the parish vividly to life. The documents in question are the Presentments, or reports, of the Churchwardens. In the sixteenth century, these were mainly concerned with the maintenance of the church fabric, such as the renewal of roof-tiles, and repair of the bell-frame and to the pews.

In the seventeenth century, however, they become more

---

4 which includes the writing of parish histories such as this one, for which the records of Coldwaltham Parish Church have provided a valuable source of reference
5 as in 1965, when Marjorie Hessell Tiltman's *Short History* first appeared

personal, and the new freedom which the Reformation
had brought with it seems to have encouraged some frank
criticism, for both congregation and minister.

In 1622, the churchwardens of Saint Giles', reporting to
the 'Midhurst Deanrye', wrote that:

> "Hee [the minister] doth catechise and some cometh and
> some are obstinate and will not; whereof James Mose is one,
> therefore we present him for his obstinacy and peremptoriness in
> that poynt ..."

In the Lord Bishop's 'Visitacion Billes' of the same year,
the churchwardens are even more explicit:

> "There is Roger Brookfield and Thomas Smyth, alehows-
> keepers, which due keepe resort in the tyme of divine service",

the sobering sequel to which adds an even more human touch:

> "Also we present Thomas Smyth and Roger Brookfield for
> that they did give us the churchwardens evill speeches, (because
> we did present them), the next Sabbath after they were presented,
> in the churchyard, in the presence of most of the parishioners."

Then, their zeal turns to the minister:

> "We present our minister because he doth not say prayers in
> due tyme; for sometymes we have noe prayer upon the Sabbath
> Day."

The seventeenth century was a troubled time for both
Church and State, and it is not surprising that the parish
registers were constantly broken at this period and, indeed,
until the end of the century.

Lists of recusants, or individuals excommunicated for mis-
behaviour or immorality, during this period have a prominent
place in the Presentments. There are also complaints of a lack
of Bibles — of great significance then, for Bible study was a
much-prized part of religious practice, as well as of general
education. Evidence is recorded, too, of a slightly resentful
attitude towards the parson's old-fashioned style of dress:

> " ... our minister doth not wear a nightcap of black silke,
> satin or velvet, as prescribed in the 74 canon, but weareth a
> wrought [embroidered] nightcap, contrary to the order set down
> in that canon."

The general effect of such petty squabbles and dissension
was destructive to the church itself, and in 1664 a sad little

paragraph reports that "our church was gone to decay, but is now in repayring".

How much repair work was undertaken at that time is not on record, but, in 1724, a great Church Inspection Book was compiled, in which Coldwaltham is described as follows:—

"St. Giles, Cold Waltham. The name of the Incumbent: Mr. Luffe of Bury. Condition of church: A Steeple a little out of repair. Book good; Chest, a silver Chalice with cover and Linen Cloth, good 3 Bells. The Chancell: Chancell out of repair belongs to Thos Knolles. No Mansion House. Families 26. No Papists nor Protestant Dissenters. Divine service uncertain. Sacrament 3 times a year, communications [communicants] about 12. No glebe."

It is possible that, as a result of the above report, the Chancel was then largely rebuilt, although it seems clear that the original piscina, sedilia, and niche for the aumbry (near the altar) were retained. This could have been the time when the old steeple was replaced by the present shingled turret and, certainly, many of the pews in the Nave were made during the eighteenth century.

However, the report on Cold Waltham painted a depressing picture of the decay of both church and hamlet. By the nineteenth century, St. Giles' was in a sad state of dilapidation and, although an organ was installed in the church in 1820, a public appeal had to be launched in 1846 to raise funds. Of the parish, the printed appeal form said:—

"Its clergyman receives £56 per annum: made up of £20, allowed as a Stipend by the Tithe Owners, and £36, arising from grants made by the Governors of Queen Anne's Bounty.

"Its population is upwards of 500; all of whom, with few exceptions, are poor agricultural labourers.

"It is without a School House, and consequentially without either a weekly or Sunday school in connexion with the Church.

"It is without a Residence for the Clergyman, who is obliged to live at a considerable distance from his Church and People.

"It is without sufficient Church Accommodation, which obliges the Labourers to crowd into the Chancel, sitting on forms and the Altar Step, to the destruction of all appearance of worship, and even of common reverence and decency.

"Under the express sanction of the Lord Bishop of the Diocese [the parish was held by Letters of Sequestration from the Lord Bishop], it is proposed to endeavour to raise funds, in order to remedy these evils."

Her Majesty the Dowager Queen (Anne) herself donated £20, and the Lord Bishop gave £20, but quite obviously the villagers were too poor to help much.

However, the appeal—launched by Rev. James Sandham, vicar of Coldwaltham for 51 years—must have been successful, for, with the money that came in, the first Vicarage (now called Stane House) was built, in Church Lane, where also the School House (the old part of the present school) was built. The church itself was enlarged considerably by the addition of the North Aisle, an organ chamber and the vestry, all of which were consecrated in 1870. The Incorporated Society for the Building of Churches helped with this building scheme, which allowed the church from then on, according to a notice in the belfry, to hold 230 people "at the very least".

The church was truly transformed during that era, for enlargement of it was complemented by extensive renovation. New black, yellow and red floor tiles were laid throughout, the Chancel was decorated, and a wooden Chancel screen was erected. New choir stalls, too, were made, as well as covers for the font inside the church and the well in the south-east corner of the churchyard. The well itself was built at that time:

> "The church was restored in 1870, and water is (in 1925, still) so scarce in Coldwaltham that, rather than fetch it for the purpose, in elaborate instalments from the river, a well was sunk in the churchyard—a most unusual state of affairs." [6]

On the well, but some years later, were inscribed the following lines, written by a Coldwaltham poet, William Hersee[7]:—

> *"This sacred well, sunk deep in holy ground*
> *Gravely cries out to every passer-by*
> *Think of the holy dead who sleep around*
> *And by well-doing prepare thyself to die."*

The painted glass windows in the church were also mainly installed in the late nineteenth century. Those in the South Aisle represent St. John the Baptist, the Annunciation, and two Nativity scenes showing the Shepherds and the Kings. There is also a small west window in the porch depicting Christ as a Shepherd. The windows in the North Aisle illustrate the Last Supper, the Agony in the Garden and the Way of the Cross; and high up at the West end, there is a small window of the Resurrection and the Ascension, and the 'Te Deum' window over the altar shows Christ reigning in Heaven. Christ is also represented in the lamb, figured between ten angel-musicians on the Victorian stone reredos.

In spite of all the work done to the church, including many improvements, while Mr. Sandham was vicar of Cold-waltham, the Victorian decoration of the Chancel was found to be oppressive by a later generation. In 1957, the Chancel was restored to its original simplicity, except for the reredos and windows. During this restoration work, an ancient doorway was uncovered, on the South side of the Chancel, believed to lead to the Priest's House across the road. In 1970, the Victorian Chancel screen was removed, in keeping with liturgical practice at the time.

After the two World Wars, memorials to those killed on active service were placed in the South Aisle, and dedicated in 1953 by Bishop Bell of Chichester. Although, for this reason, it is commonly known as the Memorial Chapel, it was the original Lady Chapel.

The North Aisle was dedicated in honour of Holy Wisdom by the Rt. Rev. Colin Docker, Bishop of Horsham, in 1984.

---

6   from *Sequestered Vales of Sussex* by John B. Paddon

7   The popularity of the poet, Robert Burns, in England just as much as in Scotland, led to a great spate of verse-outpourings by people in humble walks of life. To this group belonged William Hersee. Born in Coldwaltham on February 12th, 1786, the son of Richard, a wheel-wright and small farmer, and Elisabeth, he was taught by the local schoolmistress. He left school to help his father with the ploughing and other work. In his lifetime, much of it spent away from the parish, he wrote two volumes of verse, one in three editions, and was patronised for many years by Hayley, the famous Sussex poet, who, when Hersee met him at the beginning of the nineteenth century, was one of the most distinguished men of letters in England. For 21 years, until his death in 1852, Hersee was editor of the *Warwick and Warwickshire Advertiser and Leamington Gazette:* not a particularly romantic post for a poet, but no doubt this career was dictated by the need to support a wife and ten children.

Anyway, at least he is immortalised in Coldwaltham Churchyard's well.

*Fig. 3   Bishop Bell dedicating the Memorial Chapel, assisted by the
Vicar of Coldwaltham, the Rev. Eric Newcombe*

Although such a dedication is common in the Orthodox
Church, this is believed to be the only Anglican place of
worship dedicated to Holy Wisdom, and represents 'The
House of Wisdom' as her dwelling among mankind.[8] The
painting of Natural Wisdom, at the West end of the Chapel,
shows Wisdom surrounded by 'elemental spheres', illustrating
her role as God's purpose, or plan, for Creation; while the
picture above the altar, placed there by the present vicar,
depicts her on her throne in Heaven. The Cross below the
picture symbolises the Spiritual Word which is 'implanted'
in men when she reveals God's purpose to them and, in the
Rev. Roger Hodgson's words, "usually takes the form of a
divine imperative to fulfil that purpose".

8   Book of Proverbs 9.i

The dedication of the Chapel of Holy Wisdom marked an important stage in the development of Coldwaltham Church.

The most recent improvement to the church has been to its bells; work was completed in 1983. The bell-frame (classified as Type H by George Elphick in his book, *Sussex Bells and Belfries*) is one of the oldest in England, and the second-oldest in Sussex. Of the three bells, the two smaller ones — the treble and the second — are 24 inches and 27¾ inches in diameter, respectively, and are uninscribed. They are thought to be the work of John Langhorne, who was first mentioned in the City of London records in 1379, and was buried at St. Michael's, Cornhill, in 1406. Thus, the bells would have been cast between these dates.

The third, tenor, bell, 29½ inches in diameter, is inscribed

THOMAS HUNTER   JOHN HALE   1665   CHURCHWARDENS

It was cast by William Purdue and his grandson, Roger. Originally from Closworth and Salisbury, they had a foundry at Chichester, and during 1665 and 1666 they cast at least eleven known bells in West Sussex, including two at Chichester Cathedral.

Fig. 4   Coldwaltham bells, re-hung in 1950

The frame shows that there was an earlier treble bell, because the lip marks cut out of the braces of the trusses, to allow the bell to swing, are for a bell which was some 5½ inches longer than the present one. This was presumably a recasting of the original late thirteenth century treble, lending support to the earlier dating of the tower.

All the bells were re-hung by Mears & Stainbank in 1950 in traditional fashion, using elm headstocks, metal straps and plain bearings. At that time, they were also quarter-turned. General maintenance work and some carpentry work had to be carried out but, fortunately, the bells were able to remain in place, although they had to have their weight supported while the work was done.

Here I shall interrupt a rather long, but hopefully absorbing, account of St. Giles' Church to consider the *people* associated with it. Of these, of course, there have been thousands, and we know from the sad state of affairs before the Rev. James Sandham took things in hand, that not too many people in the past could substantially help, at least in a material way, in church affairs; and people seemed to have little impetus or guidance to lend spiritual support, either.

It must have been shattering to everybody, then, when the Rev. Sandham arrived on the scene, and his achievements over his amazing fifty-one-year incumbency have already been listed—at least in terms of church improvements.

A fitting memorial to James Sandham and his wife, Ann, was the building in 1902 of the Sandham Hall, not far from the church, which is very much the centre of community life in the parish.

The Rev. Frederick C. Clarke was also vicar for a very long period— from 1917 to 1949. In 1919, he handwrote a *Table of Fees for the Parish of Coldwaltham*, which gives an idea of just how prices have risen (Fig. 5).

When the vicar retired, a pamphlet went round to all parishioners and friends, worded:—

VICAR'S RETIREMENT FUND

The Churchwardens and Parochial Church Council feel sure that you would like to express your regard for the Vicar and Mrs.

Clarke's thirty-two years of service to the Parish of Cold Waltham and Watersfield. Will you kindly put your gift in the accompanying envelope.

The resulting gift and a lectern, in oak, commemorated Mr. Clarke's service, which ended with the Clarkes retiring and moving away from the district.

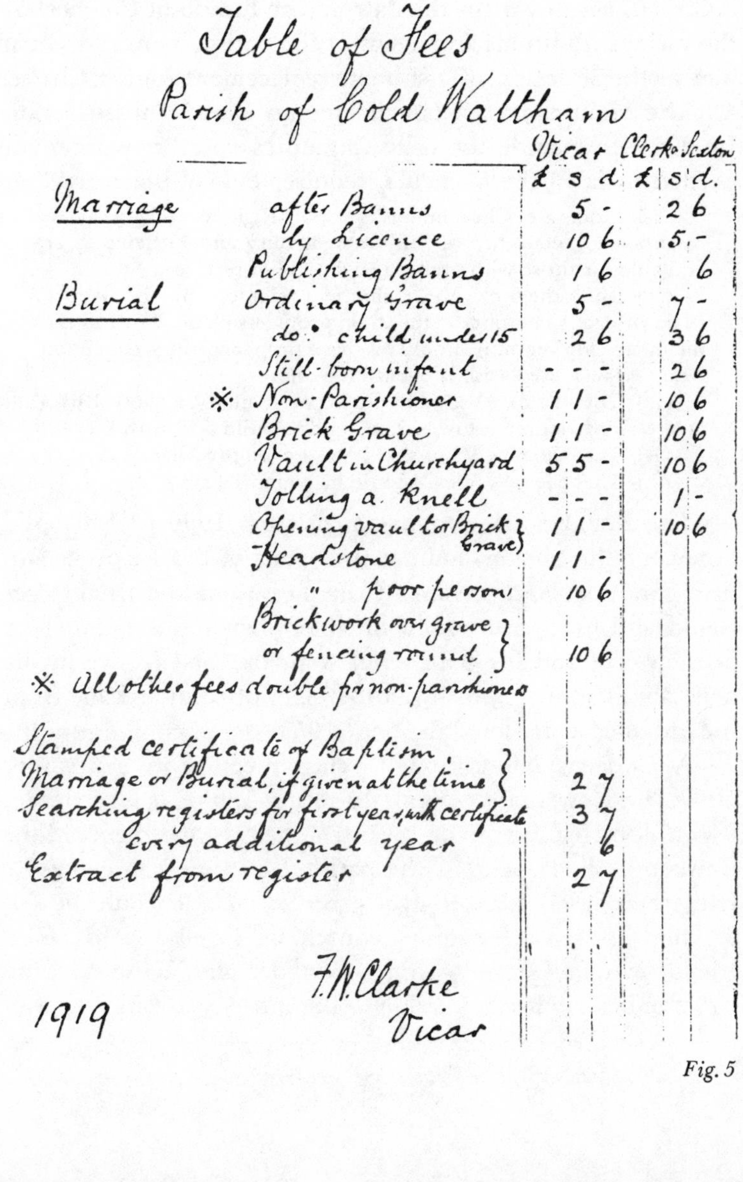

Table of Fees
Parish of Cold Waltham

		Vicar			Clerk & Sexton		
		£	s	d	£	s	d
Marriage	after Banns		5	-		2	6
	by Licence		10	6		5	-
	Publishing Banns		1	6			6
Burial	Ordinary Grave		5	-		7	-
	do.º child under 15		2	6		3	6
	Still-born infant		-	-		2	6
✻	Non-Parishioner		1 1	-		10	6
	Brick Grave		1 1	-		10	6
	Vault in Churchyard		5 5	-		10	6
	Tolling a Knell		-	-		1	-
	Opening vault or Brick } Grave)		1 1	-		10	6
	Headstone		1 1	-			
	" poor person		10	6			
	Brickwork over grave } or fencing round }		10	6			

✻ All other fees double for non-parishioners

Stamped certificate of Baptism, Marriage or Burial, if given at the time }		2	7
Searching registers for first year, with certificate		3	7
every additional year			6
Extract from register		2	7

1919

F.W. Clarke
Vicar

Fig. 5

Now, decided the Parochial Church Council, perhaps was the time for a different kind of vicar, without implying criticism of the good and faithful service of Mr. Clarke. But two long incumbencies had meant two ultimately elderly vicars . . .

'Rights of Presentation' allowed the churchwardens and P.C.C. to set down for the Patron (the Bishop of Chichester) the various traditions and needs of the parish, in order to help him in the selection of a suitable replacement for Mr. Clarke.

The Minutes of a Council meeting dated Thursday, 9th June, 1949, include the following notes on a "new vicar . . . needed to fulfil the particular requirements of the Parish":—

(i) Moderate Churchmanship, not High, especially as the neighbouring churches of Pulborough, Bury and Fittleworth are available for those who prefer a High type of service.

(ii) That the new Vicar should preferably not be over 40 years of age, since one of the main problems of the Parish is that the many children in it should receive a proper spiritual education. Also, because the Parish is a scattered one.

(iii) That the new Vicar should be, particularly, a good 'Parish' man, willing to do a lot of visiting, and to build up Parish life.

(iv) That the new Vicar should be a good preacher.

(v) That the new Vicar should be a married man.

The Rev. Eric Newcombe, vicar from 1950 to 1967, did not meet the above requirements exactly, but he proved to be a good, devoted servant of the parish, and he tried to get round and meet everybody on their own terms as much as possible. He and his wife, Eve, were the first to live in the newly-built vicarage, on the other side of Church Lane from the old one,[9] completed in about 1951.

At a Parochial Church Council meeting in September 1967, Mr. Newcombe—about to retire—spoke, it is recorded, "with deep feeling of the seventeen happy years he and Mrs. Newcombe had spent in the parish. The time had come, he felt, when he could no longer carry on. But it would be sad for him to leave the quiet church he loved and his good friends who had stood by him so wonderfully." However, the Newcombes did leave; retiring to Barnham, near Chichester.

---

9   See also Chapter 6, *Landmarks and Features*

It was agreed that a plaque should be placed in Cold-waltham Church to mark Mr. Newcombe's years of service, although initially this plan met with problems. At the time, obtaining a Faculty (Church permission) for a plaque was difficult, since plaques were then being discouraged. Notwithstanding, Mr. Newcombe's memorials in the church are a plaque, a Lectern Bible, and red priest's vestments, given by Mrs. and Miss Newcombe.

One of the things he is most gratefully remembered for is the Sanctuary Guild, founded during his time as vicar, and still flourishing vigorously today. The guild is described at length further on in this chapter.

During Mr. Newcombe's incumbency, one Faculty that appears to have been granted without problems was to place on the south wall of the Nave a bronze tablet in memory of John Edgar Braham. A Churchwarden from 1952 to 1959, Mr. Braham threw himself with great vigour into his work in this capacity. One of his principal *bêtes noires* was the absence of adequate and suitable heating in the church and, after long discussions and experiments, it was found that the form of heating most likely to prove effective in the church was low-temperature 'comfort heating', provided by tubular elements installed at floor level in the pews.

At a Council meeting in September 1953, Mr. Braham reported that the "new electrical heating system was now working . . . the time clocks had still to be installed and . . . the humming noise, which was very annoying, would be stopped as soon as a new choke had been installed! Mr. Braham thought that the main door needed draught prevention to improve the efficiency of the heating system and also that some carpeting over the grille in the floor during weekends would further assist towards this end. Mr. Braham said that there would be a meeting of the Finance Sub-Committee early in the New Year to consider how the Bank Loan to complete the financing of the heating system could be wiped off."

Obviously a devoted servant of the church and its congregation, and a practical and realistic man, Mr. Braham, with his wife, Evelyn, would have been remembered with

special affection and gratitude in the All Souls Day Requiem
in 1959, along with all those others listed, many of whom
had served the community selflessly over a long period.

REQUIEM   ALL SOULS DAY 1959

Ellen Besant
Alfred Besant
Julia Grace Austin
Roy Vickers Bardsley
Dorothy Baker
Harold Colwell
Sarah Cheesman
Samuel Cheesman
Lucy Carter
Irene Cocks
George John Charman
Tilliard Horace Collins
Charles Cooper
Walter Connor
Thomas James Dabell
Violet Annie Dabell
Annie Mary Greaseley
Arthur Greaseley
Sarah Powell
Mary Ellen Dalton
Mabel Dalton
Harold Goring Dalton
Percy Nugent Dalton
Horace Goble
Alice Gilbert
Christopher Harris
Florence Ellen Ingham
Raymond Edward Johnson
Edward Johnson
William Milne
Emile Milne
Arthur Newcombe
Emma Margaret Frere Newcombe
Thomas Puttick
Dora Peel
Amelia Pethick
Charles Rowland
Alice Rowland
Lucy Woodhouse Shedden
Duncan Shedden

Dorothy Roberts
Brian Wild
Peter Wild
Helen Evelyn Braham
John Edgar Braham
Newell Long. P.
Percy Nash. P.
Arthur Duncan Jones. P.
Arthur Amor. P.
Frederick Charles Clark. P.
Edward Secomb
Charles Secomb
Kate Cooper
Charles Chanter
Jessie Pope
Maud Cox
Winifred Jackson
Ernest Vivian Clare
Helena Shelton
Elsie Shelton
Alan Shelton
Lilian Helena Shelton
Alfred John Percy Booker
Eli Entiknapp
Amy Entiknapp
Cicily Mary Shackleton
Alfred Carter
Beatrice Alice Chanter
Ellen Parker
Alice Gregory
Agnes Mayhall
Annie Maria Dabell
William Blackman. P.
Nora Emily Green
Christian Harry MacLachlan

Florence Harley
Sybil Murdoch

(P. denotes Priest)

Once more the Parish Church Council recorded, at a meeting in October 1967, "the sort of vicar who should next be appointed". He was to be young, married, "with a wife who will interest herself in, and supplement, the work and influence of her husband in Parochial activities". The new vicar should possess "the energy and keenness to make regular visits to the homes of his parishioners – in a parish ... scattered ... with a population increased by recent housing developments". (Arun Vale and Silverdale). There were then only 90 on the Electoral Roll, out of 700, and there were only 45 regular churchgoers.

The new vicar should not be High Church. And he should take an active interest in the school, making full use of the opportunities for religious instruction. "A special effort is needed," it was recorded, "to reach the non-churchgoers, particularly the youth of the parish."

And someone should be chosen who would "lead improvements to the Sandham Hall" . . .

At last, the Council appear to have got their way, with the appointment, in April 1968, of the Rev. Ronald Chatwin. The previous February, he had expressed himself "keen to come", and the Council were very keen to have him.

Dover-born, Ronald Chatwin came to Coldwaltham after four years as Priest-in-Charge of St. Elizabeth's Church, Northgate, Crawley. Young, and married, with two small daughters, he soon proved not only popular, anxious to 'mix' and get to know people, but determined to get things done. In 1968, the new Service of Communion was introduced into Coldwaltham Church by Mr. Chatwin, and he soon won the support of his parishioners, reflected in, among other things, an increase in the number of Communicants:—

1967	1529	(including 61 on Easter Day)
1968	1562	(including 57 on Easter Day)
1969	(first four months only)	
	921	(including 132 on Easter Day)

In the Minutes of a Parochial Church Council meeting held in April, 1970, Mr. Chatwin was praised by Mr. John Boxford, in his capacity as one of the churchwardens, for "his inspiring leadership and for the programme he had arranged to celebrate the 750th anniversary of the church." (This included a garden party at the school, held on July 8th, 1970, and a Church Service on October 11th, followed by supper at Coldwaltham House.)

That same month of April, a Conference of the Parochial Church Council was led by the then Bishop of Horsham, the Right Rev. Simon Phipps.

The next Council meeting's Minutes record:—

> The Bishop finally said that 'the Church was slow to throw off its ancient shackles. The Church's members, buoyed up by their faith, must help to renew its influence by *a return to the ways of the early Christians:—* meeting in groups including non-churchgoers; helping others; entering into social activities' . . . He was glad to hear of the ways in which St. Giles' Church members were active.

During Ronald Chatwin's incumbency, the church screen was removed: perhaps another expression of his desire to communicate directly. One more example was his keenness to get the Brownies well and truly flourishing as a Pack again, and he and his wife Yvonne involved themselves in the activities of numerous community groups and clubs.

Perhaps his main community achievement was persuading John Boxford to form the Wild Brooks Society, to protect local amenities and get together local residents on a regular basis, and happily, using the Sandham Hall as a base.[10]

There are many ways in which people can actively serve their church and parish: by helping regularly at services, as churchwarden, sidesman, lay reader, organist, or choir member; or by volunteering to serve on the Parochial Church Council. Those who attend services and nothing more also, of course, support the church, as well as benefiting themselves.

In recent decades, Coldwaltham has had a goodly band of church people. Many spend hours every week involving themselves in all kinds of tasks, often menial, without complaint. (This almost eradicates the wretched memories of neglect and apathy shown by parishioners in times gone by.)

10 See also Chapter 8, *Community Life*

Many names spring easily to mind. Ian and June MacArthur (he was a churchwarden for many years; she was a choir member and secretary of the P.C.C.); Jack and Madeleine Harding (he is a choir member and former churchwarden; she is the present verger of Coldwaltham Church, with all the duties, seen and unforeseen, that that entails), and the Llewhellin sisters . . .

Edna Llewhellin ran the Village Help Scheme, described later in the book, so here I will just consider Nora Llewhellin. From 1972, when Mr. Lugmayer, a former churchwarden, presented a duplicator to the church council for the parish magazine, until 1984, Nora cut the stencils for the magazine. Mr. Ted Hibbert edited the magazine during the Interregnum after the Rev. Chatwin's departure, then he handed over to Nora, who not only edited, but typed the stencils for the magazine for nearly ten years. She has been a member of the church choir for more years than she can remember. She also organises the Sanctuary Guild, started in the early 1950s, by the Rev. Eric Newcombe, with just twelve women. Their jobs then, as now (but now with over 20 members to do them), were to keep the church brasses not just cleaned, but sparkling, and to arrange the church's flowers, making sure they were watered and fresh until the next two arrangers' turn. Mrs. Newcombe was the first secretary of the Sanctuary Guild. A monthly meeting of the Guild was, in her day, held in church, and the vicar took a shortened Evensong Service to precede it. Members then discussed the rota and other plans for the ensuing few weeks.

This arrangement has changed little, except that the Guild now meet only quarterly—sometimes in church, sometimes in members' own homes, but always with a devotional opening led by the vicar. Members pay a small quarterly subscription to help meet the cost of flowers which have to be bought when there is a shortage of garden supplies, and cleaning materials for the brasses.

Since Roger Hodgson became vicar (in November 1982), arrangements have been made (again with the help of stalwarts like the Llewhellin sisters) for the church to remain open for

Fig. 6   The altar at Coldwaltham Church, decorated for Harvest Festival
(Ann Hogben)

two or three days at festival seasons, such as Christmas, Easter and Harvest, when the church is markedly resplendent from end to end, altar to font, and niche to niche. It is always decorated by members of the Sanctuary Guild, sometimes with co-opted helpers.

All of this is still inspired by Nora Llewhellin, despite her recent retirement. But it is perhaps as a person—smiling, encouraging and always loving—that we see her most clearly.

Another representative of the parish's practical and caring (I emphasise, only one among the many) is John Boxford.

For thirty-six years, until he retired as churchwarden in 1984, John Boxford had served the parish in ways too many to number. Almost as soon as he and his wife, Peggy, and family moved to the parish in 1948, he was called upon (and was delighted to accept) to become secretary of the Parochial Church Council, and he remained in that job for eleven years.

The Boxfords occupied then (they now live in West Burton) an old house called 'Wildbrooks', overlooking the beauty spot of the same name. Appropriately, it was he who, in 1972, founded the Wildbrooks Society.[11]

In 1959, he was appointed a churchwarden, and he remained one, first, for twelve years. From this position, he stressed the need for church members to be active "in these difficult times" (1971), and urged support of the vicar (then, Mr. Chatwin) in his encouragement of house Communion groups, which still flourish in the parish today. Mr. Boxford's urging, on this score, was recorded in the P.C.C. Minutes of a meeting in March 1971, in which it was revealed that the number of Communicants during 1970 had been 2118—183 down on the previous year.[12]

When, in 1971, John Boxford stepped down as church-warden, it was recorded (at that same March 1971 meeting) that the vicar "could not speak too highly of his [Mr. Boxford's] constant self-denying work for the church he greatly loved . . . his enthusiasm never flagged. During the

11 See Chapter 8, *Community Life*
12 The number of Communicants rose in 1971, by 254 to 2372.

time the Rev. Newcombe was failing in health, and while the interregnum was in progress, he kept the ship afloat ... " (John Boxford will have liked that nautical expression, having been a Navy man.)

But they would not let him go. In 1980, he was asked to serve again as churchwarden with Ian MacArthur, when Jack Harding relinquished that position. In all, he was a church-warden for sixteen years, under six vicars!

Foundation Manager of St. James' Church of England School from 1967, he has been Chairman of the School Governors for the last four years.

Strange (perhaps not to those who know him well) that, amid his many time-consuming and exacting responsibilities, his favourite task was organising a team of grass-cutters for the churchyard. In shirt sleeves and distinctive peaked cap, he was a familiar sight on summer evenings, wielding a mower peacefully, but with dexterity.

He took over the grass-cutting duties from Charles Cousens, another remarkable church man. A slate memorial tablet on the church's north wall, at the entrance to the belfry, is touchingly inscribed:—

REMEMBER
with gratitude the
life, humour & works of
CHARLES COUSENS
1898 − 1982
for 30 years verger of this church,
caretaker of the Sandham Hall,
& in whose memory the church bells
have been repaired.

This thoughtful wording produced exactly the right epitaph for 'Charlie Cousens', much loved, loving and caring for 'his' church, constant — and funny.

Members of the remarkable Neale family are commemor-ated in Coldwaltham Church, and repose in its churchyard. Their story is too complex and too interesting to whittle down in this context, however, and we have given Mrs. Valerie Wheeler, a descendant, more space to tell that story later in the book.[13]

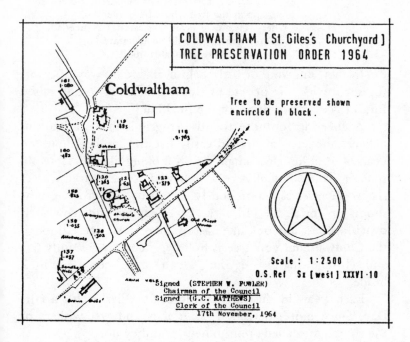

Fig. 7   Tree Preservation Order on Coldwaltham yew tree

Still out in the leafy churchyard, we soon become aware of the ancient yew tree, reputed to have been planted in King Ethelred's reign. Here again, Coldwaltham's parishioners, along with ex-parish lovers of the church and its yew tree, showed both their caring and their practical sides a few years ago, when the tree — protected by a 1982 Tree Preservation Order — was found to be in great need of a tree surgeon. The one who estimated for, and ultimately carried out, the work, Mr. Derry Watkins, of Colgate, Horsham, found much that needed doing . . .

---

13   See Chapter 9, *In Living Memory*

" 1 large Yew — Raise lower canopy over private drive, to give
          clearance to high vehicles, retaining a good overall
          shape to the tree.
                Prune back crown lightly over church roof to
          clear. Nothing too severe is required, otherwise
          the shape of the tree would be spoiled.
                Where clearance over gravestones is needed, a
          minimum pruning would be adequate.
                Clean out hollow central trunk."

In fact, knowing of little help available by way of grants
for such work, the people of Coldwaltham set to and raised
funds to cover two-thirds of the final bill.[14]

A cheering footnote to this struggle is that Mr. Watkins
believes the yew tree could easily live for another thousand
years, for, although it might go on looking like the same old
tree, it would actually be a 'renewed' one. Old yew trees
renew themselves continuously, it seems, by growing new
shoots up inside the old bark. These expand and grow their
own branches, and look like part of the original tree. Although
the Coldwaltham yew tree is hollow, then, it has a 'fully live
and self-renewing outside rim', which can be seen if you look
inside.

Each year, in the early autumn, St. Giles' holds a Gift
Day. Once more, parishioners, friends and well-wishers of
the church are called upon to help, and they do.

A recent, typical, Gift Day letter, 'To Whom It May
Concern', reads as follows:—

                                                   12th Sept. 1985
Dear Parishioner,

ST. GILES' CHURCH GIFT DAY 1985.

This year, Gift Day is on Saturday, 28th September, when
we shall be at the Church from 9.30 a.m. to 4.30 p.m. to receive
your gifts, which should be put in an envelope marked 'GIFT
DAY' and placed in the box provided. If you are unable to attend
on the day, please give your contributions either to one of the
churchwardens or to any of the Church Officers listed in *The
Parish News*.

Apart from normal running expenses, during the past year all
the repairs recommended by the architect have been completed,
at a cost of some £3000, and currently arrangements are in hand

---

14 See Appendix A: Article in February 1985 issue of *Antique
Collector* magazine.

to renew some of the very old electrical wiring in the Church, and to take down two of the largest trees in the churchyard, which have been declared unsafe, costing a further £450.

Because of your generous support in the past, we are able to meet these expenses from our reserves, although these will now become sadly depleted.

We should also mention that we have been warned by the architect that we must be prepared to renew part of the Bell Tower within the next few years.

Last year's Gift Day was a record and we hope you will support this year's appeal, in the same generous way. All your gifts will be greatly appreciated and will ensure that our beautiful village Church is properly maintained.

Yours sincerely,

DAVID BALCH   PETER WATTS

CHURCHWARDENS

The present vicar will perhaps best be remembered, when he leaves the parish, for the Chapel of Holy Wisdom, which was designed and dedicated largely through his efforts, and another place of worship, related but very different: the Woodland Church.

In search of a way to express spiritual re-birth through "Holy Wisdom and the Spiritual Word", Mr. Hodgson says that he made his Lenten task for 1985 the creation of an outdoor church, in woods beside the vicarage drive.

Although the vicar said that "Ninety-nine per cent. of the work is God's work", he had to labour quite hard, clearing tree stumps, and digging caves and ditches. The church has a central altar, 'The Lord's Table', for worship in the round, and its main features represent either events in the life of Jesus, or the Christian way of spiritual re-birth. There are the Cave of Nativity, the Water of Life, the Mount of Vision, a circular Nave with the Lord's Table, and an Easter Garden—at the furthest end.

Mr. Hodgson started the garden in January 1985, and held the first service there at dawn on Easter Morning. Apart from services and other organised events, the great beauty of the church is that it is outdoors, secluded and full of an amazing peace. Anyone is welcome to step into this peace, through a gateway of trees, to think and pray. Sitting on one of the benches, visitors can look across the glade and see the

Fig. 8 Coldwaltham's Woodland Church

Cross, so placed in its surroundings that they are always aware of it, without it being intrusive.

*   *   *   *   *

A mile away towards Pulborough, nestling behind the main road, and right off the main highway, is Hardham Church. Small, beautiful and very old. Saxon. Everything points to that assertion, at least. It has three splayed, round-headed, narrow windows of Saxon character, and the traditional British square East end also suggests that it was built before the Norman Conquest. The crude chancel arch looks typically Saxon, and on the South side of the church are the very primitive arch-stones of a bricked-up doorway.

Its founder and first patron may have been the "Godwine, a free Tenant", who held Hardham Manor in the time of

Fig. 9 St. Botolph's Church, Hardham, with eleventh-century lancet window in the Chancel

Edward the Confessor. That would make the church's date about 1050 A.D. Hardham Church is reckoned to be the earliest Saxon church in the country, which is why, from one year end to the next, a steady stream of visitors stroll and rest within it.

The church was subsequently dedicated to the Saxon "patron of ports and river crossings", St. Botolph.

Its solid structure has withstood the tests of nine centuries of exposure to the weather, and long periods of neglect. The thickness of the walls can be seen in the depth of the original lancet windows in the North and South walls of the Nave and in the Chancel. The other windows, constructed in the sixteenth century to provide more light, unfortunately spoil the building's original symmetry.

A walk round the outside of the church shows that Roman building materials — tiles and bricks — were incorporated. No doubt they were taken from the former Roman camp close by. The East window is Early English (early thirteenth century) and that in the South wall of the Chancel is Geometric in style, but in such good condition as to seem much more recent than its proper late-thirteenth-century period.

The bell cote is central, and there are two bells. One has no mark or inscription, and is thought to be much earlier than the other, which is inscribed, *"Gloria Deo in Excelsis, T.P., 1636, B.E."* The Parish Registers date from 1642, and the Communion Plate from 1570.

One of the church's curiosities, to be seen from outside, in the South wall of the Chancel, is a hermit's squint. This marks the spot where the anchorite cell must have been. One certain occupant of that, for the last days of his earthly life, was Prior Richard, in 1285 A.D.

Fig. 10 Hermit's squint in the South wall of the Chancel
at St. Botolph's Church, Hardham

Not so much curious as remarkable are the church's almost complete series of Romanesque wall paintings—among the earliest of their kind in the country, and of international as well as national importance—which are arranged round the Chancel and Nave in tiers.

Every square inch of the walls was painted, and, when fresh, the reds, greens and yellows must have been dazzling to the eyes of the country folk—who could not understand Latin and had no Bible in their own tongue—for whom they were put there. While the priest intoned Latin Mass, they could gaze round the church, absorbing from the walls, and thus learning, the message of both Old and New Testaments.

The wall-paintings date from shortly after 1100 A.D. They were nearly ruined in 1862, when the plaster was chipped off the Chancel to expose the stones. In the chipping process, a series of paintings on the theme of 'The Occupation of the Months' was, in fact, lost, except for one figure, on the South side—that of a man threshing corn with a flail.

Work began in 1866 to uncover the pictures, and treat them, first with size and varnish, then with wax and, later still, with chemical preservatives of the finest quality. At the start, not enough care was taken in the work, so that, tragically, a great deal of the original painting has disappeared forever. But when the light, or rather the dimness of light, is favourable, it is quite easy to make out the subjects of almost all the series.

All the main points in the Christian story are covered on the walls of Hardham Church. In the Chancel are the first, and most clearly defined, figures: of Adam and Eve, particularly alluring and evocative. Below them is the Banishment from Eden and, on the North side of the wall, the outline of an animal with a figure below suggests that Eve was forced to milk a cow (to survive?) when she was banished from Eden. The figures of six of the Apostles on the South wall of the Chancel were uncovered as recently as 1950.

In the Nave, west of the Chancel arch, the paintings are of the Nativity and Infancy of Our Lord. Over the Chancel arch, there is a medallion depicting the Holy Lamb, between worshipping angels. The West wall has a dramatic group of four pictures from 'The Torments of Hell'. But no amount of listing and description can do justice to those incredible illustrations. They have to be seen, in the right light, at the

Fig. 11   Wall painting of 'The Annunciation',
in St. Botolph's Church, Hardham

right time — that is, when the visitor can spend all the time
he or she wants to look, and to experience the warmth, life,
variety of character and emotion, and the humour, as when
they were first lovingly imprinted on those church walls,
almost nine hundred years ago.

Recently, the Parochial Church Council organised a
major programme of structural work. This included exterior
re-decoration, roof covering and gutters, and the installation
of an improved method of rain-water disposal, and of roof
ventilation in the form of vents in the eaves that would cause
air turbulence to help to keep the wall paintings dry.

It all cost about £30,000. Since the parish was made up
of about forty people, with only thirty or so on the Church
Electoral Roll, outside help had to be sought.

The state-funded Historic Buildings Council gave a 75%
grant. This body, now known as English Heritage (Historic
Buildings and Monuments Commission for England) was set
up by the Government, which recognised that buildings such

as this are patently part of our national heritage, and that it is clearly unfair for the burden of maintaining them to be placed on parishioners.

Locally, the P.C.C. prepared an appeal leaflet, in which it set out exactly what was asked for, and why it was needed. As a result, a City Livery Company gave a large amount of the total needed. In addition, donations came from the Historic Churches Preservation Trust, and the Sussex Historic Churches Trust. An appreciable sum was also received through covenants and donations from private individuals. Hardham P.C.C.'s appeal was deservedly successful, attracting support from both organisations and individuals. All those "who have a connection with Hardham or may have enjoyed visiting the church" were asked to help with the "enormous task of raising the necessary funds to conserve St. Botolph's Church for the future".

Now that the church is in good repair, the condition of the paintings has been stabilised. But the "enormous task" referred to in the appeal leaflet is to raise funds for the actual frescoes to be repaired, improved and conserved. The P.C.C. certainly will not be able to raise, unaided, the £100,000 needed for that.

In 1984 (April to July), the Hayward Gallery in London put on an exhibition, *1066: English Romanesque Art, 1066-1200*[15], sponsored by the Arts Council of Great Britain. Hardham Church was featured in a video film available for visitors. Maybe some of those who paced this breath-taking display—it was the first time that the great treasures of twelfth-

---

15 According to the accompanying guide (written by Margaret Gibbon, of the Department of History, University of Liverpool), the exhibition was "about the art and architecture of Norman England in the period following the victory of William the Conqueror at the Battle of Hastings. The Conquest transformed the social and political life of England and stimulated a flowering of artistic creativity which produced great ecclesiastical buildings and the wealth of objects and decoration they contained. Anglo-Saxon England, Scandinavia, Normandy and other parts of the Continent contributed to the Romanesque style in this country, though the resulting art is highly distinctive and essentially English."

century England had been assembled—will also have helped the church repair appeal. Will they help to finance the repair of the frescoes? It is going to need national and international interest by bodies *and* individuals to get together the kind of sum involved.

The late rector, Canon Frederick Kerr-Dineen, told me that slightly more money went into the church's wall box last year than into Church Service collection plates. But that is usually the case.

All the foregoing suggests that Hardham Church is now little more than a shrine. Indeed, no community lives round the church, no social life emanates from it, and the late rector lives in another village. One is tempted to think of it as a church that no longer needs people—although into the mind creeps Joan Bending's convincing argument that buildings; churches, like Watersfield Chapel, *do* need people. Yet many, many more people visit the church than worship in it, and they come from all over the world.

Tourists and pilgrims, students of architecture, and passers-by on bicycles and in cars, keep creeping through the stout wooden door into that chilly little place, and they stay long enough not only to drink in its splendours, but also to write in the book placed there for them.

What have their comments been in recent months? ... "Splendid." "Cold but nice!" "Wonderful old church." "Excellent." "Very lovely." "Heaven" (that makes one think!). "A lovely post-Conquest building." "Our heritage." "Happy to have come" (from London). "Have been before. Will come again." Those are just a few.

The parish of Hardham has never had a resident rector. It is a part of Storrington Rural Deanery and, in more recent times, has been held in plurality by the Rector of Stopham. Now that Canon Kerr-Dineen has retired, inevitably some pastoral re-organisation will be necessary.[16] Since the church is in the civil parish of Coldwaltham, some link with the church there is possible, although Hardham could retain its own parish status and regular worship could continue in the church.

Meanwhile, there are weekly and seasonal services, well attended, and the Births, Marriages and Deaths Registers are not just dusty old archives, but up-to-date records which testify that the church has these sacred facilities, and that they are used.

New burial ground was added to the churchyard while the Rev. C. Brereton was rector. The consecration took place on March 22nd, 1922, by no less a personage than the Bishop of Chichester, the Rt. Rev. George Bell. It is difficult to picture all the pomp and ceremony there must have been in that tiny church, and in its churchyard, which—even as then enlarged — does not quite amount to the proverbial 'God's Acre'. However, the Diocese of Chichester comprises both East and West Sussex: every single nook and cranny of it, and the bishop came . . .

I stood in the churchyard recently and pondered this amid the almost deafening silence there. My mind passed on to a more amusing, very recent memory. Until a few months ago (death, alas, terminated the practice), a sheep was installed to keep the grass down round the tombstones. One small boy, who visited the church with a school party, thoroughly approved of this practical pastoral solution. He wrote to the rector to say so. "Much less bovver than a Hover!" he concluded (obviously having been watching the ads. on television).

The Burial Register is of course of documentary interest. One of the facts that it reveals, for instance, is that, in the early nineteenth century, the mortality rate for babies and children was very high—11 months, 6 weeks, one day, even nine hours . . . were common ages recorded at burial. A century later, all that had changed, with medical progress and all the social and amenity improvements which we now take for granted and as our right. With reassuring regularity, ages of

16 The *London Gazette* dated March 15th, 1901, contained a report of a scheme to re-arrange certain parishes, including Coldwaltham, by way of exchange for other parishes, between the Bishop and the Dean and Chapter of Chichester, but nothing appears to have come of this.

91, 86, 82 . . . were recorded in the mid-1950s, and the age of death of old people buried at Hardham has only gone up by 10 years or so since then.

In Hardham's Baptisms Registry, on the other hand, the "Quality, Trade or Profession" of those whose children were baptised during the early part of the nineteenth century gives an indication of the work available to local residents and parishioners at that time. "Labourer in husbandry", "labourer", "bargeman", "servant", "miller", "clerk" (but only one!) are the *only* occupations listed until 1866, when "railway/signalman" and "pointsman" quietly recorded the advent of travel by train, with "bargeman", at the same time, disappearing for ever.

"Commercial traveller" makes an appearance in 1891, when Fred Cartwright and his wife Ellen had their son baptised at Hardham.

The labourers, millers and gardeners keep on appearing in the Baptism Register well into the twentieth century, joined by carters and (more and more) cowmen. In the 1930s, builders and bricklayers appear and, in 1937, the first lorry driver, Arthur Cox, who, with his wife, Ellen Molly, had their daughters, Brenda, Mabel and Jacqueline, Christened.

By the middle of the twentieth century, "cowman" had become "agricultural labourer", but there were less of them, anyway, in Coldwaltham. The professions were represented more: "engineer", "medical practitioner", "businessman", "air pilot", "advertising", "company director", "teacher", "H.M. Diplomatic Service" . . .

Although some of the baptisms were of children living outside the parish, the less frequent appearance of farm-workers and tractor drivers, in the Register, reflects the lack of employment in those jobs. The population of Hardham was changing: there were not so many people living off the land, as they had done thereabouts for centuries, and more families *living* there, but not necessarily working there; living there because they chose to. The commuter takeover had begun.

Similar trends of occupation are shown in the Register of Marriages at Hardham. One of the other facts that comes to light in this Register is just how much illiteracy there was among adults, right up into this century, with couples unable to sign the Register, but 'making their mark'—a cross—instead.

That brings us, in its way, back to the Cross of Christ, and to Hardham Church — indeed, to all three places of Christian worship in the parish—Watersfield Chapel, St. Giles', Coldwaltham, and St. Botolph's, Hardham. Those connected with one or all of these churches; with any church at all, will appreciate that staccato but warming comment, already quoted, of a visitor to St. Botolph's: "Have been before. Will come again."

Chapter 6

LANDMARKS AND FEATURES

Those who whizz through the parish without looking to left or right—perhaps indeed not having the time to do otherwise—will be unaware that, down the awkward turn-off road to the left at the foot of Church Hill if you are going towards Watersfield, lies one of the most important little nature reserves in the whole of the country and, in some respects, in the world. Just half a mile down that minor road (Brook Lane, which leads on to Greatham, then to Storrington) lie Waltham Brooks.

Until the late 1970s, these were an almost anonymous part of Amberley Wild Brooks. Many may nod in recognition of *that* name, although "Waltham Brooks" still leaves far too many people mystified.

Amberley Wild Brooks was the subject of a public enquiry in March 1978, when, as a result of strong opposition, the Ministry of Agriculture[1] decided against permitting grant aid for a proposed £340,000 drainage scheme. This could have wiped out an amazing variety of wildlife from 900 acres of rough grassland, criss-crossed by dykes and intermittently flooded in winter because this stretch of land lies in the flood plain of the River Arun.

The importance of Amberley Wild Brooks, in the lee of the South Downs, was recognised in biological terms in 1977. The area was announced to be 'Grade I', according to a status defined in the *Nature Conservation Review,* organ of the Nature Conservancy Council, which officially advises the Government in these matters.

What kind of geological and physical conditions cause the growth of such a concentration of wildlife richness? Amberley Wild Brooks has an alluvial soil, as found in other parts of the

---

1 now known as the Ministry of Agriculture, Fisheries and Food

Arun Valley, and much of the north and west of the area is overlaid with peat.

"Drainage of the neighbouring catchment through the peat results in a wide range of conditions, both in terms of nutrient quality and pH range. This in turn has led to the tremendous botanical diversity. To the untrained observer, it is just tussocky, cattle-grazed meadowland, but to the naturalists who have known the site for over 250 years, largely on account of the botanical interest, it is much more, for it supports some 400 species of flowering plants and ferns. Among them are 56% of the British water species, including 16 national rarities. In the insect line, only the dragonflies have been studied in any depth and 16 of the 38 species occur, including five that are very rare.

"Birds have been well surveyed, although only systematically since the late 1950s. Nonetheless, it is clear from the past records that the site has deteriorated; for example, in the 1920s, ... Bitterns probably bred and thus extensive areas of Phragmites must have since been lost. Its current ornithological interest . . . centres on its wintering wildfowl, in the order of 2,000-plus occurring regularly. The area is certainly of national importance for its Pintail, Teal and Shoveler (holding at least 1% of the British population of these species during recent winters). In the case of Shoveler, numbers of international significance have been observed in three recent winters. The increasing flock of Bewick's Swans is at least of national importance, and the Brooks are probably the second most important area for wintering Snipe in South-East England.

"The community of breeding birds is typical of southern flood meadows, with small numbers of Lapwing, Redshank, Snipe and Yellow Wagtail, and the site forms a valuable feeding ground for many species from the neighbouring woods and parkland, in particular for the Herons from Parham Park Heronry." [2]

Waltham Brooks, 104.5 acres in extent, is bounded on the south-east by the River Arun and on the north-west by Brook Lane and farmland. It has been common land since the Manorial System was introduced before the Norman Conquest. On October 4th, 1976, the Church Commissioners for England, acting in their inherited capacity of "Lords of the Manor of Amberley", sold most of their rights in the land[3] to the Sussex Trust for Nature Conservation for a peppercorn sum—of just £50!

---

2   from an article by Richard Porter, then South-East Regional Officer of the R.S.P.B., in the December 1978 issue of *British Trust for Ornithology News*

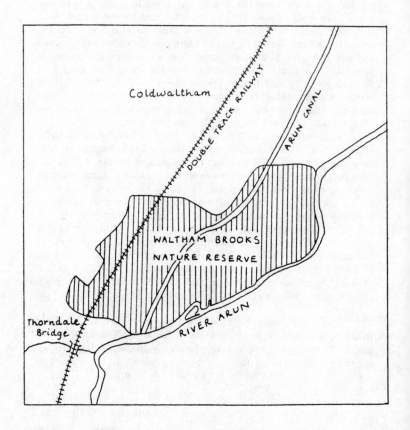

Fig. 1 Waltham Brooks Nature Reserve

Until comparatively recently, various people, including local landowners, farmers and people with land in the vicinity,

---

3 but not their fishing rights, and "excepting to the Commissioners and their successors all mines, quarries, minerals and mineral substances whatsoever (including sand and gravel and all other surface minerals) whether opened or unopened within and under the said land . . ."

held leazes to use the Brooks for grazing, but most of them lost out when they failed to register the leazes they had. Only Mr. Marten, a farmer, still has a substantial number (75), allowing him to graze his cattle there from 12th May until the floods start later in the year.

In 1979, after the already-mentioned decision not to allow a major drainage scheme to go ahead was taken, Waltham Brooks gained an 'on site' ally, when Graham Barker moved with his family to live nearby. He took over a smallholding and, shortly after his arrival, became Honorary Warden for the Brooks. For wildlife-recording purposes, Mr. Barker separated Waltham Brooks from the rest of Amberley Wild Brooks, and from then on the smaller area came into its own as a special little reserve. Mr. Barker was also given a small island adjacent to Waltham Brooks, to police and use for the reserve, and for the Wildfowl Trust (of which Arundel Wildfowl Trust is part) he prepares, on a monthly basis, a winter count for a published report on how many wildfowl have visited this reserve.

The birds which visit Waltham Brooks can be divided into various categories: resident birds, breeding birds, summer migrants, winter migrants, passage migrants, and rare visitors. Among the latter seen on the reserve are the Osprey, Pectoral Sandpiper, Black-Necked Grebe, Avocet, Spotted Crake, Wood Warbler, Marsh Sandpiper (a national rarity), Water Pipit, Marsh Harrier, Mediterranean Gull, Great Northern Diver, Blue-Headed Wagtail, Smew, Goosander, Garganey, Jack Snipe, Crossbill and Buzzard.

Resident birds, such as the Heron, Yellowhammer and Teal, can be seen there all the year round. Summer migrants, like the Redstart, Sand Martin, Swift and Spotted Flycatcher, visit the British Isles to breed each summer, flying back to the warmer climes of southern Europe and Africa for winter. Winter visitors to the Brooks include the Fieldfare, Redwing, Bewick's Swan and Short-Eared Owl. Passage migrants, for examples, the Wood Sandpiper and Curlew Sandpiper, breed in Russia and Scandinavia, heading south each autumn to escape the severe Arctic winter. They head for southern

Europe and Africa, returning home in the spring to breed, and stopping off in the British Isles during their autumn and spring passages to replenish reserves.

Each year, in total, thousands of visitors[4] are seen at Waltham Brooks, many quietly watching from the road, waiting to see at least some of the birds I have mentioned, and hoping that many more will come into their sights.

Of the winter migrants that arrive between the end of August and Christmas, and start to disperse to their breeding grounds in March, perhaps the most famous of all in the area are the Bewick's Swans, which come in such numbers as to be internationally significant. In 1979, when water was first retained on the Reserve, Graham Barker recorded fifty-five using the Brooks for their nightly roost. In 1980-1981, there were 77, and they have increased yearly. In February 1987, the Peak Count recorded 143. According to Mr. Barker, the swans start arriving on 29th October. He is as precise as that about it, and once advised some interested watchers to arrive on that very day one year. They did — and some Bewick's Swans flew in as they arrived!

If a reserve can be shown to hold one per cent. of the world population of any breed of bird, this will entitle it to be classified officially as of international importance. Having what is recognised as one per cent. of the world's Bewick's Swan population — about 125 on average — is one reason why the area has now been designated a Site of Special Scientific Interest (SSSI) by the Nature Conservancy Council.[5]

---

4 One regular visitor to Waltham Brooks to bird-watch was a former Watersfield resident, Mr. Eric Binns. See Appendix B for his extensive list of birds seen — although now more breeds are in evidence.

5 Sites of Special Scientific Interest are described in a leaflet, *SSSIs*, published by the Nature Conservancy Council, as "areas of land or water identified by the Nature Conservancy Council as being of outstanding value for their wildlife or geology. SSSIs are not the only places in Britain important for nature conservation — there are many other areas that need conserving if man and wildlife are to exist together. However, SSSIs are the cream, and many of them are of international importance."

A letter dated 7th May, 1987, to Graham Barker from the N.C.C., confirming the SSSI designation, was the culmination of eight years of lobbying by Mr. Barker, and others.

The Chapter House at Hardham Priory, now in ruins

The parish church of St. Giles, Coldwaltham

Arthur Matthews Paddon,
who bought 'Watersfield Towers' (now 'Lodge Hill') in 1905
for his beautiful Irish bride, Marion Weldon Scanlyn

Marion Weldon Paddon,
who bore Arthur Matthews Paddon three children—
John, Anthony Uye, and Julia Molly Christina ('Peta')

Old Watersfield, looking down Lodge Hill

A view of Watersfield from a field on Ruff's Farm,
showing Watersfield Congregational (now United Reformed) Chapel,
with, behind, a vague outline of the Three Crowns under erection

THE BEEHIVE, COLDWALTHAM.

*'The Beehive' (now called 'Mulberry'),
which used to be the old parish workhouse*

*The cross roads at Coldwaltham, as they used to look,
showing 'Ivy Cottage'
('Mulberry' lies behind it)*

'Laburnum Cottage' (now 'The Cottage'),
at the junction of Stane Street Lane and Sandy Lane

Two Watersfield cottages, each sitting behind the fork made by two lanes

'Pear Tree Cottage',
at the junction of River Lane and Ruff's Farm lane

The Shelton sisters, who lived at 'Applegarth', Watersfield
One of them (perhaps two) kept a guest house there

Old Cold Waltham

Old London Road,
with the Labouring Man on the left
and the Old Forge on the right

King's Lane,
showing King's Lane Cottages on the left
and the former Old Dame's School on the right

Old Cold Waltham

Those of us in these parts who get up early enough, especially on winter mornings, can be reassured, when we hear the harsh cries of swans, geese and other wildfowl, that, if they are not off for breakfast at Arundel Wildfowl Trust, they are touching down or settling down for a spell at Waltham Brooks, with Graham Barker quietly observing, and caring about, their every move. Mr. Jim Stevenson, former Education Officer at Arundel Wildfowl Trust, and now Warden for the Royal Society for the Protection of Birds, at Lochleven, Scotland, once confided to someone that Mr. Barker "knows every feather": an accolade Graham wears proudly.

Not only wildlife abounds, and increasingly so, at Waltham Brooks. Vascular plants, including several endangered species, such as Ragged Robin, Frogbit, Flowering Rush, Great Water Parsnip, Mares' Tail and Yellow Loosestrife, are now on the increase. A British Museum survey in 1980 found 277 Vascular plants (there are reputed to be over 300 now), including several endangered species.

One of the earliest flowers to bloom in the Brooks is the buttercup-like Marsh Marigold.

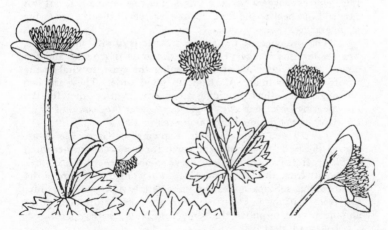

Fig. 2   Marsh Marigold

In 1984, a British Museum party returned to take some photographs for a Marsh and Bogland Plant Exhibition, held in September that year at the Science Museum in South Kensington.

Graham Barker also prepares regular reports for the Sussex Ornithological Society's annual *Sussex Bird Report,* and these are re-used by the British Trust for Ornithology.

Mr. Barker believes that 98 per cent. of all Wetlands in the British Isles have been lost since World War II, through improved drainage methods and modern farming practices. Large numbers of species associated with these habitats, both Flora and Fauna, are under threat of extinction — making reserves like this one extremely important.

Naturalist and writer, Alison Ross, who lives in Amberley, is devoted to the interests of the Brooks, and is especially enthusiastic about the flourishing state of wildlife there. She wrote recently (in her regular column in the *West Sussex Gazette*) on the necessity for conservationists and supporters of conservation to co-operate with farmers.

> "It is this stretch of wetland [Waltham Brooks] that is demonstrating how important it is for everyone to understand the necessity of co-operation. Every year there, the flooded parts of the fields get bigger. Possibly this is due to the weather, but this excuse is no help to the farmer, for every year his cattle are losing more grazing.
>
> "The presence of the farmer's cattle is of vital importance. For six months of the year when the grass is growing and the cows are enjoying it, they are keeping the grass, so vital to the wildfowl, or to many of them, in good order. They are also dunging it and thus providing an improved insect diet for the insect-eating birds, *and the longer in the year they can do this on the edges of the floodwaters, the better.*
>
> "I'll tell you why! Peewits, Lapwings or Green Plover are among the birds that probe the earth for insects and other small edible creatures . . . and they . . . have gained an enormous amount of benefit from this delightful place. They congregate here in the non-breeding seasons, appearing to be utterly negligent about life, but really packing in the proteins in the form of the little grubs and their larvae, or pupae, that they need. Numbers have increased, visibly, a great deal . . ."

Graham Barker is among those who think that cattle should be back on the Brooks, grazing, by the first day of

April (it used to be early May), and that the cattle should stay there as late in the year as the weather permits.

Apart from bird life and plant life, animal life is beginning to pick up again, undisturbed as it is, and seventeen species of butterfly were observed last year by Mr. Barker, along with several species of dragonfly. Grass snakes, adders and voles of all descriptions are making their regular home there, too.

* * * * *

How do you follow that? After spending many hours contemplating the natural richness of Waltham Brooks, then more hours trying to put my findings down, the question is hard to answer. But I still have much to say about Cold-waltham's other landmarks and features, which are numerous and varied, and so I must doff my romantic's cap and don a reporter's one, so far as possible . . .

A great spur to my progress here is the beauty of the place. This can soon and simply be seen by even the most cursory walk round it, with Fred, our dog, leading the way. How can one small parish contain so many lovely houses and interesting places?

I plan to turn the next few pages into a tour for everyone. I stroll up River Lane to the main road. Facing me, on the opposite side of the A29, is the Old Crown House—originally the village inn, then two houses, now one residence. Originally seventeenth-century, or earlier, the façade's ground floor is stuccoed and, above, it is tile-hung, with a hipped tiled roof. Its lovely casement windows, seen from Pear Tree Cottage, flash with brilliant sunlight early in the morning, just after a good sunrise. With the Old Crown House on my right and the Old Post Office—giving me a newly-painted, spick and span smile—on my left, I turn down the lane directly opposite River Lane. Next on my left, approached by an exquisite rockery of heathers and miniature flowers, is the Old Chapel, and here we stop, for an interesting story lies behind this place.

The Old Chapel was a Baptist Chapel. Money was raised by public subscription to build it, along with 'incidental'

Fig. 3 'The Old Chapel'

buildings, and the first Baptist Service took place there on August 5th, 1901. In 1949, however, the Board of Charity Commissioners for England and Wales authorised the sale of the chapel by the Baptist Union Corporation Limited, "the sale to take place within 12 months of this consent, for not less than £375"—the highest bid at an auction already held. The freehold was subsequently bought by a Miss Dorothy May Mowll, of 'The Croft', Watersfield. She then held the freeholds of both the little garage, with its bungalow and land, and the Old Chapel, making her something of a property owner in the hamlet. In 1954, by a County Council Order, consent was given to the change of use from chapel to house, subject to the approval of detailed plans for the proposed conversion to a dwelling, and General Development Consent was granted on January 6th, 1960. Seven years later, the property was bought by Mr. and Mrs. William (Bill) Innis, the present owners.

Next to the Old Chapel, on my left, are two sweet, small houses: numbers 1 and 2, Rose Cottage. Then—a fork in the lane. Within the fork, rather in the same way that Pear Tree Cottage is within the fork of River Lane and the farm lane, is 'The Cottage'. (It used to be 'Laburnum Cottage', but the present owners disliked the "poisonous overtones" of Laburnum.) On up Stane Street Lane, the left fork, we come to a really beautiful house on the left, called 'Quintins'. Its name was formerly 'Tudors', for obvious reasons, and the sixteenth-century building, with plaster infilling on the first floor and painted brick below, has curved braces on the first floor, a thatched roof topping its two storeys, and casement windows. To the right of the front door is a most beautiful rosemary bush, of great proportions, and it is one of my ambitions to grow such a bush within my lifetime! 'Quintins' is the home of the late Chairman of Coldwaltham Parish Council, Mr. J. I. M. Rhodes, and his wife, Netta. Up the other lane, one of the prettiest houses, 'The White Cottage', was recently re-thatched.

Fig. 4 The White Cottage

I have returned to the main road now. Following Fred, that unpredictable hound of annoying speed, I move towards

Windmill Hill, alias Beacon Hill[7], passing the gate of 'Apple-garth'. The first thing noticeable about this splendid sixteenth-century house is its double-hip roof, recently renovated with Norfolk Reed thatch by Mr. Jarvis, who beautified the house during the few years he lived there. The house was built mainly of brick, but local stone was used wherever possible.

Miss Shelton receives a few paying guests in her old Tudor cottage near the foot of the Downs in beautiful West Sussex. Bath, and indoor chemical sanitation. Garden of one acre. Buses through village to sea and station.

Terms :

*6/6 per day, or
To end of June £2 2s. per week
July & Sept. £2 5s. per week.
August - 7/6 per day
or £2 10s. per week
Special terms for visits
over one month in duration.*

Midday dinner.

Hot bath, 6d.

No children taken.

Fig. 5

---

7   A Roman beacon once stood at the top of this hill.

Going back a bit, Les Goble (who helped Miss Blake at the local poultry farm, as we have already seen) was born at 'Applegarth', and lived in one of the two cottages (they used to be four) with his parents, George and Eva, and his sister, Edith (Edie). Grannie Goble lived in the other cottage with her son, Horace. (He married Mabel Cheesman, another local resident, when Grannie died.) The two cottages belonged then to a Mr. Louis Horner, who sold them to the three Shelton sisters, and the Gobles moved to live at Brookview.

The Shelton sisters were known in the parish as "of theatrical fame", but one at least fell on hard times (or maybe it was while she was 'resting'), and had to rent out rooms.

In 1981, Mr. Jarvis sold the property to Mr. Tony Foster, who, since it was a Listed Building, had to apply to Horsham District Council for permission to build a garage, "for which a sample of roof tile . . . shall be submitted to and approved by the Local Planning Authority".

An historically important feature of the house came to light when it was discovered that 'Applegarth' had an elaborate sixteenth-century chimney breast. The air-ducts between the back-to-back ingle-nooks were built so that warm air would be conducted to a drying cupboard, or enclosed space, on the first floor—an old but most effective method of central heating. There is one other example of such a chimney breast, and this has been re-constructed in the Weald and Downland Open Air Museum, at Singleton, near Chichester.

Back down the main road and, just as I am about to cross the main road for home, I glimpse, a few yards away, what used to be Watersfield Store and, adjacent to it, Cherry Tree Cottage.[8] Timber-framed with a thatched double-hip roof, this house has seen a lot of re-building, with stubble, at the southern end, but it is partly sixteenth-century and very pretty.

Home now—it's time for tea. But as I stroll down River Lane to Pear Tree Cottage, I glance to my right down the long

---

8 In 1986, Watersfield Store closed for ever, and it and Cherry Tree Cottage were sold separately, both to be residences.

drive that leads to the intriguing 'Meadow House'. It used to be 'Meadow Cottage', and at one time the house was three cottages. The Cheesman family lived in one, and Mary Cheesman gained a local reputation for playing 'The Post Horn Gallop' on her trumpet, just outside the front door. 'Meadow House' now is much more a house than a cottage. The large, L-shaped building, as it has become, goes back to the seventeenth century, or perhaps earlier. It is timber-framed with plaster infilling, and the north wing is faced with stone. It has a hipped tiled roof and casement windows.

Tea will have to wait, for I have remembered that I need to see Mrs. Peggie Clark at Watts Farm Cottage. I walk past Watts Farm, which Mrs. Marion Paddon built, then lived in, after leaving Watersfield Towers. Around the same time, she

Fig. 6   Watts Farm being built in the early 1900s

built, or renovated, the cottage opposite, for her daughter, Peta, and it became known as Peta's Cottage. After other occupants, the cottage was bought in 1953 by Cecily, daughter of the famous explorer, Sir Ernest Shackleton. A great friend of the Shackleton family, a Bishop Bardsley, visited Cecily and blessed the cottage, which she then re-named Bardsley Cottage. She was not well during her short years in Watersfield, and her cousin, Mrs. Rena Norley Dodds (the present owner), lived with her and looked after her devotedly, until Cecily's death in 1957. Cecily is buried (with her mother's ashes, which she had moved from St. John's Crematorium only months before her own death) in Coldwaltham Churchyard.

On, now, down River Lane, I wander, and into Mrs. Clark's driveway. Bushes and flowers of all descriptions bloom in her front garden, and the garden hidden behind the house is a delight. For charity, Mrs. Clark opens the gardens to the public for two days each May. *Gardens of Sussex 1985,*[9] a useful information booklet, describes Mrs. Clark's grounds as "a garden of 1/3 acre, owner-maintained, with borders, roses and shrubs", but it has to be seen to be believed – a gorgeous, floral fairyland, and not just in summer.

Saying goodbye to Mrs. Clark and her garden, I throw an admiring glance in the direction of the early-nineteenth-century Baisley House, wide-fronted and solid, and a nostalgic smile at the next house on the left—and the last in this part of the lane—Silver Birches.[10] Then I go through Ruff's Farm backyard, and on down the lower end of River Lane, which ends just short of the north bank of the River Arun.

There is only one house in this lower part of the lane: 'Thorndel'. In a beautifully hand-scripted book[11] by the

---

9 published annually by the National Gardens Scheme Charitable Trust
10 For a few years, from 1973, we spent many happy weekends at this little house.
11 *Thorndel in Trisantona: The History of a House, including some history of the River Arun and the surrounding country,* by Eric and Christine Walker (June 1957, unpublished). I have not drawn more from this book: space does not allow me to; also the present owners, Russell and Jo Homan, plan to bring the house's history up to date and, perhaps, publish it.

former owners, the surrounding area is called Trisantona, the Roman name for the River Arun, which, as the authors write, "is responsible for the particular character of this part of Sussex".

Tucked away in a remote setting, 'Thorndel' was built like a Queen Anne cottage, with later additions. Inside, there are many old and unusual features, including two white columns of classical design in the sitting room, replacing what was probably once a partition wall.

Fig. 7   Old fireplace at 'Thorndel'

The house has been variously known as 'Thorndel' (its present name), 'Orchard House', and 'The Pest House'. Once it was a brewhouse, and many pieces of evidence point to this: the cave in the nearby copse, once used for smuggling (and still known as Smugglers' Cave); . . . "a nearby house ['Thorndel'] with an outdoor cellar which can be easily concealed . . . The small piece of marshland immediately in front of the building is called Wharf Meadow ... The house acted as an agency for coal and other goods handled by the bargemen and this, in conjunction with the sale of beer and a certain amount of 'illegal trade', was no doubt very profitable ... With the coming of the railway, the trade stopped and the Brew House became a small farmhouse, handed down from father to son until 1883."

The house was first called 'The Pest House' by James Laker, an assistant at the Malt House, Watersfield, the source of Thorndel's beer, but the house was never an official Pest House. These dated from the eighteenth century, the last one closing at Petworth in 1916, and they were concerned not so much with the plague as with occasional cases of infectious diseases. They were, in fact, small isolation hospitals owned by the parish. Laker stated that a former owner of the house, a Jonathan Stedman or Osborne, had lived there all his life and "practised inoculation". Perhaps it was not surprising, then, that 'Thorndel' became known locally as 'The Pest House'. ...

There are many mysteries surrounding subsequent owners of 'Thorndel', and apparently their presence can still be felt in and around the house, although a family, including young children, give the place a 'normality' that perhaps it has not known for a long time.

*   *   *   *   *

Back I go up River Lane to Pear Tree Cottage. I lean on the wall of the alluring house where I live, inevitably casting a glance up the lane to the right, leading to Ruff's Farm, once Besleys and Torepsoes Farm, where the Ruffs—Stan, and his stalwart son, Charlie—live and work. You would think that, having known them for fourteen years, I would not need to glance towards their house, but I do so, several times a day—wondering if all is well with them.

Even without the Ruffs in it (and we are all drawn as if by a magnet up into that farmhouse kitchen, at some time or other, if only just to buy eggs), the house is a fascinating, dignified old place. It was built in the early nineteenth century of Pulborough stone ashlar, with red-brick window dressings and quoins. Its tiled roof, now spankingly renewed, gleams in the sun, and it has a lovely front doorway (through which no one, to my knowledge, ever passes!), with fluted pilasters. If you drive down Beacon Hill looking at the hamlet in the valley, almost the first thing you are aware of is this farmhouse, on the right; solid, large and cared-for, its paint gleaming, and — if you are lucky enough to go through the hamlet in March — you will see the field before the house ablaze, or awash (depending on the light), with vast patches of daffodils — two round patches and one, diamond-shaped — planted there over a hundred years ago.

Almost all the houses I have described so far are Grade 1 or Grade 2 Listed[12] and, after tea, as I walk up Lodge Hill, I approach yet another listed building: Rosemary Cottage. Just before it, I pause and look back to where the village pond used to be, on the roadside, more or less opposite the butcher's shop.

What a pity that Watersfield's pond is now no more. Several bronze coins were found in its mud, many stories surround it, and numerous people stood beside it, but none guarded it more jealously than old Grannie Clark—apparently a short, stocky old lady "with a beard". In 1922, a dispute took place about the footpath, or right of way, round the pond. Grannie Clark is said to have stood menacingly at the five-bar gate alongside where she lived at Brockhurst Farm, threatening anyone and everyone who approached. Those coming over Lodge Hill to Watersfield would stop on the brow, if they caught sight of her. They simply would not descend; so fierce was her temper, and so unpredictable her ways. (Whatever bit of a heart of gold she had, they say, was reserved for children, whom she loved . . .)

---

12 Grade 1 Listed Buildings are "buildings of exceptional interest (less than 5 per cent. of the Listed Buildings are in this grade)". Grade 2 Listed Buildings are "of special interest, which warrant every effort being made to preserve them. (Some particularly important buildings in Grade 2 are classified as Grade 2*.)"

Fig. 8 *Watersfield pond, with Rosemary Cottage behind and the Malt House Cottages block, which contains Rowland's the butcher's, along with the parish Post Office*

One day, to try to sort things out, a site meeting was arranged and seven members of Coldwaltham Parish Council grouped themselves round the pond — with Grannie Clark. Someone got on the wrong side of Grannie and, from then on, it all went wrong . . . She was so upset, she seized a pitch-fork and got five of the parish council members into the pond. The other two were squared-up against the adjacent barn, where Grannie Clark 'kept them in place' menacingly. The local 'Bobby' was sent for (from Fittleworth) and, until he came, the five sodden councillors felt they were safest in the water, and would not come out!

Eventually, Grannie Clark fenced off the village pond, thus absorbing it into her property. Possession, they say, is nine points of the law. The pond has long since dried up.

From memories to present-day reality. Rosemary Cottage is still there, a timber-framed, sixteenth-century house with painted brick infilling, the south end refaced with stone rubble—now painted—a hipped, thatched roof, and casement windows. Recently an extra porch, sympathetically designed, was added unobtrusively to the existing one.

Up the short but steep Lodge Hill now — a landmark in itself. At the top, I turn left, at a sign for Lodge Hill Residential Centre. To reach this, I have to go up a very hilly drive indeed (not liked by my old car!). Lodge Hill—first, by its very position — holds an aura of intrigue for the parish's inhabitants, who have little to do with its activities. There are exceptions, as when young James Barton, who used to live in Watersfield, won a place in the West Sussex County Boys' Choir. He attended a couple of courses just up the road, at Lodge Hill. Yet most of the people who stay there have nothing to do with the parish. The manageress, Mrs. Millard, is resident, and the centre's secretary comes from Storrington.

A fascinating history helps to give Lodge Hill's house its aura. In November 1828, the Lodge Hill estate was leased by the Bishop of Chichester (implying that, in those days, it still belonged to the Anglican Diocese), on behalf of the Church Commissioners, to a Robert Watkins, Esquire. Fifty years later, the estate was sold to a London solicitor, Mr. Murrough, who built the basis of the present house in 1879, named it 'Watersfield Towers', and lived in it for a number of years. In 1901, it was bought by a Captain Campbell. Then, in 1905, the house became the property of Arthur Matthews Paddon, a brilliant young man of wealth and position, to be home for himself and his beautiful Irish bride, Marion Weldon Scanlyn, a Gaiety Girl. No expense was spared, at this stage, in refurbishing the house. Battlements embellished the towers, the interior was panelled, and a bevy of servants, inside and out, kept the place in immaculate order. Acres of gardens were laid out for Marion's pleasure. She was always dressed in superb gowns (still remembered by 'Nan' Cooper, in Cold-waltham), and every luxury was lavished upon her by her husband, who loved her with a consuming passion. Arthur became a highly respected and successful barrister and, in law circles, was expected to 'take silk'. They had two sons— first, John, then Anthony — and then they had a beautiful, blonde, blue-eyed daughter, Julia Mollie Christina, known as 'Peta'. But tragedy struck the family from all directions, and it would need another book to explain all that.

*Fig. 9   'Watersfield Towers' photographed from the main drive,
when the Paddons lived there*

The Paddon connection with the house was terminated in 1935, when it was bought by a retired army man, Captain Waller. Under his direction, the estate expanded. The purchase of land from the Leconfield Estate extended the grounds west-wards. Captain Waller and a business associate, a Mr. Chorley, obtained backing from the Earl of Iveagh, and formed a company called The Lodge Hill Estate Limited. Next, 'Watersfield Towers' opened its doors as a country hotel.

However, with the advent of World War II, the house and its thirty acres were requisitioned by the West Sussex County Council. The hotel was turned into the headquarters of the A.R.P. (Air Raid Precautions). As such, it served until 1945.

A year later, the house and land were bought for £30,500 by West Sussex County Council, to provide "a venue for educational facilities, especially for young people". The Lodge Hill Committee was formed and, at this stage, the house was re-named Lodge Hill Residential Centre.

Forty-odd years have gone by, and now it flourishes "as a venue for numerous county, regional and national organisations. School parties spend weekends studying drama and music; teachers and students of all ages and disciplines train in adult education courses; there are conferences, holidays, meetings and seminars. As an education centre, Lodge Hill enjoys a great, and growing, popularity".[13]

Leaving Lodge Hill and making the main road again, I turn left towards Coldwaltham, then right, as if heading for Waltham Brooks, discovering an ancient farmhouse called 'Widneys', on my right.

An article in the 10th August, 1986, issue of *Country Life* puts 'Widneys' historically on the map:—

> "In Sussex, neither the projecting hammer beam nor the larger dormer is common, and in West Sussex they are, in my experience, entirely absent. This may well account for the large number of Wealden houses in West Sussex and Surrey that have been built up so that they are not immediately recognisable as such. Time and again jettied wings have been underpinned with brick, and the wall of the recessed hall brought forward. Widneys at Coldwaltham is an excellent example of this treatment, where local stone, and some flint from the nearby downland, has been used in addition to the brick. Here two particular features usually remain: the curved struts in the wings and the hipped roof with its gablets, giving a clue to the original building. Very occasionally the treatment is more drastic, and the house has been given a complete outer casing in brick."

'Widneys' is a beautiful house, and was used—with the permission of the present owners, Mr. and Mrs. Leslie Jones— in a national advertisement campaign by a well-known wood-worm, dry rot and rodent control firm. Their advertisement

---

13 The hordes of children who used to descend on Watersfield Store, to spend pocket money on sweets and sticky buns, miss the shop now that it is closed. But, fortunately, they have the Rowlands' shop instead.

started off: "This delightful Knapped Flint Timber Cottage in Sussex . . . is *not* on the market!"

I am leaving 'Widneys' now and returning to the main road, up the steep hill in the Pulborough direction, past the pretty flint-and-brick Church Cottage, where the Post Office used to be, on my left and, on the right, the cosy red glow of lights from Barn Owls Restaurant. Almost opposite the entrance to Church Lane is the Priest House, which was built in about 1220 by Hardham Priory, to house the priests serving Coldwaltham Church, nearby, across the road. Reputed to be one of the oldest dwelling houses in the country, it has a rectangular structure of squared blocks of Wealden sandstone, material also used in building Coldwaltham Church tower and Hardham Priory. The walls are all of eighteen inches thick.

Fig. 10   The Old Priest House

Mrs. Marjorie Hessell Tiltman writes, in *Cottage Pie*[14]:—

"A clergyman, in those days, would as lief have lived in a pig-sty as in a Tudor cottage with thatched roof and tiny leaded windows, and a neo-Gothic stone building of handsome proportions

---

14   published by Hodder & Stoughton, 1940

(built across the road, behind the church) took over its functions.[15] The original priest's house then fell on evil days. Rough partitions were erected to divide it into two cottages; the old stalls upstairs were plastered up to make separate bedrooms. But as it was neglected, so it decayed. Birds nested in the thatch and the rain dripped through. The rats frequented the outhouses; dry rot attacked the beams, the plaster fell away, the rafters fell in, the old green glass in the windows fell out. Fungus grew on the wet wood; dirt covered the floors; it became grim, desolate and squalid, until, finally, it was condemned as unfit for human habitation.

"At this sad moment, it was bought by a man who specialises in such restorations. It was stripped till it was a skeleton. It was re-thatched, re-plastered. The great fireplaces were opened up, disclosing cupboards over them. The deep well in the kitchen was bricked up for ever and a modern cooker placed over it for a tombstone. The nettles and other weeds have been rooted up from the garden, which has been replanted with many of the flowers that must have grown there four hundred years ago. Now, tragic or comic as it may be, admirable or lamentable, in the dining-parlour, retiring-room and study of the old Tudor priest, meals are served to twentieth-century motorists by two efficient girls dressed in flowered cretonne."

The cretonne has gone, and the Old Priest House has for some time been a licensed restaurant.

Resisting the temptation to stop and gaze at every pretty house, which would be totally time-consuming and would deprive you, the reader, of any element of delighted surprise you should be left to experience when you walk round the parish, I move on to Hardham, where, on the right, just before St. Botolph's Church, I see the roofless but graceful ruin of an old building. It is the ruin of the Chapter House, which, with the Refectory, now a private house, is all that remains of the complex of buildings connected with Hardham Priory.

---

15 The "neo-Gothic building" was the old vicarage, and is now called Stane Street House. It has its own claims to fame. According to the late Rev. Eric Newcombe, Cardinal Newman visited the house, probably spending the night there, when it was still the vicarage. Going back further, the architect behind the building of the house (in 1830) "exercised the stonemasons' skill", as Mrs. Mary Stuart-Douglas, the wife of the present owner, put it, by designing windows that were all different—perpendicular, trefoil, Norman, round, and so on.

In the garden is a magnificent old cedar tree. When measured in 1984 by the Walbe level, it was found to be 9 feet, 4 inches in diameter.

Imposing on the skyline in any sort of weather, the Chapter House's masonry somehow holds together, apparently protected from decay by a narrow strip of tough tile roofing along the wall-tops. The arcading on the west side is so elegant that all should stop and look at it.

From the ancient, ecclesiastical to the modern, functional the gap is short, and I have only to proceed a few hundred yards before a sign leading to the latter: HARDHAM WATER TREATMENT WORKS.

Although the parish is predominantly a residential area, except for the few small working farms dotted about the district, industry did creep into it in the early 1950s, when the Rother Pumping Station was built in Hardham.

The North-West Sussex Joint Water Board formulated a plan to improve supply facilities in the area, badly needed because of the rapid growth of Crawley New Town (among other factors).

Rother Pumping Station was built on the east side of the River Rother, near its confluence with the Arun, not far from where Hardham Mill once stood. This site was chosen because it was one of the few places in the area where a building could stand close enough to the river to ensure easy abstraction of the water, without being so low as to be troubled by flooding, and where it was feasible to construct a weir across the Rother to prevent 'back-up' of saline water at high tide.

Geologically, the site had specific advantages, too. The works were built above the Hardham, or Wiggonholt, syncline. This is a natural basin of porous sandstone[16] about 90 metres thick at its deepest point, and sealed off by the impermeable Gault clays above and the Atherfield clays underneath. The syncline, which extends from Wiggonholt to Fittleworth on an east-west basis, is, at its widest, about four kilometres across. From boreholes sunk into this sandstone aquifer, near the works, supplementary or alternative supplies of water can be drawn—when the river is low, for example, or if gross pollution were to occur.

---

16   the Folkestone sands mentioned in Chapter 2 (p.22)

Once built, Rother Pumping Station, opened by the late Duke of Norfolk on July 24th, 1954, served the Horsham and Crawley areas, along with Pulborough, Hardham, Coldwaltham and Watersfield. Prior to that, Coldwaltham Parish was served by bore-hole sources at Smock Alley and Nutbourne, via public water mains laid in 1934. Before that, people drew their water from wells.

By 1959, the station's maximum output was three million gallons per day (mgd) and Mr. Holt, in his study, sounded a warning note that, even though "this may be at some future date increased . . . it must not rise above a certain maximum proportion of the outflow of the Rother, which is twenty-two million gallons a day".

All this must have seemed very exciting and progressive in 1954, although it did not provide many local people with jobs: few, in fact, were needed to man the station. But soon the pumping station was inadequate to supply demand, and, in the early 1970s, the Sussex Division of the Southern Water Authority (successor to the North-West Joint Water Board) recognised the need for an additional water treatment plant at Hardham, to supply properly the fast-growing population areas of Crawley and Horsham, as well as meeting the needs of increasing industry in West Sussex.

The new Hardham Water Treatment Works started being constructed in 1979, in preparation for three projected stages to provide an ultimate capacity of 136 MLD[17] (30 mgd). The first stage was commissioned in 1984, and its completion was marked in July 1985 by a special ceremony conducted by Ian Gow, M.P., then Minister for Housing and Construction. Capacity at that stage was 34 MLD (7½ mgd), although a maximum of 68 MLD (15 mgd) was achieved.

A new weir, constructed downstream of the river intakes to provide an adequate depth of water, was designed to allow fish to pass upstream. The raw river water is drawn via a submerged intake through coarse screens, and pumped to the contact tanks. Here, alum is added, as this improves the

17   136 megalitres (million litres) daily

settling characteristics of the water, before it is passed to the clarifiers — rectangular tanks through which the water flows from the bottom to the top. During this process, particles in the water coagulate in a filtering layer held in suspension against the upward flow of water. Material from this layer is continuously bled off into sludge consolidation tanks for thickening, pressing and subsequent disposal.

Then, the partially treated water is passed to the rapid gravity sand filters for the removal of any remaining particles, and discharged, after chlorination, into the clear water storage tanks, from which it is pumped into supply.

Bore-hole water on the site is clear but slightly acidic, and contains metallic salts. It is treated by aeration and the adddition of chemicals before passing to the filters and being blended with other treated water. When this process has been completed, the water is fit to drink — or, to put it more officially, "the treated water meets the EEC quality standards for drinking water".

All these careful and complex processes of improving our water are controlled at the touch of buttons. Introducing computerised monitoring and control of the plant has revolutionised the daily round, and left even fewer 'jobs for the boys' locally — there is only one Coldwaltham employee in the place. Some of the other people who live locally and work at the plant live in Water Authority houses, and these include those displaced when the Area Office moved from Horsham to Hardham in 1981. In 1954, there were four plant attendants, and two groundsmen; in 1957, eight plant attendants, two groundsmen and a superintendent. Now, a total of nine people are employed at the plant, although its size, importance and capacity have grown dramatically.

Hardham Water Treatment Works is in fact the first major works in the country specifically designed to be controlled by computer. Automatic sensing devices monitor flows and composition of the water and various stages of the treatment process, and report back to the central computer, which adjusts flow rates and chemical quality by means of valves and dosing pumps to achieve the desired final quality of the water. As with any new system, an extensive period of checking and calibration was undertaken, to ensure that the system was reliable.

Some miles upstream of the works, near Fittleworth Bridge, automatic sensors check river-water quality, to give early warning of possible pollution, so that the intake works can be shut down until the danger is past.

The Area Office, now based at Hardham, controls the supply of water to most of West Sussex, north of the South Downs, from Midhurst to the A23, the London to Brighton road. The only large towns served are Horsham and Crawley. Coldwaltham is predominantly rural, however, and most of the industries around are small users of water supplies.

In all, the population served is about 200,000, and the mains distribution network from Hardham includes many miles of 32-inch- to 8-inch-diameter pipelines and a number of service reservoirs and booster pumps to ensure continuity of supplies at an adequate pressure. Present peak demand from the works is about 65 MLD, 14 mgd, although 15 mgd was achieved, when needed, during 1984.

But things will not stop there, at Hardham. The availability of supplies and the capacity of the works for economical expansion make it eminently possible to extend the supply area beyond its present boundaries, if demand increases.

Passing on from the functionally acceptable to the practically beautiful, we come to Winter's Farm, the last house in the parish before the road sign takes us into 'Pulborough'. This lovely timber-framed, three-bay house, with its crown post roof, was built about 1500, with an open hall, possibly a smoke bay, inserted c. 1600 and the chimney built some fifty years later. In the early part of this century, the house may have been used as two or three separate dwellings. Two doors in the east wall, and another blocked up, point to this.

Originally, Winter's Farm belonged to Hardham Priory. The house fell into disrepair and was used as a farm building until, in 1958, it was bought and extensively renovated. For the past 27 years, it has been the home of Mr. Gordon Smith and his family. Mr. Smith is a churchwarden of St. Botolph's.

Fig. 11 Winter's Farm

As well as being the *last* house in the parish, it is of course also the *first,* when you leave Pulborough, and its beautiful façade smiles on the passer-by, and introduces him to the many other delights of Coldwaltham, just along the road.

Chapter 7

AMENITIES

Until the middle of the nineteenth century, Coldwaltham children attended the 'Dame' school in King's Lane, Coldwaltham, in a thatched cottage which is now a private house.

But, in 1848, largely through the efforts of the Rev. James Sandham, then vicar of the parish, Coldwaltham School was opened. It was dedicated, according to the commemorative plaque, as "the fruit of Christian love", on March 15th in that year, "to the glory of God and the training of Christian children". It was built in Church Lane, not far from the church and vicarage.

This "Little School behind the Church", as it was described in old Parish Magazine articles, had its foundation stone laid thirteen years later, in 1861— *"Laus Deo, Amicis Gratie, MDCCCLXI"*. Under the stone is a well and, until

Fig. 1 Coldwaltham School children of many years ago

the early 1960s — that is, for a century — all the water needed for the school had to be pulled up from this source.

It was slightly re-named — "Coldwaltham Church of England School" — when a second plaque went up. This, unveiled by Mr. R. Martin, Vice-Chairman of the West Sussex County Education Committee, marked "the occasion of the official opening of the rebuilt school, on October 5th, 1962".

There is dissent over why the church school run under the auspices of *St. Giles'* Church should have as its patron *St. James* (the school's official title is now St. James C. E. Controlled School). Mrs. Sheena Maskell, headmistress of the school from 1983 to 1985, is of the logical opinion — one shared by others in the parish — that it is because St. Giles, as patron of the lame and infirm, is hardly, with due respect to his memory, suitable to be patron of a school for lively youngsters.

From 1897, a school register was kept, and in it can be read again and again the names of families who have lived in the area for generations — Hawkins, Puttock, Harris, Hedger, Scutt, Maynard, Norman, Ruff, Clark, Rowland, Dudman, to name but a few.[1]

The register reveals, too, that the parish was still spelt 'Cold Waltham' as recently as 1953 (entry: Peter Wild, b. 2.3.48, of the Post Office, Cold Waltham). In a Parish Magazine article dated January 1957, headmaster Mr. S. Norris proudly records that fifty-seven children were on the registers at the end of the preceding term, and the average attendance in November 1956 of 95.7% was "the highest in the district". That same month, "Electric lighting was brought into the classrooms, and what a blessing it is". In 1958, a school crossing patrol was established, at the junction of the A29 with Church Lane. Mrs. Wyn Morum was the first Lollipop Lady to man the patrol.

---

1 Tudor Court Rolls, Exchequer Accounts and Church Registers reveal lists of old West Sussex names which are still common among families today. They include Allewyn, Bishop, Bowyer, Boxall, Eager, Ede, Hillman, Payne, Pullen, Streeter, Tanner, Tychenor (Tickner), Tribe, Vincent, Wakeford, and many others.

Fig. 2   Mrs. Wyn Morum, first Lollipop Lady of Coldwaltham

Nothing can improve the wonderful, if slightly inaccessible, site, secluded from the main road, surrounded by trees and fields and gardens, but since 1957 the school has certainly developed in scope and area. In 1957, a sandpit was built, the school was painted, and "the open fires which many parents will remember . . . disappeared, and although," writes Mr. Norris, "we will miss the friendly glow of the coal fires, we will appreciate the increased warmth from the more efficient coke stoves".

It was also in 1957 — obviously a red-letter year for the school — that its Parent Teacher Association was formed, following a suggestion put to parents by Mr. Norris. The Association held its first meeting in November, and has shown itself among the most active and supportive in the county ever since. In 1964, the P.T.A. started raising funds for a school swimming pool, and by 1965 the children were splashing about in it! The County's grant was £300, half the total cost of building the pool. It is the sole responsibility of the association, except for the pump. In 1975, the association found the money to buy a new pool liner. During the summer holidays, the P.T.A. provides voluntary helpers so that children can use the pool as much as possible.

by Mark Streeter.

Fig. 3 Cover of 1984 Coldwaltham School Sports programme

The association organises functions throughout the year to fund various projects. In 1961, the association even bought a bell rope for the church. For their school, over the years, they have found the money for musical instruments, carpets for the hall and infant classroom, a sewing machine, Lego building bricks, sand for the sandpit, cooking utensils, a colour television and tape recorder, computer and software, a computer trolley, bookcase and chairs for the reading area, books, calculators, a Z-Bed, science and maths equipment, and a school garden seat.

In addition, the association raises funds for the cost of coaches, and all the ingredients for the end-of-term Christmas parties are bought by them. They organise the costumes for school plays, and have taught themselves to apply grease-paint to excellent effect!

The P.T.A. has helped to paint the school—in 1984, the head teacher and a parent together decorated the inside. In 1984, too, members were behind their children in the Garden project. This involved (parents helping) digging and planting a vegetable garden (the children eventually ate their own produce for lunch), and planting ten trees round the playing fields.

Only two sobering events have marred the happy, peaceful life of those under the roof of Coldwaltham School. During World War II, a bomb fell at the back of the school, and a piece of it is still visible, embedded in one of the windows. Fortunately, no one was hurt. Then, in 1985, a disquieting rumour began to circulate about the school's possible closure, or amalgamation with Bury School, or with the school at Fittleworth.

A report on the three schools was considered by West Sussex County Council's Primary Education Committee at a meeting on December 16th, 1985. Under discussion were details of the buildings, staff and numbers of pupils, and "the various options open to them for the future provision of primary education in this area of the county".

At that meeting, it was also decided to defer from the 1987-88 'Starts Programme' the setting-up of a project to provide a new school at Fittleworth. The next step would be "local consultations", and a further report should be made to the Sub-Committee in May 1986.

Among the consultations were school meetings, and public meetings, in each parish. In Coldwaltham, they were heated and anxious. The overriding fear was that Coldwaltham School would be closed. Dwindling numbers of pupils and limited access for coaches to bring children from the other two schools, if the three were amalgamated, were against it.[2] All would definitely be resolved at a meeting of head teachers, chairman of school governors, chairmen of parish councils, "and others". In the meantime, parishioners with children at the school waited with bated breath in the wings, but ready to 'face the footlights', if need be . . .

At a meeting in June, the official decision was final: Coldwaltham School was not to be closed!

On another exciting note, Coldwaltham School has several times been televised during the past few years. On a practical note, the school's lunches, prepared daily at Coldwaltham for all three primary schools under current discussion, are renowned for their tastiness. One of the cooks, Mrs. Edith Pavey, who retired in the summer of 1985, had been cooking school lunches there for no less than thirty years.

When they reach ten, Coldwaltham schoolchildren usually move to the Herbert Shiner School, opened in 1961 in

---

2 Considering the situation in their 'Consultation Document' on the three schools concerned, the County Education Authority laid down their current "Policy towards Rural Schools":—

" . . . during the 1950s and 1960s there was a rationalisation of provision, when a number of schools were closed to establish a pattern of schools with reasonable numbers on roll.

"Secondly, in the Rother Valley area there was a reorganisation which was completed in the early 1970s and resulted in a three-tier system of 5-10, 10-13 and 13-16 schools. The age of 10 rather than 9 was chosen as the age of transfer so that village schools would remain of reasonable size.

"During the late 1970s and early 1980s, numbers on roll declined. The policy of the Education Committee during most of that time was in favour of village schools remaining open, and the kind of rationalisation favoured by some other [Education] Authorities, involving many closures, was not favoured.

"Towards the end of that period, however, it became clear that a small number of schools had reached such low numbers that there had to be grave doubt about their viability in education terms . . . "

Petworth, and from there, at thirteen, they may go to Midhurst Grammar School, travelling on the special buses provided daily.

*   *   *   *   *

In 1965, when Mr. Holt wrote his study, the main source of employment for Coldwaltham residents was still the land. There were still about a dozen working farms, and thirty to forty people worked on them. Mr. Jim Jupp's market garden in Coldwaltham gave work to six regular workers, augmented by casual workers at seasonally busy times.

Most other work was outside the parish — at Pepper and Son's limeworks at Amberley, A. G. Linfield's market garden at Thakeham, Spiro-Gills' engineering works at Pulborough, and the various local garages, including several in Pulborough.

Lodge Hill Centre provided work for at least twenty people — in the office, the kitchen, and the grounds. The Rother Pumping Station, as it used to be called, more or less ran itself, with the help of three or four staff working in shifts to keep things running smoothly.

In the earlier part of the twentieth century, Hardham Flour Mill was operating, and there was Hardham Brickyard (which produced the bricks for, among other houses, those of Golden Terrace in Pulborough). The Redhill Tile Company had used the quarry in Watersfield, beside Champs Hill, but closed down in 1943. There was a coalyard in Watersfield, too, down River Lane, at Watts Farm. It was run by the Heasmans, who lived there and worked what was then a small farm, as well as selling coal.

In 1927, a company called Marley rented land from Mr. Hicks, a Storrington farmer, to make tiles. Subsequently, Marley bought a large piece of land from Mr. Hicks for development of the business. Local people were delighted, because work became available to many who were being displaced by mechanisation, especially in agrriculture. Marley grew to be the largest employer for miles around. This situation continued until 1981, when the tilemaking operation was terminated. Other products were manufactured, and storage was carried on, but Marley finally closed down their entire operation in Storrington in 1983. One Coldwaltham resident for whom this was a blow, since he was so near to retirement age, was invited by Marley to go three times a week for a few months to their Cirencester place. No doubt the memory of those dawn drives from West Sussex to Gloucestershire, and late-evening returns home, will remain with Mr. Reg. Pavey, of Brookview, for a long time to come. (At least he had his wife, Mrs. Edith Pavey, and her superlative cooking[3] to come home to!)

There used to be thatchers living in the parish, but only one remains, Mr. Neville Galley, retired. "It is significant," the W.I. 1965 scrapbook wryly comments, "that he lives in a bungalow with a tiled roof!" The Dudmans have had a contracting and building business for many years, mainly a family concern. But apart from this, and concerns like the pubs and restaurants, and the garage, there is little local employment on offer.

The number of commuters to London and other places, as we have said, has grown considerably since 1965. Many people have moved to the parish because they like to live in the country, but want to remain working in town—whichever town it is. Gatwick Airport is conveniently close, too, and a few residents work there.

During May 1965, work started in the parish on the mains drains scheme and, at that time, regret was expressed that the drains had not been installed before the houses in Arun Vale and Silverdale were built, for their owners had the double expense of septic tanks and mains drainage connection charges. The West Sussex Water and Drainage Division (now, fortunately, shortened to the more endearing Southern Water) provided even better facilities when, from April 1983 until 1985, it worked to reinforce water mains in the Coldwaltham area, a step necessitated by the increase in population and thus in water usage. The new mains, completed in the autumn

---

3   see page 129

of 1985, are used as a gravity supply from the new reservoir
on Bury Hill, the construction of which was finished just
before that of the mains. Mains were laid from Bury Hill to
Tripp Hill, Fittleworth, with 'branch feeds' (subsidiary pipelines) to Coldwaltham and Bignor, and the pipes were mostly
laid on private land.

The parish is served by three telephone exchanges, which
seems odd when you remember the small size of this place. Of
the three exchanges, Pulborough covers most of Coldwaltham,
although parts of it come under Bury and Fittleworth, and
Bury also covers the whole of Watersfield. Pulborough became
an automatic exchange in 1962; Bury joined the automatic
sector in 1965, and Fittleworth followed suit in August 1966.
The parish has three public telephone boxes, one in each
hamlet: on the Old London Road, near Hardham Church; on
the A29, beside Brookview Estate, Coldwaltham, and in the
forecourt of the Three Crowns, Watersfield.[4]

The Post Office, which has 'moved around' in the parish,
from King's Lane, Coldwaltham, to Watersfield (where it was
first at the Old Bakery, opposite the garage; then at the old
Watersfield Stores) is now run from premises adjoining the
butcher's shop.

Newspapers used to be delivered from Monday to Saturday
by Mr. Bill Merritt, of Sutton, a familiar but fast-moving
morning feature as he whizzed from one house to the next.
He was known to cover River Lane in two minutes flat. His
successor, from 1985, is Mr. Denis Hollingsworth, of Petworth.
Also delivered without fail are the Sunday papers, by Mr. Ian
Scutt.

A fishmonger from Shoreham used to call every Friday,
but his place has now been taken by a Storrington fishmonger,
who delivers weekly, on a Wednesday. A local man, Mr.
Charlie Williams, used to deliver fruit and vegetables twice

---

4 Near the Three Crowns forecourt, beside the Watersfield bus shelter,
is another useful amenity: a noticeboard. (There is also one near Arun
Vale.) The Watersfield board (at least) was originally put up, in 1967, so
that the times of Divine Service at Coldwaltham Church could be posted.

Fig. 4   Coldwaltham Post Office

a week in Coldwaltham. Now, every Thursday, a van from Wisborough Green brings fruit and vegetables round.

The parish has always been well provided for, as far as food is concerned, and at one stage it even had its own bakery. How exhilarating it must have been to walk one's dog, or one's self, early in the morning along the lanes or to the pinewoods, passing the Watersfield bakery, with the aroma of freshly-baked bread to put thoughts of breakfast into one's mind! The bakery was run on the same premises as the old Post Office, by Mr. Fred Pennicott. His wife, Martha, ran the Post Office. The late Mr. Bert Pennicott, Fred's son, was a carpenter,[5] and his sister, Mrs. Ruby Mills, who died in 1985, was an accomplished amateur musician. She used to play the organ for worship in Watersfield Baptist Chapel, and

---

5 When I mentioned Bert Pennicott to Stan Ruff, he took me out to look at a seat in the garden, beside the kitchen door. Bert had apparently mended the seat many years before by inserting two new slats, and his giving of new life to the old seat was clearly registered by a then much younger Mr. Ruff.

join in village musical evenings, especially with the Rowland family. Mrs. Ruby Mills' two daughters, Mrs. Gertie Andrews and Mrs. Liz Barnard, who live in Petworth, remember how devoted she was to her husband, as she had been to her father.

*Fig. 5   Watersfield Bakery, now Old Post Office Cottage,
with Fred and Martha Pennicott outside*

Those who wanted to get away from Coldwaltham used to be able to kennel their dogs at Hollow Farm, Bury, with six-foot, formidable, sadly, the late Miss Barbara Stapeley.

People who wanted a dog of their own could, until 1976, apply to a Miss Joyce Braham—if they required a Skye Terrier. The then Miss Braham, who lived at Greenacres, Watersfield, bred Skye Terriers there for twenty years. From her first puppy, she bred her first champion, in 1965: Happyhill Hokey Cokey. That same year, she bred two further litters, and among them was a bitch which was exported to the United States. At that time, Miss Braham also kept what was then the only pedigree Jersey herd in the area.

There are two riding stables in Coldwaltham. One, at
Coldwaltham House, Watersfield, is run by Mrs. Esmé Jack.
In addition to standard livery and riding facilities, Mrs. Jack
has a roomy indoor riding school. For a number of years, she
gave riding lessons to spastic children from Ingfield Manor
School, Five Oaks, near Billingshurst, but now they are able
to use the riding facilities of a school much nearer to base.
Princess Anne, President of the Riding for the Disabled
Association, used to come down to watch the children there
and, long before that, her aunt, Princess Margaret, had riding
lessons with Mrs. Jack.

Based at Waltham Farm, Mrs. Joan Baxter, daughter of
Mr. Roy Cooper, also has a small riding school for adults and
children. Mrs. Baxter has a school contract with S. Michael's,
Petworth.

The parish had two general stores, Watersfield Stores,[6]
opposite the Three Crowns, and the one incorporated in
recent years in the butcher's shop, which was set up in 1931
by Mr. Beaumont (Beau) Rowland, coming from Northchapel,
and run later by his son, Mr. Reginald Beaumont (Reg)
Rowland. Since 1972, the butcher's shop has been run by his
son, John, whose wife, 'Birdie', has run the parish's Post
Office alongside for the past ten years.

Watersfield Stores dated back further, and has had a
somewhat chequered history, although it was the pride and
joy of Mr. Edward Unsted, who built and ran it in the early
1920s. Sadly its last owners could not get enough custom,
since many parishioners had by then formed the habit of
going to the Rowland establishment, where they could buy
meat, vegetables and groceries, and use the Post Office
facilities, 'all in one go'. Other people—at least, those with
transport—tend to shop daily in Pulborough, and make major
weekly shopping trips to Storrington, or further afield, to
Horsham, Chichester, Rustington, or Worthing.

There has been a garage at Watersfield for as long as
anyone can remember. It used to be nothing more than a

6 which finally closed down in 1986

Fig. 6 The Croft Garage, Watersfield, when it belonged to Moses Harris

primitive square old petrol pump and shack, run by the late
Moses (Mosey) Harris, who, in 1945, passed on the goodwill
in the garage to Miss Dorothy May Mowll. In 1948, Moses
Harris sold the garage and land round it to Miss Mowll, who
continued to carry on the business of "motor engineer and
garage proprietor", as the Deeds say, until she admitted into
partnership, in 1955, Mr. Eric Bell, of West Wickham, Kent.
He was to help her run what was until then known as the
Croft Garage, under the changed name of "Parish Brothers",
presumably because of her close relationship with Mr. Fred
Parish. Miss Mowll had for about five years held the freehold
of both the garage, with its residential bungalow, and the old
(Baptist) chapel, in Stane Street Lane.

The Partnership Deed stipulated that Mr. Bell was to devote
"his whole time to the business, managing and controlling of
the workshop department", and Miss Mowll would give "what
time she thought necessary", and "promote its success". The

same document also gave Miss Mowll the power to "appoint Mr. Frederick Parish, or others, to manage, conduct and supervise the business, in conjunction with Mr. Bell". Sixty per cent. of the net profits were to go to Miss Mowll; forty per cent. to Mr. Bell, and all losses would be borne in the same proportion. Following registry of this Partnership Deed, a Declaration of Trust was drawn up between Miss Mowll and Mr. Bell.

In 1954, a County Court Order[7] had changed the use of the old Baptist Chapel, owned by Miss Mowll, "subject to the approval of detailed plans for the proposed conversion to a dwelling house within three years".

About three years later, the partnership between Eric Bell and Miss Mowll was dissolved, and the former was assigned all Miss Mowll's share in the business. In 1960, Eric Bell sold the garage to Shell-Mex & B.P. and John P. Scammell Ltd., estate agents, for £850 and, in 1968, Eric Bell, Shell-Mex and Messrs. Scammell sold their joint interest in the Old Chapel, as it is now called, to Mr. and Mrs. William (Bill) Innis, who have lived there ever since. Mr. Bell then ran Tripp Hill Garage, in Fittleworth, until his death in June 1987.

For three years, from 1960, the garage was run by Paul and Eric Massey, until it was bought by its present owner, Mr. John Northcott. A tremendous parish outcry greeted Mr. Northcott's subsequent attempt to streamline and enlarge the garage premises. But Planning Permission was sought, and granted, for the pulling down of the bungalow (where Mr. Northcott at first lived with his family) and for the construction of a showroom. Apart from operating as a petrol station and car repair workshop, it became a well-patronised Saab car agency between 1971 and 1980, and in 1984 it took on the Honda agency for the area. In 1986, the garage expanded yet again. The workshops were re-built, the car sales showrooms renovated, and the garage offices and shop were improved.

---

7 The County of West Sussex (Area of Special Interest) Order, 1965

The centre of most of the parish's social and community
life is Sandham Hall, named after the Rev. James Sandham,
who was vicar of Coldwaltham for fifty-one years. When he
died, the Rev. Sandham left the land to his niece, Miss Mary
Louisa Sandham, and a Trust Deed dated 7th May, 1903,
records her gift of the land "with the building erected or in
course of erection thereon". The vicar and churchwardens
were appointed administrative trustees, to take charge of the
property, for its use in a number of ways, as is usual in the
case of a church, or parish, hall.

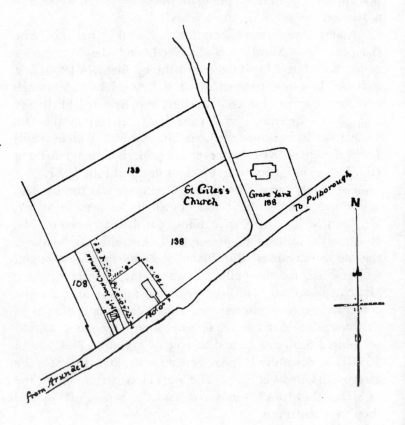

Fig. 7   Plan of Sandham Hall site

Sandham Hall was conveyed by the Diocesan Trustees, who were later replaced by the Chichester Fund and Board of Finance (Incorporated). But the effective managing trustees have always been the vicar and churchwardens.

The Deed further restricted the use and management of the hall by "providing that the property was held upon such trusts, etc., as the vicar and churchwardens shall from time to time direct, subject to certain safeguards, in particular that it shall be an ecclesiastical charity and that until the vicar and churchwardens otherwise direct, shall be held upon trust for the use of the vicar and churchwardens, or their nominees or licensees for the numbered purposes set out in the Deeds."

The "purposes" are worth listing in full from the Trust Deed:—

"Upon trust to permit the same and all or any buildings or building which now are or may hereafter be erected on the said premises or any part thereof to be used by the Vicar and Churchwardens or their nominees or licensees as the case may be for all or any of the purposes following, that is to say:—

1. For the celebration of Divine Service in accordance with the rites and ceremonies of the Church of England.

2. As a school or schools for the education of children, and adults or children only of the labouring manufacturing and other poorer classes in the said parish according to the principles of the Church of England.

3. As a residence or residences for a teacher or teachers of the said school or schools.

4. As a class room, meeting room or lecture room for confirmation or communicants classes or for other religious instruction or for secular instruction.

5. As a place of meeting for clerical meetings for social conferences of the Clergy for District Visitors for Committees of any societies, parochial or otherwise, connected with the Church of England, and for meetings to be called in aid of, or for the benefit of, any such societies.

6. As a place of meeting for a club or clubs of the labouring manufacturing and other poorer classes in the said parish.

7. As a lending library or as a place of entertainment.

8. For letting out to hire for such rent during such period and on such terms as the Vicar and Churchwardens shall think fit.

9. For any other meetings or for any other objects ends and purposes as the Vicar and Churchwardens shall think desirable."

When Sandham Hall was built in 1903, by a local builder, the late George Charman[8], the Rev. Owen Phillips was vicar,

Coldwaltham

and the churchwardens were Harry Cayme, of Pulborough, and Frederick Millyard, of Watersfield, so that these three were the first effective trustees of the hall.

The hall's 1947-48 balance sheet reveals the variety of events taking place there. It was, one might say quite literally, a godsend to the parish.

Sandham Hall

1st Oct 1947 to 30th Sept 1948

Receipts	£ s. d.	Expenditure	£ s. d.
Dances, Whist Drives and Entertainments	26 11 0	Deficit	6 14 2
W.I.	3 19 0	Cleaning	10 15 0
ditto. Canning	2 10 0	Coal	3 7 8
Meat Pie Scheme	1 1 0	Theatre Licence	1 1 0
Rother Players, Rehearsing	3 0 0	Rates	7 16 11
Private Parties	3 3 0	Fire Insurance	2 17 8
Parish Council	1 5 0	Public Liability Insurance	13 6
Rogues-Vagabonds, Rehearsing	1 7 0	Electric Bulbs	6 10
Table Tennis Club	6 15 0	Playing Cards	1 8 0
		Electricity (3 Quarters)	3 6 6
		Repairs	5 0
		Sundries	2 9
			41 15 0
		Balance in hand	7 6 0
	£49 1 0		£49 1 0

Fig. 8   Balance sheet of Sandham Hall, 1947-48

Quite a sensible suggestion put forward in 1963 by Coldwaltham Parish Council was its taking over the running of the hall, so that grants could be obtained to allow improvement of the kitchen and sanitary arrangements. In 1951, a building licence had been secured for sanitary "improvements", and toilets had been added. Presumably, before that it was very primitive indeed. Also in 1951, a store shed had been erected. But all this was not enough, given the increasing use of the hall's amenities by growing numbers of people.

The idea of a secular group taking over what many considered, and many still consider, to be a "church hall"

8 Mr. Charman also donated the hall's swing doors—very much the 'in thing' then.

led to a fierce controversy. It didn't rage for long, but it raged nonetheless.

Parish councillor, Mr. Peter Parish, having researched the position and examined the relevant papers, discovered that the money for building the hall had been raised by public subscription, but there was no written record of where the money had actually come from.[9]

The vicar and churchwardens would not agree to the parish council's taking over administration of the hall, and the matter was dropped, but reluctantly by some. At the time, Mr. Eric Bull, landlord of the Labouring Man, was also, more relevantly, chairman of the parish council. He was quoted in the local press as saying: "It was never our idea to take over the hall, but we did want to do something to see that it was used more."

Mr. Parish was less self-effacing. He spoke of another hall in West Sussex being in exactly the same position. The Diocesan trustees in this other case were also opposed to handing over the hall to the parish council. "Yet," argued Mr. Parish, "in other parts of the country, we can see Diocesan trustees only too willing to sell to parish councils at a nominal purchase price of one penny."

Mr. Parish thus made this a county, and not just a local, problem, but Mr. Bull's diplomacy won the day.

"We had better go into this more deeply," he advised his colleagues at a meeting. "We may still be able to do something for the hall—or build another."

In fact, nothing has happened since those heated meetings in 1963. The hall remains self-supporting, and receives no financial help from any quarter for its maintenance. Fortunately, the loyal and long-labouring parishioners of Coldwaltham keep on decorating the hall, inside and out, without a murmur, trimming hedges, maintaining the car park and, recently, extending the park and erecting a splendid fence, with funds raised from events and appeals.

---

9 £375 was raised by subscription, all but £25 of the total needed to build the hall. A Victorian Smoking Concert was given to raise the final £25. Unfortunately, fire destroyed the detailed records of all this.

There was one occasion when the hall was used as a school: in 1961, when St. James's C.E. School was awaiting completion, but, apart from that, most of the activities have been social. Up to 1965, these included meetings of the Darby and Joan Club, Women's Institute, Mothers' Union, Village Produce Association, Youth Club, Guides and Brownies, and whist drives.

In 1965, the Sandham Hall Olde Tyme Dance Club was formed by the vicar, the Rev. Eric Newcombe. This ran with great success until 1977, when it had to close down through lack of funds. However, in 1981 another Old Tyme Dance Club was formed, under the leadership of Mr. and Mrs. Mike Wood of Pulborough, and this is still going strong.

By the end of the 1960s[10], the hall had fallen into sad disrepair — it was not looked after by volunteers in the way it is now — and in 1970 it was decided to make an effort to obtain funds for an extension for toilets and other facilities, and to re-build the kitchen. A lottery fund was formed: The Friends of Sandham Hall, with over 100 members, and an additional parish-wide appeal was made. Money came in to the extent that renovations to the hall were completed by 1975, without recourse to the parish council, or any other source, for financial aid.

A human touch to end this little saga of the much-loved and well-used Sandham Hall: when the old floor was ripped up in 1963, and a new one swiftly fitted[11], Mr. Chris Harris discovered an old but intact box of matches among the joists. They could well have been left there, he believes, by his wife Jean's grandfather, Mr. Thomas Goodger, who helped to build the hall.

---

10 Mrs. Mary Maynard remembers a meeting at the hall in 1968, after which she remarked to her husband: "I'll never set foot in that place again!" Nevertheless, she has helped to run the hall, including its bookings, for over fifteen years.

11 To help raise funds for the new floor, sections of the old floor were sold to parishioners at 35/- a yard ... This was in November 1963. A month later, Mr. Chris Harris removed the old floor, and in January 1964 a party was held for those who had laid the *new* floor.

*Fig. 9 Coldwaltham and Watersfield outing
in the late 1940s or early 1950s*

The Women's Institute, a regular user of the Sandham Hall, has also been a great source of social and instructive activity in the parish, and of just plain friendship. I have written fully about the local W.I. in the next chapter, but perhaps here, for interest's sake, I will just quote what the institute wrote for its 1965 scrapbook:—

"The membership of our W.I. now stands at fifty-six, with an average attendance of thirty-two members. Our programme of speakers ranges from Floral Decorations to Cookery, Travel, Guide Dogs for the Blind, Road Safety and Beauty. We usually have two garden meetings in the summer but this year both of these meetings had to be abandoned because of bad weather.

At each meeting, we run a monthly competition and our enterprising sales table is a great help to our funds. During the year, we had a jumble sale, three raffles and a coffee morning in aid of County and [local] Institute funds.

Each year, our branch raises funds for, and organises, a summer outing for all the people in the village who are over sixty. Quite a large portion of the funds is contributed by the W.I. The rest is collected by us from private donors and from other local charitable institutions. This year, our senior citizens enjoyed an outing by coach to the Pier Pavilion, Worthing, for the Summer Show, followed by a substantial tea."

Books are important to many who live in an out-of-the-way place, and Coldwaltham has long been well served in this respect. A travelling library van has operated for many years, first out of Horsham and, more recently, from Pulborough. The van now calls, each Monday morning, first at the Three Crowns, Watersfield, then at Brookview estate and, finally, at 1.40 p.m., it stops at the Labouring Man. The van driver is accompanied by a library assistant, who takes in books and issues them, and the van carries a wide selection of titles.

In addition, both Storrington, five miles away, and Pulborough have good libraries, with bonuses in terms of hours when open—all day Saturday, and one late night a week each. But even going back a few years, an enterprising and community-minded lady called Mrs. Cattermole, who lived at the Old Malt House, Watersfield, made available to the parish a comprehensive stock of some 400 books, brought in, and changed five times a year (in 1965 at least[12]), by the County Library at Horsham.

The parish fares less well in transport matters. Just a few years ago, there were frequent daily buses to Pulborough, Worthing and Horsham, but now buses through Coldwaltham are few and far between. Until 1986, the 288 Southdown bus, on Wednesdays, ran from Slinfold via Coldwaltham to Chichester, and back. Now, London Country Southwest run a similar service, the 972, between Dorking and Chichester, via Coldwaltham. The 297 Chichester - Horsham, Thursday service also takes in Coldwaltham. The reason for the cutbacks is given as "the change in the nature of the rural population". The most significant "movement of people" now, says Southdown, is that of children, and adequate provision is made for them with hired buses.

Things had started deteriorating by 1965, and the W.I. scrapbook for that year records that "buses all stop at Pulborough Station, although there is only one fast train each hour from Victoria and only one bus each hour from the station", and "The bus does not always wait for the train.

---

12   W.I. Scrapbook for 1965

Often unfortunate travellers to our village arrive at Pulborough station, therefore, to find no means of reaching their destination, unless they take a taxi or walk."

Now, the train service is better, although there are no local buses to meet the trains! During the morning and evening rush-hour periods, there are up to three trains an hour. Between times, trains run half-hourly and, off-peak, for just a short time, hourly. On Sundays, there is an hourly service.

I have always thought that curtailed Sunday rail services are a pity, but I notice the lack much more, living in a rural area. Many people come down to see family and friends, not only in Coldwaltham, of course; all over the country, at weekends. Many would much rather take a train, if there is one, than drive down. But all of them have to check carefully what Sunday trains there are to take them back, and whether engineering works on the line will restrict the service still further before they leave.

Fortunately, there is a good taxi service from the station, although it is usually necessary to telephone for a taxi, and there never seem enough to go round.

Like many small places, Coldwaltham is well served when it comes to public houses and eating places. Watersfield, indeed, used to have two pubs. The Swallow Inn, on Beacon Hill, was just a small place. In October 1940, George James (Jim) Pescod, who had moved his family down from Redhill, Surrey, after they were bombed, became licensee of the Swallow. When he died, in 1946, Mrs. Pescod took over the pub. First, it was only licensed to sell beer, then a wine licence was granted, provided she didn't dispense spirits. The Swallow was famed for its darts team, which held the Darts Hospital Cup for 32 consecutive weeks — a record said never to have been broken in the 1950s. Mrs. Pescod ran the pub until it closed on May 20th, 1957—a date clearly remembered by her son Jim, because it is his birthday. Friary Brewers owned the Swallow, but when they took over the Three Crowns, from Henty and Constable, they felt that there would not be enough business for two pubs, so the Swallow had to go.

Figs. 10 & 11   The Three Crowns

first at the Old Crown House,

then across the road

The Three Crowns used to be housed in what is now called the Old Crown House, on the opposite side of the road from where it now is. Marjorie Hessell Tiltman wrote of the old pub: "It is a good inn, full of old memories and touched with reports of the smuggling that went on in every river port near the coast at one time,[14] and the smell of ale and shag [tobacco] has crept into its beams and its walls for ever."[15] Past licensees of the old pub included the Turners, then, in the 1920s, Moses and Emma Harris. It is said that when the Harrises arrived in Watersfield they were so penniless, they didn't know whether to go to Fred Pennicott, the baker, to get oats for the horse, or something for themselves. Next, Louise (née Harris) and Arthur Turrell took over the pub, and Mr. and Mrs. Tom Lock were the last tenants of the old pub and the first tenants of the new, which was built about 1930. There used to be an apple orchard where the forecourt to the Three Crowns now is, with the village green behind.

The 'new' Three Crowns has also had many licensees. The last but one, Mr. Dave Pettit, organised the making of a lovely garden to one side of the pub, with an exciting, beautifully made log hut for the children. In his time, too, a small family restaurant was added, with good meals available, including excellent Sunday lunches—a tradition carried on by subsequent licensees. There is also a pool room attached to the pub—a great asset, especially on long winter evenings.

The other parish inn is the Labouring Man, on a loop of the Old London Road in Coldwaltham. An Edwardian pub, some eighty years old, it used to have a thatched roof, but the whole place was burned down in 1906, and had to be rebuilt. Mr. and Mrs. Sam Greenfield had the pub at one stage, then Mr. and Mrs. Bill Laing, but perhaps its best known licensee was Mr. Malcolm Bull, a former Chairman (and among the most diplomatic, it is said!) of Coldwaltham Parish

14 from *Cottage Pie* by Marjorie Hessell Tiltman
15 It is even hinted by some of the older people that smugglers themselves used the old Three Crowns to drink in. To bear this out, right down River Lane, just before the river, there's a secret little hollow with a cave in it, still called Smugglers' Cave.

Council. The pub is now owned by Mr. Bill Davis, of Cold-waltham.

Between the Three Crowns and the Labouring Man, at the top of Church Hill, is Barn Owls restaurant and hotel. John Batten, writing about it in a 1976 issue of the *West Sussex Gazette,* describes it as "a tall Victorian house with three perky dormers".[16]

Barn Owls used to be called Oxford House and, at the beginning of the twentieth century, it was lived in by William ('Shottie') and Eliza Harwood,[17] who ran a smallholding there.

After World War I, it belonged to the Misses Lydia and Ellen Henly, and it was then called 'The Gnomes'. The Henly sisters took in 'summer visitors', many of them friends, for board and lodging, as well as continuing the practice of making cream and butter, which graced the tables of the guests and were sold to the public as well.[18] Lydia and Ellen, obviously an indefatigable pair, also ran Waltham Farm until 1911. There, in addition to a coach house, they had loose-boxes for horses and calves, and a cowstall for their ten cows. The sisters retired to the White Cottage in Sandy Lane, Watersfield, in 1948.

After that date, a number of people bought the property, and its name was changed first to Brown Owls, then to Romans, and finally, in 1980, to Barn Owls, when it was bought by the late Mr. John Peel, in partnership with Mr. Fred Testka, who was in charge of the running of the place, and of the cooking. In 1982, Pat and Marion Hellenberg took over

---

16 Mr. Batten went on to note that "Close by is a pillar box and a stamp machine, which made me think 'full marks for the Post Office' until I saw it deliver stamps for a fivepenny coin, and wondered how you'd make up today's 6½p or 8½p value!" The little post box and machine are still there, but the machine has been adapted, more than once, and now helpfully issues 50p stamp books for those in such need.
17 see also Dorothy Smith's account in Chapter 9, *In Living Memory*
18 Mr. Vic Reading, now retired and living in Brookview, worked as a boy for the Misses Henly. When I asked him if he had lived 'in' or 'out', he said: "Definitely out! I slept in the chicken shed, near the house, and primitive it was, too. No, I definitely lived 'out'." Mr. Reading recalls that, at one time, Oxford House was run as a guest house by a Mr. and Mrs. Greaves, who called the place 'Crossways'.

the place, and have located the little round-house where butter used to be churned. The Hellenbergs take in not just 'summer guests' but all-the-year-round paying guests, in addition to running a good restaurant specialising in organic foods. Two kind gestures they make to the parish are holding its monthly Village Lunch Club there for all to come to, at a low cost, and welcoming in, during a night before Christmas, a large and weary band of parish carol-singers, to consume limitless mounds of home-made mince pies and coffee. For this, the cold-nosed and cold-handed band are only too glad to serenade diners with a few favourite carols.

On April 1st, 1933, a Deed was drawn up between the National Playing Fields Association and Coldwaltham Parish Council. It concerned Captain John Alban Head's bequest of "a Playing Field in the Parish of Coldwaltham in the County of Sussex."

The NFPA were appointed Trustees of the lands which, the Deed says, were granted "for the benefit of the inhabitants of the Parish of Coldwaltham and the neighbourhood."

Coldwaltham Parish Council applied to the West Sussex County Council to be vested with the powers of the Open Spaces Act 1906, and such powers were duly conferred upon them by an Order of the County Council dated 24th February, 1933.

Under the terms of that Act, the NFPA have the power to transfer the lands to the council "by a free gift for a limited term"—and they, in fact, transferred the lands for 99 years, with certain provisions.

On March 27th, 1933, the council accepted the gift, and the Deed was executed on the council's behalf by the then council chairman, Everard Holland, his signature witnessed by Tilleard Horace Osman Collings and George William Ruff, two council committee members.

The lands consisted of six acres "with the rights of way appertenant thereto". The council would hold the lands from 25th March, 1933, and they had "at all times thereafter [during the 99 years] to give effect to the trusts" affecting the lands, and "observe and perform the conditions on and subject to which the National Playing Fields Association hold the same" . . . and keep the lands and any buildings "which are now or may hereafter be erected in proper repair and condition", as far as the income received from the association permitted.

Captain Alban Head left an amount of £1200, the annual interest from which was to be used in maintenance.

The Deed stipulated that a Committee of Management should be formed. It would consist of:—

> three members of the parish council appointed by the county council, who would hold office for up to three years (less, if they ceased to be council members);
> one representative of the West Sussex Playing Fields Association appointed by the association, to hold office for three years;
> one representative each of the "Cricket, Football and Stool-ball Clubs of Coldwaltham" and "of any other club or clubs in the said Parish approved hereafter by the council, each such Club representative to be appointed by his or her club, and to hold office for three years"; and
> three people appointed by the council from outside the council's own members for three years (at the outset).

All these members of the Committee of Management should be eligible for re-appointment. If any breach of the Covenant occurred, the National Association of Playing Fields, or anyone authorised by them, could repossess the lands forthwith.

Lastly, the Deed of Covenant stated: "It is hereby certified that the transaction hereby effected does not form part of a larger transaction or a series of transactions in respect of which the aggregate amount or value of the property transferred exceeds £500."

Over the years, there has been much controversy over the use, and lack of use, of the Alban Head Playing Field, and indeed over the prevention of the field's facilities being used by those entitled to. Attempts have been made to build tennis courts, by public subscription — but not enough enthusiasm could be engendered by Mr. Roy Wardell, whose idea they were. There have been fights to keep horses off the field, which have been won, fights to stop dogs fouling it, which may not be won, fights to curtail the number of activities going on — and they are lamentably few — by local residents who did not want their peace disturbed.

But, at the end of the day, on the positive side, there is this most beautiful stretch of land. We walk our dogs along the edge of it (or they walk themselves), into the pinewoods behind. We still remember the excitement when the sports pavilion went up in 1967.[19] And we proudly watch our football and cricket teams getting better and better in a setting which must be hard to beat, in terms of scenic peace.

Of all the amenities in the parish, this is perhaps the greatest, with the greatest potential for recreational development for *all* those stipulated in the 1933 Deed: that is, the inhabitants of the Parish of Coldwaltham and the neighbourhood.

---

19 one of the many achievements of the parish council, through its Playing Field Committee

Chapter 8

COMMUNITY LIFE

Spread out though it is, and dissected by the busy A29, which buzzes continuously with traffic, Coldwaltham is a close community.

Fig. 1 Summer outing from Coldwaltham

For centuries, many activities have centred round, or have been influenced by, the church, which is described in Chapter 5, but the Wildbrooks Society organises much of what goes on, in various spheres.

In 1971, John Boxford, who had been one of Coldwaltham Parish Church's wardens then for 12 years, was approached by the vicar, the Rev. Ronald Chatwin, to set up some kind of club that would bring parishioners together. It should be non-religious and non-political, and its main aim would be to "get a community spirit going", as the Rev. Chatwin put it to Mr. Boxford.

Tentative feelers were put out. Would people be interested? Would they support such a club? What sort of things would they like to see the club doing, and catering for? An initial meeting was announced, to be held in the vicarage, and the response was tremendous. No fewer that eighty-seven people turned up. "They had to sit on the stairs, in the kitchen, wherever there was space," recalled Mr. Boxford. People thought the idea was excellent, and their choice of social activities then was, first, visits to local theatres and cinemas; second, discussions and debates, and third, talks, walks and other outings. The main hobby turned out to be gardening. Times have not changed much!

Thus, in March 1972, the Wildbrooks Society came into being. Why was it called 'Wildbrooks'? The founders wanted to call the society something that would from the outset weld together those living in, and around, the parish. The beautiful Wild Brooks area borders on the south all three hamlets in the parish, and so it was felt that no more appropriate name could be found.

The society's stated objects, at its inception, were:—

(a) To improve and conserve the good appearance and general amenity of the villages of Coldwaltham and Watersfield and the civil area of Coldwaltham Parish for the benefit of their inhabitants.

(b) To build up a 'Community Life' by fostering social and cultural activities, providing a means of meeting together to discuss and further the interests of the inhabitants.

(c) To encourage high standards of planning and architecture in new developments.

These were worthy aims, and not much was asked of individual members in return: in 1972, the subscription was a mere "fifteen new pence". In 1976, the subscription went up to 30p and in 1984 to 50p, but these amounts were minimal measured against the benefits available, which included numerous causes taken up for the parish by the Wildbrooks Society.

The first-recorded of these was the threat to local footpaths. In June 1973, the society wrote to Chanctonbury

Rural District Council (based at Storrington), asking that it be put on the Register "in order that we may receive any proposals [pertaining to footpaths] which may affect the parish of Hardham, Coldwaltham and Watersfield."

In the same letter, the society expressed concern that some public footpaths faced closure at that time, including one on the south side of Watersfield. The society also pointed out, to show its weight, affiliation to the Council for the Protection of Rural England, and its intention (as in 1973) to join the Federation of Sussex Amenity Societies.

Next, the Wildbrooks Society got to grips with a major road-development problem in the parish. In July 1973, the then Honorary Secretary, J. H. (Harry) Sanders, wrote to the West Sussex County Council, ready to do battle. His letter reads:—

> "Our society was formed . . . to look after the amenities of the villages of Coldwaltham and Watersfield. We are very concerned at the proposed alterations to the route of the A29 as it affects these villages. This is not a By-Pass of Coldwaltham but a route to take the road through the edge of the most densely populated residential area of the village. It is so sited on the South East facing slope that the best views from the village over the Arun valley to the Downs will be quite spoilt by having a four lane Motorway in the foreground.
>
> "We feel the reason for the surprising decision of the planners to route the new road in such a way as to completely spoil the amenities of the village for so many people is because the map upon which the new route is planned is quite out of date. It fails to show three new Housing Estates through the edge of which the . . . road is planned to pass. Enclosed is a map showing the approximate position of these new Estates marked in red.
>
> "We should therefore be grateful if you would be so good as to see that our protest against this new route for the A29 through Coldwaltham is recorded with the right authorities.
>
> "The Housing Estates affected are Arun Vale, Silverdale and extensions to the Brookview Council Estate. The proposed route is so close . . . that some of the bungalows will have to be demolished to make room for a four-laned motorway because of the nearness of the Railway on the other side."

Imbued, on behalf of the society, with a strong crusading spirit, Mr. Sanders used this same letter to draw attention to heavy traffic on the A29 at Coldwaltham . . .

> "May we also add a request that if it is possible to do some-

thing to stop the very long and heavy lorries continuously using the A29 through the village, we should all be very grateful. Is it possible that they could be restricted to the A24, which has dual carriageways?"

The blows were somewhat parried by the County Surveyor, to whom were addressed various other letters, both on the question of re-routing the projected A29 By-Pass, and that of removing heavy traffic from the same road.

However, the Wildbrooks Society had made their points. Their presence had been felt. Coldwaltham Parish Council lent its support to the By-Pass protest, too, and wrote on the subject (not quoting the Wildbrooks Society's campaign) to the County Surveyor.

The By-Pass was to have been built about ten years later, by 1982, but *it was not built.* A letter dated 5th February, 1976, from the County Surveyor to the Honorary Secretary of the Wildbrooks Society brought the news officially:

"The scheme for the by-pass has been rescinded"!

In the meantime, having heard a rumour that the By-Pass project had been abandoned, the society now proved itself to be opportunist as well as crusading, and leapt in with another amenity bee in its bonnet: What was going to happen to the land which *would* have been the site of the proposed By-Pass? Land between Silverdale and the railway, and also between Arun Vale and the railway had been partly cultivated by local residents but, early in 1976, they had received notice to quit.

The Parish Council once more showed support, writing to the County Surveyor about the Notice given:

"The Council hope that these notices will be cancelled in view of the imperative need for more food to be grown and further, that land not being cultivated as allotments will be made available for this purpose as we are receiving an increasing number of enquiries for allotments . . .

"It is felt that the County Council will be sympathetic to the increasing desire of people to indulge in *the healthy and reasonably profitable exercise of gardening.*"!

Back to the traffic situation on the A29 went the society. If the By-Pass had been constructed, although it would have meant upheaval for the residents of the three estates implicated, it *would* have helped to solve the heavy-traffic problem, because the existing stretch of the main road would have become a mere service road for Watersfield and Coldwaltham. Alas, more and more lorries were thundering through the parish, even longer and heavier, it seems, than in 1973 — and now it looked as though things would just get worse.

Dangerous driving was another traffic problem and, in 1978, with commendable tenacity, the Society wrote to Coldwaltham Parish Council, then chaired by Mr. Chris Harris, on this score. Members wanted the 30 m.p.h. speed limit, which was already in force in Watersfield, to operate in Coldwaltham as well, reinforced by the extension, both to north and south, of the double white lines over Church Hill. They also proposed the introduction of a roundabout at the junction of the A29 and Brook Lane (leading to Greatham and Storrington and much used as a short cut by Fittleworth to Storrington traffic). Pedestrian crossings were proposed, too, at Church Lane, Coldwaltham (leading to St. James C.E. primary school) and in Watersfield, near the store.

Coldwaltham Parish Council again involved itself, but the joint petition met with no success. At least, however, the West Sussex County Council, according to a letter of 9th July, 1979, undertook to provide "larger warning signs ... on the A29, to give greater emphasis to the existence of the crossroads at Brook Lane."

It is doubtful whether many of the parish's residents realised just how much the Wildbrooks Society warriors were doing to protect and serve them at that busy stage of their existence.

Just a few months later, on December 15th, 1979, John Boxford, founder-member of the society, and chairman for 11 years, again took up the matter of reducing the speed limit in Coldwaltham hamlet to 30 m.p.h., in line with that in Watersfield.

Replying to Mr. Boxford, the West Sussex County Engineer and Surveyor showed little hope, but sympathised ...

"I would just mention that in the very detailed report submitted to the June meeting of the Committee in response to your Society's request earlier this year, reference was actually made to the elderly people visiting the surgery at The Pines [near the Brook Lane crossing], youngsters attending the Youth Club situated in Fittleworth Road, people attending the various functions in Sandham Hall, and children going to school in Church Lane. Thus the [Roads and Transport] Committee were acquainted with most of the 'social conditions' which is the new evidence you would like us to submit in support of a change in the speed limit and extension of double white lines."

The Scrutiny Panel—which decided whether or not to pass on such problems to the Road and Transport Committee—decided "a further report was not justified".

On the Panel's behalf, the County Surveyor had to write back:

"The problem of communities being bisected by busy main roads is an extremely difficult one to overcome in real terms, but, with the large amount of experience available throughout the country on both how well speed limits are respected and double white line systems obeyed, it is apparent that at Coldwaltham, with both of these devices, possible dangers would not be obviated. In the circumstances, it is preferable for pedestrians to exercise care knowing what the traffic behaviour is really like, rather than introducing measures which might create the impression that conditions are more like those found in busy urban situations."

Ah well.

In 1983, the Stopham Bridge project gave cause for concern. The chairman of the society wrote to the district council for assurance that, while the old bridge was closed and the new bridge being built, there would be no question of diverting all traffic via Coldwaltham and Watersfield. He received a reply to the effect that this possibility had been turned down on "environmental grounds".

That same year, Mr. J. H. Sanders died, aged 83. He had been a tower of strength and activity in the society, with Mr. John Boxford (who only gave up the presidency in 1983), since its inception. Harry Sanders had already retired when, in 1972, he became Hon. Treasurer *and* Hon. Secretary of the Wildbrooks Society. He held both these posts for 11 years, along with that of organiser of the Worthing shopping coach (mentioned later in this chapter) from its very first run, in 1972, until 1981. The contribution he made is appropriately praised in the society's records.

Object (b) of the Wildbrooks Society—"To build up a 'Community Life' by fostering social and cultural activities, providing a means of meeting together to discuss and further the interests of the inhabitants"—was by no means forgotten. Indeed, it is perhaps here that the society has, over the years, been of the most lasting and constant value to its members and friends.

Ever since its inception in 1972, a monthly event has been organised, usually in the Sandham Hall. These have been varied, and still vary, but most are well attended. Debates are ever-popular. Random examples include:— "That the way parents have brought up their children is responsible for the decadence of the standards of life today"—December 1972; "That the Affluent Society is not a happy one"—December 12th, 1974; and "That this house is of the opinion that we have become too soft in our present-day treatment of criminal offenders"—February 11th, 1976: one likely to be revived, surely, in view of the climate of current public opinion on the subject.

Illustrated talks have always been popular, on topics of local as well as 'headline' interest . . . "Vegetable gardening"; "The Wildfowl Trust, Arundel"; "Parish footpaths: What we can do to help" (no doubt this one was an attempt to rope in as much support as possible for the society's defence, and offensive, against possible closures!). A talk on "Simple Precautions against Nuclear Attack", on the night it was given an airing, November 10th, 1982, led to forthright and fiery exchanges.

Two annual favourites are the Twelfth Night party, in Sandham Hall, and the Garden Plant and Produce Sale, also held in the hall. Here parishioners and friends can buy a range of goods from home-made cakes and crab-apples to garden tools—but, especially, plants to replenish their flower and vegetable beds, and window-sills, before the cold weather sets in.

There have been regular walks, often across the nearby South Downs, theatre trips to Worthing, either by coach or in a fleet of neighbours' cars, and musical evenings. A popular event was "An Evening's Delight", produced by Maud Hodgson, the vicar's wife, hosted by the vicar, in relaxed, armchair mood, and "presented by members of the society for the entertainment of all", in December 1984. The vicar introduced poems of his choice. Several were of local significance and one, by Padraic Colum, which I was asked to read, had a particular poignancy. Padraic Colum, along with many other famous poets and writers (Hilaire Belloc, Francis Thompson, D. H. Lawrence, to name but a few), visited the home of that special poet and person, Alice Meynell, and her distinguished editor and journalist husband, Wilfred Meynell, who lived in nearby Greatham (where their descendants still live). Many present, on hearing the poem, identified with the joy and delight of living in a cosy Sussex cottage (like mine), in an area of almost indescribable beauty, and never failing to appreciate it.

I print the poem in full,[1] so that everyone can understand exactly what I mean—and because it is lovely in its own right!

The Old Woman of the Roads

O, to have a little house!
To own the hearth and stool and all!
The heaped-up sods upon the fire,
The pile of turf against the wall!

To have a clock with weights and chains
And pendulum swinging up and down!
A dresser filled with shining delph,
Speckled and white and blue and brown!

I could be busy all the day
Clearing and sweeping hearth and floor,
And fixing on their shelf again
My white and blue and speckled store!

---

1 permission to reproduce this poem applied-for from Administrator of Padraic Colum's estate

I could be quiet there at night
Beside the fire and by myself,
Sure of a bed, and loth to leave
The ticking clock and the shining delph!

Och! but I'm weary of mist and dark,
And roads where there's never a house or bush,
And tired I am of bog and road
And the crying wind and the lonesome hush!

And I am praying to God on high,
And I am praying Him night and day,
For a little house—a house of my own,
Out of the wind's and the rain's way.

Padraic Colum

Direct spin-offs from the activities of the Wildbrooks Society include several which assist and enhance the life of the community.

Working parties of volunteers regularly trim the church-yard hedges and decorate the Sandham Hall, alleviating financial pressures on church and hall, and helping to keep both establishments spick and span.

From the start, the society had realised that a shopping coach to Worthing would help and be pleasant for residents, and in May 1972, with Mr. Harry Sanders then in control, the first monthly coach to Worthing was run, by volunteers, from Coldwaltham—stopping in Watersfield, at the Three Crowns, and intermittently en route — to Worthing. On the coach, people who see each other perhaps only seldom get the chance to chat and exchange gossip. Apart from those who just like the company, the trips are patronised by older residents who cannot, or do not want to, drive (the coach is much more economical than a car, for only one) and by anyone who fancies an occasional day out, a 'good shop', or just a stroll along the sea-front. In 1974, demand was such that two coaches had to be laid on for each trip, but now it is back to one again.

An instance of many requests for the society to participate in events organised by other bodies in the parish was the summer fête held in Watersfield in 1976 . . .

THE WILD BROOKS SOCIETY

Summer Fete - Watersfield Playing Fields

SATURDAY - 19TH JUNE, 1976

We have been asked to run a Tombola Stall in aid of the Funds to build new Shower facilities at Watersfield Playing Fields.

This is a really worthwhile effort, and everyone will want to make it a success.

As our contribution, everyone in the Wild Brooks Society is asked to provide one prize for the Tombola Stall. If each person does this, our stall should be a success.

An expensive prize is not necessary, but if you happen to have more than one item which you think would do - Don't Hold Back!

Please take your prize to Mr. Cruttenden, The Old Post House, Cold Waltham who is organising the Stall.

If this is inconvenient, your Area Representative on the Committee will be pleased to call and collect it, if you will let him or her know.

Area Representatives:-

Old Coldwaltham	George Stokes
Silverdale	Jack Harding
Arun Vale	Dorothy Youngs
Brook View	Tom Barber
Watersfield	Madge Dickerson and
	Heather Page

FINALLY - PLEASE BOOK THE DATE FOR THE FETE IN YOUR DIARY.

This is the 1976 "VILLAGE OCCASION" which everyone will feel they must attend.

Fig. 2

But a definitive highlight in the society's social history was its involvement in the Royal Jubilee, in 1977.

*The Wildbrooks Society organised
the 'GRAND JUBILEE Procession"*

JUBILEE DAY CELEBRATIONS
TUESDAY -   7th JUNE, 1977
COLDWALTHAM, WATERSFIELD and HARDHAM

TIME TABLE

10. 00 a.m.   GRAND JUBILEE PROCESSION
                   This will assemble in Loop Road by Mr.Roy Cooper's Farm,
                   Old Coldwaltham.

10. 30 a.m.   Short OPEN AIR SERVICE in field adjoining.

10. 45 a.m.(approx) PROCESSION moves off.

11. 15 a.m. to   PROCESSION arrives at ALBAN HEAD PLAYING FIELDS,
11. 30 a.m.   WATERSFIELD.

11. 30 a.m.   PRIZE-GIVING and presentation of JUBILEE CROWNS to
                   children under 16.

                   BAR opens - soft drinks and ices available.

                   It is hoped that EVERYONE in the villages of COLDWALTHAM,
                   WATERSFIELD & HARDHAM will turn up for the PROCESSION from
                   Cooper's Farm, DRESSED in "CARNIVAL RIG" with FLAGS,
                   RATTLES and PLENTY of COLOUR, and that MOST will enter for
                   one of the FOLLOWING CLASSES, a JUBILEE MUG PRIZE being
                   awarded to the best decorated or most original : -

                     1. Tractor & Trailer.   6. Pedestrian & pram
                                   float.   7. Pedestrian & wheel-
                     2. Commercial vehicle   barrow
                     3. Motor car   8. Family of 3 or more
                     4. Motor bike   9. Lady
                     5. Bicycle   10. Gentleman
                        11. Boy (not over 16 on 7th June)
                        12. Girl (not over 16 on 7th June)
                        13. Horse and rider
                        14. Horse drawn vehicle.

                   MORE THAN ONE CLASS MAY BE ENTERED FOR,   and
                   final judging will take place after a PARADE of
                   EACH CLASS on the PLAYING FIELDS.

                   The PROCESSION will be accompanied by the very best
                   BAND MUSIC from loudspeakers on a decorated vehicle.
                   All SPECTATORS along the route are invited to join the
                   end of the PROCESSION as it moves along to ALBAN HEAD
                   PLAYING FIELDS, Watersfield.

                   IF THERE ARE ANY QUERIES ABOUT THE PROCESSION PLEASE TELEPHONE
                   JOHN BOXFORD, "FOGDENS", WEST BURTON - BURY 611.

12. 45 p.m.(approx)+CHILDREN'S PICNIC LUNCH at PLAYING FIELDS, WATERSFIELD+

                   Snacks available for adults at BAR

1. 45 p.m.(approx) FABULOUS, FASCINATING, FANTASTIC   ...   TREASURE HUNT!
                   Starting at WATERSFIELD PLAYING FIELDS - for both
                   CHILDREN and ADULTS   -   MANY PRIZES!!!

+ N.B.   THIS NOTICE CANCELS the 3.30 p.m. CHILDREN'S PICNIC PARTY at ST.JAMES'
          SCHOOL, COLDWALTHAM, MENTIONED IN THE MAY ISSUE of the "PARISH NEWS" +

7. 00 p.m. to)   EVENING ENTERTAINMENT - which will include Supper,
10. 00 p.m.   )   children's singing and other entertainments. It is
                   hoped to hold this in the SANDHAM HALL.

8. 00 p.m. to)   DISCOTEQUE with 'Sun Disco' at YOUTH CLUB HUT,
11. 45 p.m.   )   COLDWALTHAM   -   with Bar.

Fig. 3

Another scheme which has developed under the aegis of the society, and which is indubitably one of the most important in the parish, is the Village Help Scheme.

Early in 1975, a talk was given to the Wildbrooks Society by Peter Varcoe, Liaison Officer at the Social Services Department of West Sussex County Council. His talk was on the need for 'help schemes' throughout the country to relieve pressures on overworked social workers, and to give help that could not be provided by the Statutory Services.

At the end of this meeting, it was unanimously decided to start such a scheme "to provide voluntary aid for the aged, the handicapped and others in need of emergency assistance in the villages of Hardham, Coldwaltham and Watersfield".

Edna Llewhellin agreed to organise the setting-up of the scheme, with John Boxford as chairman, and help from an *ad hoc* committee and the Social Services Department.

In April 1975, a letter went out to all residents, outlining ways in which help might be given.

1 Visiting the aged or lonely
2 Reading to the blind
3 Sitting for a while with the aged or the handicapped
4 Doing light handyman jobs
5 Assisting with the completion of forms and correspondence
6 Fetching pensions, prescriptions, shopping, etc.

IN AN EMERGENCY

7 Cooking meals
8 Giving *emergency* help in the house
9 Caring for infants or supporting new 'Mums'
10 Providing transport—hospital visiting, etc.

People were asked to identify ways in which they would be prepared to offer their services. It was made clear that in no way was the scheme to replace help already available from voluntary agents or good neighbours.

In August that same year, at a meeting of those who had offered to help, everyone agreed that the area should be divided into sectors, with two or three people to act as contacts, and organise requested help. The sectors were Watersfield, Brookview and Church Lane, Arun Vale and Silverdale, Old Coldwaltham, and Greatham. (Subsequently, Greatham was dropped from the scheme, as over a period of more than two years there had been no call for help: it was a "well-integrated, self-supporting community". But the Scheme reassured Greatham that, if it needed help in the future, it would get it.)

On the first day of November, 1975, the Scheme was started, on a six-month trial basis. It got off to a slow start, but gathered momentum during the early months of 1976. Since then, 400 recorded requests for help have involved about 1,000 separate instances of service.

A petrol allowance is given to drivers, because transport is the greatest need. This is paid from funds which are raised at an annual Coffee Morning held at a local house, 'Champs Hill', Coldwaltham, and always well supported. Those being helped give donations if they can, particularly when a considerable amount of transport is involved. New residents are acquainted with the help that is available.

In June 1979, the Rowntree Research Unit at the University of Durham undertook "A Review of Good Neighbour Schemes in England", and circularised the organisers of all such schemes that they could trace—over 3,000 altogether.

Replies to their questionnaires were received from over 1,000 organisations, and it was decided to look in-depth into about a dozen of the schemes. Coldwaltham's Village Help Scheme was one of the rural organisations selected and, recalls Edna Llewhellin, who has remained in charge of the flourishing service since it began,[2] "for about a week we were 'invaded' by three members of the Research Unit!"

A handbook describing the role of 200 of the schemes considered to be successful was published by the Volunteer Centre, and a paperback, *Action for Care,* reviewing schemes in general, was published.

Coldwaltham's Village Help Scheme has now been in action for over a decade. Changes of officers and committee have taken place over the years but, says Miss Llewhellin, "all have served unstintingly and it is to their keenness and the generous giving of time by helpers that the scheme owes its success."

---

2   but retired in May 1987

Perhaps the smallest recipient of help was an injured starling, which in 1981 "was fed with brandy by Edna Llewhellin and Hilary Hibbert, and soon recovered and took flight" (from the Minutes of a Wildbrooks Society Committee meeting on August 19th, 1981).

When the Wildbrooks Society first welcomed members, early in 1972, it also provided them with a list of local organisations, which gives an idea of how much was going on in the parish at that time (Fig. 4, overleaf).

Names change, but many of the organisations then in existence live on.

Coldwaltham and Watersfield Women's Institute is a special case in point. A carefully-typed report on the branch's earlier years, from March 1933 (when it was formed),[3] shows that this branch soon became active and useful. The report came from Miss Heather Page, whose mother, the renowned Mrs. Doris Page, was a founder-member, along with Mrs. Dorothy Secomb. These two served as president and honorary secretary respectively, from 1933 until 1951.

Reading the report, it is evident that some issues that are controversial today were already being debated then: for instance, funds for tennis courts (periodically asked for, but still not erected) ... "£4. 4s. (four guineas) was given to make Tennis Courts on the Recreation Ground." What happened to those four guineas, given in 1933?

During the World War II years, the W.I. excelled itself in real help and caring ... "At the outbreak of War in September [1939] practically the whole of the Institute Committee were also members of the W.V.S. Committee, and throughout the War years we all worked together very smoothly. As we were a Reception Area for Croydon, our population was greatly increased. We welcomed all the evacuated mothers as visitors to our monthly meetings."

Compassion and practical activity knew no bounds. Five guineas of Institute funds were invested in War Savings

3 *A Short History of Coldwaltham and Watersfield W.I., 1933-1950* (unpublished)

T H E   W I L D B R O O K S   S O C I E T Y

The Society welcomes you to its membership and hopes that the following information about Local and District activities will be useful to you and your friends.

The Parish Council	Clerk: Mr A.G. Johnson, 'Dalatho' West Chiltington Common, Pulborough.
Churches:	Church of England. St Giles Goldwaltham The Rev'd R.E. Chatwin, The Vicarage, Coldwaltham. Pulborough 2146
	Congregational. Watersfield Chapel and Fellowship. Miss E. Wilson, Redwood, Maple Leaf, Coldwaltham. Pulborough 2767
School) Parent Teachers Ass'n)	St James' Church of England School Headmaster Mr G. Stevens
Womens' Institute	Mrs S. Over, 26 Arunvale, Coldwaltham Pulborough 2776
The Other Half	Mrs A. Mount, The Willows, Watersfield Bury 576
The Youth Club	Mr O. Lammas, 27 Brookview, Coldwaltham
Guides and Brownies	Mrs E. Cordier, 23 Silverdale, Coldwaltham Pulborough 2556
Brookview Playground Association	Mr R.N. Wardell, 24 Brookview, Coldwaltham
Friends of Sandham Hall	Mr H. Youngs, 54 Arunvale, Coldwaltham Pulborough 2434
The Wildbrooks Society	Mr J.H. Sanders, 1 Silverdale, Coldwaltham Pulborough 2899
Darby and Joan Club	Mrs Y. Chatwin, The Vicarage, Coldwaltham Pulborough 2146
Over Sixty Outings	Mrs E. Street, 7 Brookview, Coldwaltham
Cricket Club Watersfield	Mr A. Goodchild, 10 Brookview Way, Coldwaltham
Football Club Watersfield	Mr C. Brown, c/o 'Three Crowns' Watersfield
Bowls	Mr C.F. Englefield, Downside, Coldwaltham Pulborough 2448
Old Tyme Dance Club	Mrs B. Clark, Brockhurst Farm, Watersfield
Sandham Hall Oil Painters	Mrs E. Cordier, 23 Silverdale, Coldwaltham Pulborough 2556
Whist & Beetle Drives	Held at Sandham Hall. See Notice Boards and Parish Magazine for details
Alban Head Playing Field Watersfield	Mr M.J. Bull, The Labouring Man, Coldwaltham. Pulborough 2215
The Sandham Hall	Hon. Booking Secretary, Mrs M. Bull, The Labouring Man, Coldwaltham Pulborough 2215

Fig. 4

Certificates in 1940, and £4 went to start a Wool Fund for 'comforts' for the Services. Watersfield Chapel was offered to W.I. members "at a nominal rental of 1/- per annum. We put in the electric light in the Chapel, a new fireplace and a lavatory; this was paid for by gifts and special efforts. A member . . . presented us with a piano. During the winter, socials and whist drives were held in the afternoons for the men of the Searchlight Battery" (stationed near the village).

Two activities of prime usefulness during the War years were the setting up of a Fruit Preservation Centre in the Sandham Hall, and a Meat Pie Scheme. These were not modest endeavours. The output of 300 lb. of fruit canned and 1,000 lb. of jam made in 1940 increased, in 1941, to 634 cans of fruit; 268 lb. of rosehips (sent away) and, again, 1,000 lb. of jam made. In 1942, 1,609 lb. of jam were made, 2,000 lb. of fruit were canned, and the rosehips collected weighed 1½ cwt. The canning continued well after the war, when food was still in short supply, and a record 11,121 cans of fruit and tomatoes were canned in 1948.

The meat pie fund was equally successful. It started in June 1942 and, between then and November, 14,395 meat pies were sold (some in the Sandham Hall, but most in Watersfield Chapel) at 4d. each.[4] In 1950, when the Meat Pie Scheme finished, it was recorded that during the time of its operation, from June 1942 to July 1950, 135,024 pies had been sold to "the people of the village" (that is, the parish).

Paper salvage during World War II was run by the Women's Voluntary Service, but staffed by W.I. members, who, during those years, raised £64. 7s. 8d. for the British Red Cross and £17. 0s. 9d. for the S.S.A.F.A. (Soldiers', Sailors' and Airmen's Families Association) from the sale of waste paper. Sorting rivets which had been swept up from the aircraft

---

4 There is a touching story of a little girl who was sent up to the Chapel one morning with a note from her mother, saying she did not want any pies. The girl, by mistake, pinned the note, which read, "NO PIES TODAY", on the Chapel door, so that for a little while those coming for pies, on reading the notice, went away pie-less. Finally, the mistake was discovered and business returned to normal!

factory floor, to be melted down and re-used in the munitions factories, was yet another war chore the W.I. took on. The rivet-sorting took place first in one, then another, building in Sandy Lane, Watersfield.

Doris Page, founder-member and president for all those years, was leader *par excellence;* the sort of person every community needs, and not enough have. Possessed of apparently indefatigable energy, she worked in innumerable ways, some important, some minor, to help people. Apart from heading the local W.I. for all those years, in April 1939 she was made Produce Leader for the Pulborough Group of Institutes[5] and in 1943 she became Group Chairman, remaining so until 1950. In 1949, it was also recorded that "our president is a Foundation School Manager [of St. James C. E. School, Coldwaltham] as well as Vicar's Warden [Church-warden]".

The list of responsibilities she breezily took on, and seriously carried out, is endless. One of my neighbours remembers that when she moved into Coldwaltham, many years ago, a neighbour said to her: "Dodge that Mrs. Page. She's a marvellous organiser, and she's bound to try to rope you in for something!"

In Chapter 9, *In Living Memory,* I have reprinted in full a tribute to Mrs. Page, after her death, written by the Rev. Ronald Chatwin, then Vicar, and published in the December 1973 issue of the Coldwaltham *Parish News.* Thus, in this chapter on *Community Life,* in that called *In Living Memory,* and among the Appendices, Mrs. Page has her place, and we make no apologies for so diffusing her 'stardom' within the book.

A visible memorial to her, in the form of a church notice-board, with a bronze plaque, was erected in the church in 1975.

---

5 comprising the branch institutes of Coldwaltham and Watersfield, Pulborough, Pulborough Meadows, Fittleworth and West Chiltington Hayling. The Group, at a March 1986 meeting, was re-formed and now consists of Coldwaltham and Watersfield, Storrington, Sullington, West Chiltington and Thakeham.

Mrs. Page was also connected with Coldwaltham and Watersfield Village Produce Association — which is now no more, although in 1965 it was still going strong and had a membership of 120. Its two main annual activities were a Spring (Bulb) Show, held in the Sandham Hall, and the Flower and Produce Show, always held on the third Saturday in July, on the Alban Head Playing Field in Watersfield. Mrs. Dorothy White, one of those closely involved in the running of the association, has fond and clear memories of the summer show:

> "It was a great excitement and success every year. We had a marquee set up, and I was down in it every year at 8 a.m. on the day of the show, with a picnic lunch to see me through. I got the money prizes ready, and I was also a steward to the judges during the show. Eventually, we had three marquees — one for fruit and flowers, one for home produce and other things, and one for the treasurer.
>
> "There were lots of sideshows, too, including 'bowling for a pig'. Ted Norman [of Brookview] organised the sideshows."

(Mr. Chris Harris remembers the man who looked after the coconut shy, shouting, "Coconuts as big as water-butts!")

In a Women's Institute scrapbook produced to mark its Jubilee year, 1965, Coldwaltham and Watersfield W.I. mention that year's summer show:

> "This year it was held on July 31st, which proved to be a lovely sunny day. In spite of bad weather through the summer, the judges commented on the excellence of the exhibits ... Sports for the Children were organised by Mr. ['Darkie'] Pollard and Mr. Rowland. The youngsters also enjoyed a substantial tea and Punch and Judy show ... Mr. Peter Parish presented the Association with a silver challenge cup."

Col. Jean Berry, A.T.S., of Coldwaltham, took on the chairmanship of the association in the later 1960s, but, well meaning and efficient though she was, the parishioners found her "bossy", and "her ways were not liked". At this stage, the organisation "fizzled out": extremely sad, in view of the number of excellent gardeners there have always been in the area.

No doubt they would like to see a revival, to be able to show in their own parish, with pride, their produce and

170 *Coldwaltham*

flowers and compete with (mostly!) friendly parishioners for show prizes and cups, as in the old days. For years, everyone has had to go either to the Pulborough Shows, which are excellent, or to Rackham Fête and Show (Rackham is a small village about three miles along the road) to get the right sort of recognition for their 'green-fingered' industry. However, it is always a great pleasure to attend this jolly event, held at the foot of a small chalk cliff, with a giant slide to enthral children (of all ages), whose excited screams echo up the slopes. A very high standard of show exhibits encourages people from many miles around to take part.

By 1971, Coldwaltham and Watersfield Village Produce Association had ceased to function, but Marjorie Hessell Tiltman has immortalised the show and, in the process, Mrs. Page, in one of her books:[6]

"The great social event of the month is taking place . . . event of the year we might almost say . . . the local horticultural show.

"It is to be held in the Rectory field, and the Rector himself is chairman of the somewhat indefinite committee. For some months past, the booklets with details of THE SHOW have been displayed by the local tradesmen. These booklets contain the rules, lists of the divisions, schedules and classes (of which there are one hundred and seventeen) and the prizes, of which there are three hundred and sixty!

"It is a brilliant day. The field, perched high on a ridge above the village, looks blandly down on the winding street, on the brooks beyond it, with the cows and sheep grazing on them, the Downs in the distance. The sky is a most un-English bright blue, and the gardens of the cottages at the back, of the Rectory itself and of the few plutocratic houses in the vicinity, are still in high flower, still three or four weeks off the inevitable August dilapidation.

"And the visitors behave as if they were incredibly pleased with life. The ladies carry parasols, wear dresses of figured *crêpe-de-Chine*, adjusted now as always to a decorous ankle-length, with feather boas and gold chains or beads about their necks and kid gloves on their hands. The villagers are got up in their Sunday best, a bright blue being a strong favourite. And the children—in this year of nudism, nature cults in general, and laundry prices in particular—wear starched cotton dresses, very full and very frilled!

"Our friend Mrs. Cudlipp has been there for some time already. She is at her best on such occasions, omniscient, omni-

present. The visitors, all very much the reverse, wander vaguely
about, not exactly sure of where they want to go. It is Mrs.
Cudlipp's duty and pleasure to tell them, to divide off the sheep
from the goats, to whisk unmanageable children in the direction
of the Fair which is blaring merrily away at one end of the field,
to get the boys interested in the sideshows, where the buskers
decorously but reluctantly tone down their voices in deference to
the presence of the Rector, the Rector's lady, the Rector's family,
the Rector's curate, to shepherd the several maiden ladies towards
the refreshment tent for a ninepenny tea before it is packed to
overflowing, and to get the exhibitors in the great tent, which is
over a hundred feet long, instead of clustering round the narrow
opening like a swarm of bees.

"The tent smells of dried grass, of flowers, of fruit and
vegetables. At a rough glance, it looks as its predecessor fifty to
a hundred years ago must have looked. Not for our conservative
corner of Sussex is the anguished cry of the gourmet for the
vegetables of youth and tenderness; not for them the announcement of the London Allotments Garden Show Society that in
awarding prizes the judges are recommended to consider quality
in preference to size. Marrows, lettuce, carrots, broad beans,
beetroot—they would all do justice to a race of supermen; not to
a French cook!

"The section devoted to Flower Decoration is monopolised
by competitors who have obviously never heard of either Miss
Spry or the Japanese School, but who follow the dear old tradition
of one bowl in the centre and one in each corner, with sweet peas
and gypsophila stuck in them for choice.

"By far the most attractive exhibits are in the industrial
section—the jams, the jellies, the honey in comb or in bottles, the
bottled fruits and pickles. The cakes, breads, supper dishes and
sweets alike look heavy and unappetising, and the low standard
is only eclipsed by the various handicrafts, which are deplorable
from every point of view except that of workmanship . . . "

Soon after World War II, Doris Page, along with Mrs.
Kirwan, started the Darby and Joan Club. It fell to Mrs. Page,
as leader, to organise "a rota of ladies, with cars, to transport
the elderly to Sandham Hall, where meetings were held, and
provide tea and cakes."

When the Rev. Ronald Chatwin became Vicar of Coldwaltham, his wife, Yvonne, took over the running of the
club, which then had about 18 members. When the Chatwins
moved to Rottingdean, Mrs. Mary Maynard became leader, and
eventually the name of the club was changed to the Monday
Club. "Apart from whist and cribbage," writes Mrs. Maynard,

Fig. 5   Darby and Joan tea party, probably in the 1950s

"Scrabble has become very popular and out come the dictionaries if there is any doubt about a spelling!" At Christmas, the club has a dinner outing "somewhere local", and there are periodical outings to Worthing and Bognor. Mrs. Margaret Deverill now looks after the Monday Club.

The Other Half, a club run for young wives, thrived during the time the Chatwins were in Coldwaltham. In 1970, Mrs. Chatwin reported "the best year yet", with increased membership and enthusiasm. That year, the club gave almost £100 (still a lot of money then) to the Sandham Hall Building Fund, and other bodies, including the Church of England Children's Society; ran a keep-fit class — open to all — and provided active help in making the Women's World Day of Prayer "a fine occasion" (quote from the Parochial Church Council Minutes of a contemporary meeting).

The present vicar's wife, Mrs. Maud Hodgson, among seemingly dozens of parish activities, re-started the keep-fit[7]

---

7   It closed in 1986, through lack of support.

class in 1982. She also started a Young Women's Club, and was instrumental, with her husband, in setting up a Village Lunch Club, held monthly on a Wednesday, at Barn Owls Restaurant.

For younger people, more seems to have gone on in the 1960s and 1970s than now.

In 1972, the 1st Coldwaltham Brownie Guides were being run by Mrs. Parish as Leader, with Mrs. Cordier as Assistant Leader. The Pack numbered fourteen. At the same time, the 1st Coldwaltham Guide Company was being led by Mrs. Cordier, assisted by Mrs. Betty Clark. There were six Guides and two "due to join", and it was noted that Guide "training was not easy with so few".

The Brownie Pack at Coldwaltham was taken over by Mrs. Freda Hawkins, soon after she came to live in the parish,

Fig.6 Coldwaltham Brownies, with Brown Owl, Mrs. Freda Hawkins, and helpers, being presented with the Wealden District Shield in 1973 by Mrs. Smith, District Commissioner

in 1973. Although the Pack never reached the allowed maximum of twenty-four, seventeen children regularly attended meetings, and the catchment area was extended to take in Bury and Bignor, so that girls from those villages could join in the variety of events that Mrs. Hawkins was laying on.

Only four months after the re-organisation of the Pack, came a swift, exciting triumph for the Brownies. They had entered a 'Know Your Tree' competition for the Wealden District. For this, they made bark rubbings, plaster casts and leaf pictures, planted saplings, and studied one tree in depth. The judges, impressed by all the work the Brownies had put in, awarded them first prize.

By March 25th, 1973, there was a full Pack of Brownies at Coldwaltham, including five from Fittleworth. That year, a Brownies' Nativity Play was performed in church, and one of the children[8] was asked to read out the numbers of the accompanying carols . . .

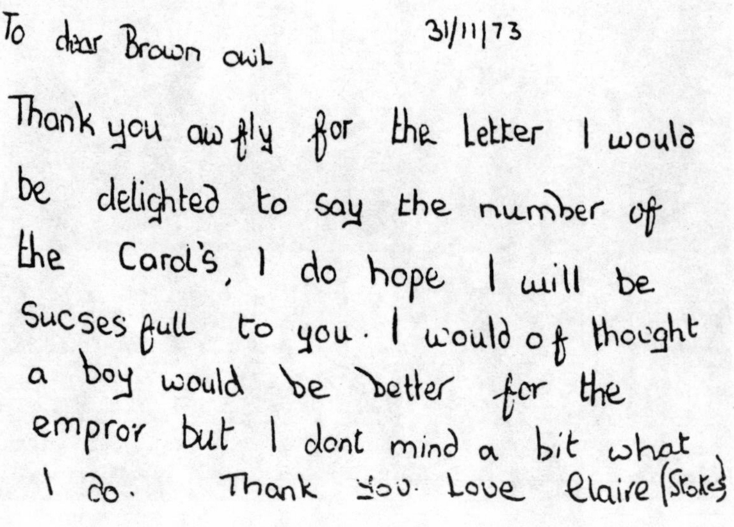

To dear Brown owl   31/11/73

Thank you awfly for the letter I would be delighted to say the number of the Carol's, I do hope I will be Sucsesfull to you. I would of thought a boy would be better for the empror but I dont mind a bit what I do. Thank you. Love Claire (Stokes)

Fig. 7

The Brownies had their own church service each Sunday, at 9.30 a.m. (taken by Mr. Chatwin, before he rushed off to take a service at Hardham Church, after which he hurried back again for Sung Eucharist at Coldwaltham).

When a Farewell Service was held for Mr. Chatwin, on May 12th, 1974, prior to his move to Rottingdean, there was a parade of sixteen Brownies, including his daughter Yvette, who carried their banner to the Sanctuary.

Fig. 8   Farewell to the Chatwins: Ronald, Yvonne, Yvette and Monique, shown with the then Churchwardens: Edward (Ted) Hibbert (left) and Bryan Mount (right)

When they reached ten, the Brownies became Guides—in Pulborough, Petworth or Billingshurst. But there was always

8   Claire, now 23, and an air hostess with Saudi Airways, based at Heathrow Airport, is the daughter of the late George Stokes, and of Mrs. Margaret Stokes, who recently moved from Coldwaltham to Washington.

a good number of Brownies on hand in Coldwaltham to
enjoy everything that was organised for them, or by them.
Events included singing Christmas Carols to the old people at
Stopham House, trips to London, to see 'Cinderella on Ice' at
the Wembley Stadium (1973) and the Changing of the Guard
(April 1974), a Sausage Sizzle at North Lodge Camp, Lodge
Hill, Watersfield, where Coldwaltham Pack were the hostesses,
being runners-up in a Brownie Challenge Cup 'Make a Toy'
competition (July 1974), and decorating the church porch,
during Harvest Festival, with a collage of 'Breakfast on the
Shore after the Resurrection'. For Cancer Research, the
Brownies held a Sponsored Silence during November 1974.

Mothering Sunday, on March 9th, 1975, saw the Brownies
laughing and chattering and picking primroses along the
disused Fittleworth railway line, before their special church
service, the theme of which that day was 'Christ, the Light of
the World'. Each Brownie (some were in costume) lit a candle
for a different country and the Rev. Martyn Hughes[9] lit one
for China, which, that year, allowed Girl Guides for the first
time.

It was International Guiding Year in 1975, and every
Brownie Pack was allotted a country. At Coldwaltham it was
India, and an Indian lady—'Indira', living in Pulborough—was
invited to come to the meeting. The Brownies garlanded her
at the entrance to Sandham Hall car park, then put their
hands together and bowed in traditional style. Indira was
touched. She took the meeting that day with everyone sitting
cross-legged on the floor, and showed them how to put on,
and wear, a sari.

For Brown Owl and Mrs. Peggie Boxford, then District
Commissioner and Young Leaders' Adviser for Guides, the
highlight of 1975 was the 22nd Conference of the World
Association of Girl Guides and Girl Scouts. It was held at
Sussex University, in Brighton, and Mrs. Hawkins and Mrs.
Boxford were asked to act as hostesses, ferrying the many
international representatives wherever they had, or wanted,

9   then curate at St. Mary's Church, Pulborough

to go. Brown Owl and Mrs. Boxford arranged flowers in 120 yoghourt pots (suitably decorated by the Brownies), which were placed in the delegates' rooms.

For the Brownies themselves, however, the highlight of that year must have been winning the District Shield again.

Sadly, this golden three-year period for Coldwaltham's Brownies ended in 1976, when there were fewer children of the right age to join the Pack, and its numbers dwindled rapidly. But that joy and bustle is still well remembered, and a girl working until recently in a Bury garage summed it all up when she told Mrs. Hawkins recently: "They were wonderful, those times, and I learned such a lot."

A Youth Club was started in Watersfield in 1958 by Mr. Eric Bell, who at the time was working at Watersfield Garage with the joint proprietor, Mr. Fred Parish. The garage had use of the deconsecrated old chapel in Watersfield, as a store room for car spares. Mr. Bell, who that same year bought the garage, cleared out the chapel[10], and it became the club's premises. Unfortunately, some of the children damaged the chapel and, in 1961, the club had to be closed.

The club was started up again in 1963, in the Sandham Hall, by Mr. John Enticknapp. Two years later, Mr. Enticknapp gave up the leadership. At first, no one came forward to replace him, but, within a few months, the Rev. Ronald Chatwin agreed to become chairman, and Mike and Shirley Smith took on the joint leadership, encouraged by Jeff Smith, then Chanctonbury Area Youth Officer.

Because of complaints, again, that members were spoiling facilities in the hall, it was decided to find alternative club premises as soon as possible. Through his work as a builder, Chris Harris heard of a pre-fabricated classroom hut for sale, at Paulsgrove School, near Coates, for £100.

During the 1973 Easter Holiday, a group of helpers dismantled the building, and then Mr. Alfred Buckman laid

---

10 Mr. Bell, Chairman of Coldwaltham Parish Council for 12 years, remembered that, while cleaning up the chapel, he discovered a full immersion pit for Baptisms.

on removal lorries from his firm to transport five loads of material back to Coldwaltham.

Permission was given for everything to be stored on the piece of West Sussex County Council land where the hut stands today. (Local members of the county council, the late Mr. Alfred H. Bowerman and Mr. Ludovic Foster, put in a good word for the project at meetings.)

When it came to re-building the hut, there was a mere £20 in the kitty towards the estimated cost of £2,000! A house-to-house collection in the parish brought in £300 and eventually, with fund-raising events and donations making up the balance, the time came to start work. John Worman Limited, local builders, laid the concrete base and did the heavy work. Roy Wardell was responsible for carpentry and Rodney Elliott for electrical work. Altogether, 1,000 working hours were spent on the building, most of the work from then on being undertaken by the late Owen Lammas and Chris Harris. They spent every spare minute they had on the job, and Chris's wife, Jean, remembers that she carried Sunday lunches across the road for what seemed a very long time! Last but not least, (the late) Mr. George Stokes, then chairman of the Youth Club, dealt with all the paperwork.

All kinds of features were added to the original classroom. They included two old doors from a branch of Barclays Bank, and a seat from the jockeys' changing room at Goodwood Racecourse — which was converted into a bar counter! The club was officially opened in March 1976 by Linda Gainsbury, Chanctonbury Area Youth Officer and an enthusiastic supporter of the scheme.

From the outset, the whole community took great interest in the club, supporting it not only with good wishes but by attending all the fund-raising events. These laid down a pattern for the club's programme of events through the years: concerts, especially folk concerts, at the club (but sometimes held in Coldwaltham School), bring-and-buy sales, beetle drives. The bring-and-buy sales, well stocked and cheerfully manned by local youth-club parents and friends, and members themselves, are still among the most successful and friendly of all social gatherings in the parish. The parish council and, more recently, the British Lions support the Youth Club financially, but local residents continue to patronise all that goes on. Of these, by far the most supportive are the older people; it is especially touching that the old should help the young. In gratitude for such help, the club has held a Senior Citizens' party every Christmas since 1979.

On Monday evenings, juniors and seniors both have use of the club premises – the juniors until 8.30; the seniors until ten o'clock. On Wednesday evenings, only the seniors meet. Apart from Chris Harris, who has been deeply involved in the club since it restarted in Coldwaltham and has been chairman for several years, Gordon ('Dig') Streeter has also been a tower of strength since 1979. He now runs all the sessions, junior and senior, helped by Mrs. Pat Wardell on Monday nights. Since 1979, too, his wife, Mrs. Pauline Streeter, has been a member of the club committee. Now secretary and treasurer, she also takes on any role as necessary, and gives unstintingly of her time.

Money continues to be a problem. The club is situated on the edge of the Western area administered from Chichester by the West Sussex County Council, and the council provides a small grant based on the number of members aged fourteen to twenty-one. The grant has just been increased slightly, but much of it – £50 – has to be given back to the county council in ground rent.

The parish is immensely lucky in having the use of a large and beautiful playing field, in Watersfield and well away from the main road. The two main uses of the Alban Head Playing Field,[11] as it is called, are for football during the winter months, and cricket in summer.

Founded in 1950, Watersfield Cricket Club has grown from strength to strength, due in large part to a band of loyal and dedicated older players, and their policy of encouraging and helping young players to improve. Its fixtures programme

---

11 The Alban Head Playing Field is dealt with in greater detail in Chapter 7, *Amenities*.

is well organised, and 1983 and 1984 were especially successful seasons. In fact, 1983 was the club's most successful one
since 1976, with only three defeats in seventeen games played.
The climax of the 1984 season was, without a doubt, winning
the Clymping Plate, through a splendid all-round team effort.

On Sunday afternoons, when most of the cricket matches
are played, the bordering pinewoods (and further afield,
even across the main road in River Lane) resound to shouts
of delight, amazement, derision or encouragement – as the
moment dictates. Tea, served in or outside the little sports
pavilion at the wood's edge at the interval, helps to spin out
the pleasant match hours, along with friendly inquests after
play.

One of the people most closely associated with the
Cricket Club—ex-secretary, team secretary, player and general
mainstay – is Gerald Clark, who, until his recent marriage and
move to Fittleworth, also lived (in Sandy Lane) closer to
the field than any other player. He was Club Member of the
Year for the 1983-1984 season, and in 1985 was made vice-
chairman of the Alban Head Playing Field Committee. Like
many other C.C. members, he 'spills over' into the ranks of
Watersfield Football Club, of which he is currently manager
and a player.

Another pillar of strength in the Football Club is Rodney
Elliott: committee member for fourteen years, chairman for
the past three, and a member of the Alban Head Playing
Field Committee for over nine years[12]. Mr. Elliott's company,
Elliott & Henley, have sponsored the club for the 1985-86
season[13], a generous gesture from one (not forgetting his
partner) who has given countless hours over the years to both
clubs.

Affiliated to the Sussex County Football Association,
West Sussex Football League, and Worthing and District
Football League, Watersfield Football Club thrived especially

---

12 Mr. Elliott was the first player-member to be made a chairman
(1983-85) of the Playing Field Committee.
13 In 1983-84, Gray & Rowsell were the club's sponsors.

Fig. 9   Watersfield Football Club, 1983 season:—
Back row, l. to r., H. R. Elliott (Chairman), D. Horne, T. Sutton,
A. Merrick, R. Stokes, D. Clark (Capt.), G. Spicer,
M. Spicer, T. Spicer (Linesman)
Front row, l. to r., S. Wardell, G. Clark, P. Budd,
I. Denyer, K. Clark, C. Budd

in the 1970s. For the 1972-73 season, its members won
the Guy Walker Sportsmanship Trophy. In 1973-74, they
were the champions of West Sussex League Division 3, and
1974-75 saw them become West Sussex League Division 2
champions.

What about the 1980s? At first, Watersfield footballers
seemed to be marking time, and in the 1983-84 and 1984-85
seasons, to quote one player, they "didn't quite make it".
The 1985-86 season, however, made up for all that. By mid-
January 1986, the team had had their tenth consecutive win
(3-1, against East Preston Youth Club). They had reached
the quarter-final of the Chichester Bareham Trophy, and, by

April, they were clear leaders in the West Sussex Division 3 South. More glory came in January 1986, when Keith Clark was selected to play for West Sussex in the Inter-League Competition. The reserves also had a successful season, and reached the finals of the Worthing and District League Division 3 competition. The F.C. are creeping up again.

Soon, a very special kind of light—floodlight—will shine down on the club. West Sussex County Council have just granted planning permission for floodlighting to be erected on Alban Head Playing Field by Watersfield Football Club, subject to four conditions:—

"1 The development [erection of the floodlight system] must be begun within five years;

2 The floodlights shall at all times be angled to light the training pitch only, in the interest of local amenities;

3 The floodlighting shall be used on Tuesdays and Thursdays only, for a maximum of two hours, no later than 9.30 p.m., in the interest of local amenities; and

4 This permission shall enure for the benefit of Watersfield Football Club only, not for the benefit of the land. Permission would not normally be granted for such development in the location, but in granting permission, exceptionally, the West Sussex County Council have had regard to the particular circumstances."

Whatever those "particular circumstances" are, the floodlighting facility, once in operation, will no doubt take the F.C. even further up the road to success.

*   *   *   *   *

Finally, this chapter takes a look at other 'roads'—those that run through the parish, main and minor, and connect parishioners with the outside world. The need for transport has always been a major matter of interest here. In the old days, a coach and horses took people to Pulborough Station. Later, hourly buses between Horsham and Bognor Regis passed through Coldwaltham. Number 69 buses ran each way —north and south—every hour, even in 1965, all stopping at Pulborough Station, so that train travellers could bus it back to the parish. Unfortunately, the service was discontinued "for economic reasons".

In 1975, Age Concern was anxious to find transport to the shops where there was no regular bus service, and an association was formed in Pulborough to fill this gap. Coldwaltham parishioners watched with special interest as it developed.

In fact, it started life with one borrowed vehicle, one morning a week. Then, in 1978, the Community Minibus Association (West Sussex), as it was called,[14] borrowed an old ambulance from Chichester and, as the ambulance had to pass through Coldwaltham, the scheme from then on took in the parish. The indomitable British Lions lent their fund-raising support and raised the money to buy a new minibus. Mrs. Caroline Jeffries, the wife of a local G.P., in Pulborough, and the late Mr. Bert and Mrs. Margaret Deverill, in Coldwaltham, began to "canvas for customers", as Mrs. Deverill put it. Old people in Bury wanted to be part of the service, too, and go to Pulborough to shop, so Bury was included in the same run. Little by little, other villages acquired their own buses, but all operated under the umbrella of the Association, which continued to be based in Pulborough.

Over the years, many hundreds of pounds have been raised to subsidise the Association's services, and in Coldwaltham the special annual summer event (always, so long as I can remember, successful—whatever the weather) is Mrs. Deverill's coffee morning and bring-and-buy, held in her home and garden, in Arun Vale.

The local service provides transport on Friday mornings to and from Pulborough, with the added pleasure of coffee in Pulborough when the shopping is finished, in a small back room at the village hall, giving those who want the benefit of a small, friendly social gathering. Mrs. Deverill recalls that "one gentleman who hadn't been out of the house for seven years until the minibus arrived to pick him up, thereafter became a most regular customer!"

---

14 see also *Minibus: the Story of the Community Minibus Association (West Sussex)* by Leonard Phillipson, with a Foreword by Lavinia, Duchess of Norfolk (Marehill Press, 1986)

Every other Tuesday, in addition, a minibus comes to Coldwaltham, to take shoppers "somewhere"; usually to Storrington. There is also a shoppers' bus from Pulborough to Horsham, which operates on two Mondays in the month and allocates three seats to Coldwaltham residents.

Coldwaltham's five drivers and escorts, as in all the other villages, work on an entirely voluntary basis. There are now eight minibuses, with one in reserve, serving areas covered by Pulborough, Petworth, Storrington, Billingshurst, Barnham and Steyning. Coldwaltham's Mrs. Deverill has seen the scheme progress quietly but dramatically over a decade, and more and more Coldwaltham people taking advantage of the buses. The president of the Association, who from the outset has been Brigadier Sir Geoffrey Hardy-Roberts (a former Master of the Queen's Household), has witnessed the changes, too, and monitored them. He always manages to persuade interesting and influential people (no doubt stirred by the immense community spirit and spirit of independence involved in running a project of this sort) to attend, and actively take part in, the Association's Annual General Meeting. In April 1984, it was Anthony Nelson, Member of Parliament for the Chichester Division, who addressed the meeting, with, as a friendly guest, Richard Luce, then "another Sussex M.P." At the 1985 A.G.M., held in May, Lavinia, Duchess of Norfolk, in her first year as Lord Lieutenant of West Sussex, presided at the Annual General Meeting—as she had done, to quote Brig. Hardy-Roberts, "in 1976, with flattering faith in our future."

Impressive support has always been forthcoming, as it should be. The reasons why are perhaps best expressed by the president, in his Association report for 1983 :—

"A service of the kind that our Association provides takes individual users to and from their own homes. This, I suppose, is not something that the operators of a municipal bus service could contemplate; and yet it is immensely appreciated by those who are most deprived and whom we seek to help, namely :

the handicapped of all ages;

the old and infirm;

young mothers who cannot leave their children in care of a neighbour for more than a few hours while doing the

weekly shopping;
and indeed any others who are beyond walking or cycling
distance of shops, libraries and churches, who have no cars
of their own and no kind neighbours to give them lifts."

In this selfsame 1983 report, the president defends,
praises and epitomises the strength of all strong community
schemes, for which there will always be a need . . .

"I have heard it suggested that the creation of Village
Community Bus Schemes in other areas could be stimulated if
County Councils were to offer regular subsidies to meet some or
all of the running costs. But I have also heard that it would be at
variance with the practice of such Authorities to bear even part of
an Association's regular expenses without insisting on a measure
of bureaucratic control. In my opinion this would inevitably stifle
the spirit of voluntary service and independence, which is just as
vital for the members of an organisation such as ours as is petrol
for our vehicles.

"Since it has long been the practice for voluntary organisations
to carry responsibility for many kinds of important service to
communities, I can see no reason why a community transport
service should not be one of them. And since an organisation
such as ours is accustomed to receiving regular small grants from
District and Parish Councils without any stipulation by them to
participate in the management of our affairs, I suggest that the
larger Authorities could safely do the same with somewhat bigger
grants"!

Many will share the Brigadier's belief in "the spirit
of voluntary service and independence". Money can buy
much, but it cannot buy that—although it may enhance and
encourage it. People not only need to be helped; they need
to help.

Chapter 9

IN LIVING MEMORY

The final chapter of my book is devoted, mainly, to the memories of older members of the parish, who, despite their age, clearly recall how things used to be in the district — sometimes better, sometimes worse.

Mrs. Dorothy Smith

My parents, Walter Henry and Jane Selina Winslade, first came to Coldwaltham about 1901, to live at No. 1, King's Lane Cottages, Hardham. At the same time, my maternal grandparents, William ('Shottie') and Eliza Harwood, moved to Waltham Farm, nearby on the London Road — now Old London Road.

In 1906, my grandparents moved to Oxford House, on Church Hill, Coldwaltham. Today it is Barn Owls Restaurant, but then it was a smallholding. They kept sheep, pigs and cows in the long building nearby, which is now a separate, private house. What was their grazing field is now the Arun Vale Estate.

Also in 1906, my parents moved to the Old Parsonage, now called the Old Priest House, where I was born that same year. The Old Parsonage then was two cottages, and Grannie and Grandad White lived next door. I had one brother and three sisters, and I was the second youngest. Now I'm the only one left.

My brother, Walter William, joined up at seventeen for the First World War. There was a recruitment wagon at the Swan, Pulborough, and he was the first to jump up on it. He joined the Royal Sussex Regiment, but was killed in France, aged 19.

Father was a builder in Pulborough and Coldwaltham, and when I was two we moved to a house built by father in London Road, Pulborough.

Fig. 1 Trottie Woods

My earliest memories are of two personalities in the parish. I was just a tiny girl, but I plainly remember Trottie Woods.[1] She was in her forties, and lived with her mother in Sandy Lane, Watersfield. Trottie always dressed in red, summer and winter, with a red flannel petticoat, and she wore men's boots. She always walked in the ditch along Watersfield Common (now no more). She kept two cows in the Brooks, and used to go down and milk them.

The other personality was Mr. Richard (Dickie) Dallyn, who lived at Hardham House. He was Mr. Jake Dallyn's grandfather, and the family had farmed there for many years. Dickie Dallyn was already an old man. He had a grey pony, and used to sit on it, and say: "Come on, Sam. Sam. Come

---

1 "Trottie was not so daft as she made out, and did you know that there were 500 safety pins in her clothing when Nurse laid her out? And, 'they' say, £40 in gold sovereigns stuck onto candle ends." (from a letter from Peta Matthews, daughter of Arthur Matthews and Marion Paddon, written to Marjorie Hessell Tiltman)

on, Sam." When they got to the Labouring Man, the pony
would just stop, all on its own, and stay there without being
tethered while Mr. Dallyn went in for a drink. They used to
go to the Swan at Pulborough, too. And even if he was put
on his horse, at the end of the evening, facing the horse's tail,

Fig. 2 Grannie Harwood

he seemed to get home all right! One night, coming home from Pulborough, his horse stopped to drink at the pond opposite Hardham Priory. As he lowered his head, over Mr. Dallyn went, splash! into the water.

In 1907, Father helped my uncle, George Harwood, build 'The Pines' for Grannie and Grandad Harwood. We stayed with them for a year while my father built the bungalow here in London Road ('Moorings') for the family. Father also built 'The Homestead', now 'Ashridge', in Old London Road, where the family lived from the early 1930s to 1941.

During our stay at 'The Pines', my Grandad ran the sandpit nearby, quarrying it for building sand. A tile company (the Redhill) had a factory in the quarry for making their lovely black, red and mixed black-and-red roofing tiles. Father had a steam engine to take the sand to Hardham Halt, and load it on the train.

I also remember the coalman calling while we were at 'The Pines'. Grannie Harwood was upstairs, but there was this parrot called Polly, who never stopped talking. The coalman called out, "How many?" Grannie didn't hear him, but Polly answered, "Two, please!" Two were delivered, then the coalman knocked for payment. Grannie came down, and opened the door. "But I didn't order any today," she said. "Yes, you did," said the coalman, "you said, 'Two, please,' clear as anything." "Oh, lord," said Grannie, "it must have been that dratted parrot!"

Father had a pony and trap, then a motor-bike with a wicker sidecar. Later on, he had a Ford car. He gave up building in 1915, at the age of thirty-six, and became chauffeur-gardener to the Meynells, at Greatham, until he went to do war work at the old Ford Airfield, built in 1914-1918, where Ford open prison and the industrial estate are now. He returned to work for the Meynells in 1918.

As well as local men being employed at the quarry, some were employed by a Mr. Eames at Hardham Mill, where the Pumping Station now is. The Mill was painted by a local artist, T. Harrison Miller, RA, who had his studio almost opposite the Labouring Man. He married a Miss McKechnie,

Fig. 3   Annie Winslade, Dorothy Smith's youngest sister,
with their father's Ford, and wearing his cap,
with their mother in the back

who lived a little further down Old London Road, at Wayside
Cottage (now Church House), but he kept the studio. He did
a large oil painting of Hardham Mill, and one called 'On the
Rother', and he presented them to the village, in memory of
his wife. They were hung in Sandham Hall, but only one is
left now—the other disappeared.

Our baker in the 1920s was Mr. Fred Pennicott, who also
ran the old Post Office, in Watersfield.

There was a Post Office in Coldwaltham then, run at 'The
Post House' by a Mr. and Mrs. Roberts, and Mr. Roberts'
brother. It was also a general store. My husband, Frank,
remembers it being there in 1925. When the Roberts died,
the Post Office moved to the top of Church Hill, to what is
now the house next but one to Sandham Hall. It was run by
the Besants until about 1930, then it was amalgamated with

Watersfield Post Office, which moved first to where Waters-field store now is, then across the road.

The shops were good then, and there was no need to go farther afield. 'Shopping local' was more than sufficient. There was a general store, in a hut beside the Labouring Man. And Olivers, grocers and drapers in Lower Street, Pulborough, came one week to Coldwaltham with a horse and covered cart, and Greenfields, the grocers, then at Storrington where Cullen's now are, came the other week. I can also remember the forge being worked in Coldwaltham, and loved watching Mr. Andrews at work.

Joseph (Joe) Joiner was Verger of Coldwaltham Church[2], and lived with his sister, Esther, and brother, Benjamin, in Ivy Cottage, Coldwaltham — but it was always called 'Joe Joiner's Cottage'. Joe would sit on a chair in church and ring three bells—two by hand and one with his foot.

We had to pump the church organ in those days. When (the late) Mrs. Edie Puttick, who became Mrs. Harold Colwell, and I were young, we were the only girls in the choir. We weren't allowed to sit with the boys, but sat either side of the organist.

I remember also, when we were girls, the road to Greatham [Brook Lane] was gated. There were gates where the council estate [Brook View] now ends, and one this [Coldwaltham] side of Greatham Bridge. When the charabancs, as we called them, came to visit the area, Annie, my younger sister, and I would dash to open the gates, when we were visiting Cold-waltham from Greatham, and the passengers would throw us out pennies.

Later, Annie married Ernest Colwell, who worked for our father. Ernest's father started a fruit farm at Ashurst, but it isn't there now.

We drew all our water from wells in those days, but things progressed . . . The main road was improved in the 1930s. Even before that, there were regular buses. They started in

---

2 Joseph Joiner was Verger and Sexton for 50 years, from 1873, and died in 1927.

1927, and ran every day from Horsham to Littlehampton via Coldwaltham. Even in 1971, buses were still frequent. Not like now. The estates [Arun Vale and Silverdale] were built in Coldwaltham, on land owned by George Charman, who lived on a farm opposite the Old Priest House with his sister, Ethel. There were two big black wooden barns on either side of the road: one where the entrance to Silverdale is, the other opposite.

Fig. 4   London Road, Pulborough,
with Dorothy Smith in the foreground

When we moved back from Pulborough, I went to Coldwaltham School. The headmistress was a Miss Wally, and Miss Ford also taught there. Then I returned to Pulborough School. We went by bike and, when the roads were flooded, we had to wait for a farmer and wagon to come by and give us a lift. Or we would leave our bikes by the roadside, and walk along the wire fence. Then it got better, when they lifted the road four feet and put in five culverts, and built the new bridge in 1925.

In 1922-24, I was courted by my husband, Frank William Smith. We both worked in Worthing, where he was a building

Fig. 5 Miss Ford

craftsman, and I was a cook. We travelled up to Pulborough together for Christmas 1922. It cost 1s. 8d. return on the bus from Worthing to Pulborough. We were met at Pulborough by my father, with the pony and trap. I remember that, while I was waiting for the bus back, I bought a pair of Russian boots from Olivers, for 19s. 11d. They had just come into fashion.

Sometimes, when we visited my family, we cycled from Worthing. It took us 1½ hours. The Rev. Frederick Clarke married Frank and me in 1928. We moved away to live, but I kept in touch with the village all my life until, in 1979, when my husband retired, we returned to live in the bungalow built by my father, 'Moorings'.

Reginald Beaumont Rowland

I was born in Roffey, Horsham, where my father, Beaumont ('Beau') Rowland, was a successful farmer. In 1931, when I was seventeen, the family moved from Northchapel (where Father had a butcher's shop) to Watersfield. I was delighted, because I had been bicycling over to Watersfield to see friends since the age of thirteen, and I liked it here.

I stayed on in Northchapel, though, for three months, to give the new owner a smooth takeover, then joined my father in Watersfield in the butcher's shop he had set up there. It had been the village grocer's, owned by Mr. Edward Unsted, but in the early 1920s he had built Watersfield Stores, a bit further down the road in the village, on the opposite side. I was Father's 'right hand man' in our shop, and we were helped for a while by Mr. Eddie Mills. His wife, Ruby Mills—whose father, Mr. Fred Pennicott, ran the baker's and the Post Office — and my father both played the piano. I remember many enjoyable evenings with sing-songs round the piano. There was no television to distract us then.

In the village, everyone had parties, and everyone had their own party piece. We used to drink home-made wine, and quite potent it was, too!

When we made the move to Watersfield, my sister Marjorie was thirteen, and my brother, Bernard, six. I also had two other sisters. One, Kathleen, was in service and had lived away from home for as long as I could remember, and the other, Violet, lived in Duncton. My sister Marjorie married my best friend, Mr. Leslie (Les) Goble.

When we first came to the village, I clearly remember Captain Alban Head. He lived in Watersfield at a house called 'Greenacres' (now 'Swallowfield'). In those days, thanks to him, Watersfield was the only village for miles around that had Sunday cricket — and very special cricket at that, with members of the county team, like Wensley, Bowley, Maurice Tate, Cook and 'Titch' Cornford, all taking part. On Saturdays, there was village cricket — a free-for-all, including me and Captain Head! A family called the Coxes lived at 'Quintins', up near the playing field, and their son Leo played cricket with us; and another son later. After matches, we used to have tea at their house. Later, we had tea at the Three Crowns.

In addition to giving the recreation ground for the Parish's use,[3] Captain Head gave an annual sum to maintain it. Before World War II, Bert Boxall was chairman of the Playing Field Committee, and after the war I was chairman.

I spent five or six years running the business with my father, then ran it on my own for a few months with my mother (Rose, née Connor) until war broke out.

In 1937, I married Irene May Upton, from Mare Hill, Pulborough, who also helped me in the business from then on.

Then, in 1939, I got my call-up papers. I applied to a tribunal in Worthing, saying I had to run the family business, but they wouldn't exempt me and I was called up within a fortnight, anyway. My wife somehow ran the whole business for 5½ years while I was away. This included a week when the van driver let us down, when she took over the van and drove it round to supply all our customers. On one occasion, without really knowing how to drive, she backed into a ditch at Sutton, and was rescued by a lorryful of Canadian soldiers. They not only drove with her for the rest of that day's run, but made sure she had lessons, and accompanied her on the round for the rest of the week, until another van driver was found to take over.

When meat ceased to be rationed, in 1947, our business took off. I had seen enough 'rough' meat during the war, and I vowed from then on to supply meat that was nothing but the best. During the rationing period, people had been allowed to keep their own pigs — one for market, one for themselves. We had our own, and a kiln in the garden. We made our own bacon and pickled pork. There were three 180-noggin wine barrels, I remember, and they were always kept full.

We had three sons and a daughter, Pat, the eldest. She lives in Hailsham, but Alan, Ron and John all live in the

---

3   It is called the Alban Head Playing Field, after the donor.

parish. My children and their families have been marvellous to me, especially since my wife died in 1985. When the children were young, we had a weekly trip to Brighton Hippodrome, and stopped for fish and chips on the way back. My children still say: "Do you remember . . .?"

After the war, I bought the shop, and most of the adjoining block of cottages, from my father. We had an agreement that I would pay him £1 a week. When the two cottages at the end were vacated, I knocked them into one for my family, and my son John, who has run the butcher's shop since 1972, lives there with his family. His wife, 'Birdie', has run the Post Office on the same premises for the past ten years. There is a general store there now, too.

In the 1960s, we acquired the last cottage in the block from Mrs. Morris, a niece of Captain Alban Head. The cottage was next to the butcher's shop, so we could expand, and we started a delicatessen—cold meats and so on—a great success. (My grandson Mark[4] and his young family have the flat that runs over the expanded shop.)

We ran the delicatessen in collaboration with Mr. Gee, who had Watersfield Store then, and the Post Office, until he retired and went to live in Malta. Mr. Cox ran Watersfield Store after that, for a few years.

Opposite our shop used to be the village pond. Grannie Clark claimed the ground, and the pond was filled in, in the early 1960s, and fenced. In the old days, the old threshing tackle was stopped there, for the boilers to be filled up.

The Youth Club was first started in Watersfield, in the Old Chapel—which was more or less in rack and ruin then—before it was rebuilt into a private house. Mr. Eric Bell, who ran Watersfield Garage, was chairman of the club. That was about 25 years ago. We had one night for the boys, and a leader used to come over from Chichester, and one night for the girls, run by my wife and Janet Dunstan. After a number of years, it fell through. Later on, Chris Harris, from Coldwaltham, took it over.

---

4   see end of Mr. Rowland's memoirs

Perhaps this is the best place to say something about Mark Rowland, who is a source of great pride to the parish for his achievements in athletics. It all started when he won the Sussex Schools Athletics Championships in 1980. Three years later, he won the 800 metres and 1500 metres in the Sussex Athletics Championships. Next year, he won a bronze medal in the Southern Counties Track Championships at Crystal Palace in June, and in November he won the Sussex Cross-Country League six-mile event in 29 mins., 48 secs.

Inevitably, with so many successes charting steady progress behind him, in 1985 he made his international debut alongside fellow Phoenix Athletics Club (Brighton) member, Steve Ovett. The occasion was a meeting against the United States team, televised live from Birmingham. Mark came in second. That same month of June 1985, Mark had his Great Britain debut at Gateshead, running in the 1500 metres against Steve Ovett. Steve has been Mark's mentor for some time, and they regularly train together in Brighton. Perhaps one day Mark will wrest the 1500 metres world record from Steve? Also in 1985 — Mark's greatest year yet — he went to China with the England Men's Under-23 team, and was winner at the Nanking meeting — one of forty English athletes in his team — for all events except the hammer. In 1985, again, Mark won the 1500 metres men's event in the UK Championships in Antrim, Northern Ireland.

In March 1987, he came fourth in the 3000 metres in the World Indoor Athletics Championships, at Indianapolis. His latest triumph (in June) was to win the 5000 metres, running for England, at the Dairy Crest International Meeting at Portsmouth.

*   *   *   *   *

Another Coldwaltham man who brought fame recently to the parish is Peter Gorman, the international and national canoeist. In the 1970s, this dedicated sportsman won dozens of trophies at home and abroad, training nightly on the River Arun, regardless of the weather. Now living in Guildford,

Peter is team coach of the British Marathon Canoeing team, and, as his mother, Mrs. Olive Gorman, puts it, "he is putting something back into the sport by encouraging and coaching others". Earlier this year, he became Commodore of Wey Canoe Club.

Mrs. Doris Mary Page
An obituary by the Rev. Ronald Chatwin
published in the *Coldwaltham Parish News*
for December 1973

Without doubt we shall never again see the likeness of Doris Mary Page, who died at her home, 'Highfield', Bury Gate, on October 30th, leaving a record of fifty years' devoted service in the parish where she came to live shortly after her marriage in 1921.

The private family Funeral Service was followed by internment in Coldwaltham churchyard, and immediately afterwards came the parish tribute at a Service of Thanksgiving for her life and work. Her contribution to our community life was prodigious and unstinting; no opportunity was passed over, no cause too small: churchwarden, parish councillor, parochial church councillor, Founder member and President (for twenty-seven years) of the Women's Institute, school manager, leader of the 'Darby and Joan Club', Sunday School teacher, Honorary Librarian, member of the Sanctuary Guild. With all these activities one may wonder if there was time for anything else, but her relaxation, apart from a large garden, was as a guide at Parham House, where she took infinite pains to inform visitors of the history and value of the treasures of that manor. A visit to 'Highfield' nearly always included a conducted tour of the garden, and one found one's arms full of flowers or plants as a parting gesture, for Doris Page maintained that flowers and a garden were God's gift to be shared.

Until her terminal illness two years ago, few people in our parish remained outside the orbit of her interest; some thought her 'nosy', inquisitive, but it was all done with kindness and a desire to promote a sense of 'belonging' to the community.

The parish paid tribute on 5th November by filling the church — both with people and flowers; organisations were represented and some people were there just because she was a friend to all; Mrs. Roger Wilson, the Bishop's wife, came to honour a friendship of forty years; some could claim but three or four years. At the Thanksgiving Service it was said of her:—

"Doris Page was born and brought up in an English Rectory, and there she learned the virtues of abstemiousness, self-discipline, fortitude and courage that later became the characteristics of a woman who ruled our two villages for some fifty years. Such was that discipline that her 21st birthday, falling on Good Friday, was considered more a misfortune than a celebration on that solemn day of the year. But that discipline was there when at a Martinmas Market just two years ago she had to be bodily removed from her stall, physically incapable of carrying on any longer, and that was her last parish function."

"She worked, she struggled, she fought; she was a leader amongst women—men always knew when they were beaten!"

"Doris Page cared about people's happiness—cared enough to get hurt in the welter of village politics; she brought people together to communicate to them her vision of the Kingdom of Heaven; her life *was* other people, and so she tended our common life, enriching it, fertilising it with love and devotion. The scores of letters and postcards that poured out from 'Highfield'! We lesser mortals do our best with the aid of the telephone; but not she. Always she cared."

Our sympathy in their loss goes out to Mr. Geoffrey Page and to Heather and Robin. Heather gave up her own career to nurse her mother with great tenderness and devotion.

R.E.C.

Mr. Darkie Pollard

Mr. 'Darkie' Pollard came to Coldwaltham from Aylesbury, Buckinghamshire. He says he was first apprenticed to a duck shoer. When pressed, he further revealed that this meant he helped a man to shoo ducks in the right direction!

At first, Mr. Pollard lived in one of the (then) three Meadow Cottages, in Watersfield.

Apart from serving long on the parish council, until he retired from it, in 1985, at the age of 86, he has a particular claim to parish fame, for it was he who, over many years, walked the local footpaths to ensure they were kept open. He recalls that, one evening, he was having a pint in the Three Crowns with Mr. Tom Lock, the landlord, and Mr. Bill Ruff, the farmer, and they were talking about the footpaths.

Mr. Pollard challenged Mr. Ruff: "If you don't walk the footpaths, you won't be on the parish council next election—because I won't vote for you!" They started to talk about Footpath 2411, opposite the butcher's, and leading to where the house, 'Beltane' (now called 'Saunders'), stands, in Sandy Lane. Darkie was challenged to walk that path one Maundy Thursday, and the following day, Good Friday, he walked it. Mr. Lock had promised him a pint of beer if he made the walk, and Mr. Ruff likewise promised another pint when he 'signed him off' at the end of the walk. Mr. Lock turned up to wish Mr. Pollard 'Godspeed', but Mr. Ruff was not at the finishing point, so Darkie asked the resident of 'Beltane' if he had noticed him (Darkie) in the vicinity . . . Fortunately he had been seen, and so two tasty pints of free ale came his way that evening.

After that, Darkie, who had been a "serious" walker since a boy, trod all the parish's footpaths on a regular basis. There was no better authority on them. At one stage, Mr. Phil Hedger (who, tragically, died young, just a few years ago) used to walk the paths with him, with his two small sons.

The footpath between the main road and 'Beltane' was going to be closed, but Darkie, then a member of the parish council, objected. The county council tried to get him to withdraw his objection, but he would not budge. One footpath got closed, so far as he knew: the one from the Labouring Man to near the Smiths ('Moorings', in Old London Road)—a path a mere 200 yards long. They tried to close the path between Watersfield cricket playing field and The Ridge. Mr. Pollard observed that a bungalow was in fact being built right on the footpath, and he complained to the building foreman, with the result that the bungalow was moved off the footpath!

Then there was the saga of the footpath down by Watts Farm, Watersfield. The late Mr. John Paddon told Mrs. Murphy, who lived in Watts Farm Cottage, that the privet hedge to Mrs. Whitefield's garden, next door at Watts Farm, was built on a public footpath. Mrs. Murphy went to court about it, and lost — to the tune of so much money that she was forced to sell up and leave the neighbourhood.

Darkie Pollard's longest walk was a 20-mile event for charity. He walked from North Turkey Farm, Washington, to Seaford College (boys' school), Petworth, for the Red Cross. In the process, he raised nearly £50 (a lot of money in 1978), and the Duchess of Norfolk signed his sponsors' card, and personally gave him one pound more. He still has that pound note, having substituted another to make up his sponsored total.

Another of Mr. Pollard's clearest and fondest memories concerns the Boxing Day Shoot. According to him, it went back "donkeys' years" before he arrived in the parish and started to take part. He remembers taking two caps on the shoot: a good one, to wear; and an old one — to throw up in the air and shoot at.

The Shoot members met at the Three Crowns, went to the Labouring Man, on to nearby Timberley Farm, and back to the Three Crowns for lunch. The lunches were quite amazing, he remembers. One year, Mrs. Lock made a rabbit pie with fourteen rabbits and four pounds of pork: it was so enormous that it had to be taken to Bunny Ayres, the baker at Sutton, because the pub's oven was not big enough!

After that (one wonders how!), the Boxing Day Shoot set off again, and there are reports that at this stage many of the men actually rolled down River Lane. (Mr. Reg. Rowland aids Mr. Pollard's memory here.) After rolling down River Lane, members of the Shoot would nonetheless get themselves together by the time they reached their first stile. Before mounting any stile, in fact, they would 'break' their guns,

Fig. 6 Boxing Day Shoot

extract the cartridges and, having mounted the stile, would re-charge their guns. (Quite a remarkable feat for anyone in their condition, 'in their cups' and bursting with one of Mrs. Lock's major confections.)

The Shoot used to bag rabbits, pheasant and snipe, and one year they shot a bittern, which must have been a special endurance test, since bitterns wave about from side to side — their natural gait — and the men trying to shoot it must have been weaving about even more ... One year, Lord Leconfield's gamekeeper invited the Shoot to the back of the cricket field, and they got twenty-two rabbits.

Or did they see double?

Mrs. Lil Dunford

I am 78 years old. My parents were Edith Lilian (née Hayler) and John Charles Farhall. I have a surviving sister,

Rose, and a brother, Peter. They both live in Slough now, but I see them quite a lot.

When I was eight months old, we went to live at the Forge Cottage, in Old London Road. Dick Andrew ran the actual forge, but he didn't live there.

After that, we lived in the Old Priest House, known then as 'The Old Parsonage'. It was two cottages then. There was a well in the scullery but the water was bad. We had to fetch water from a pump right down Brook Lane, at Butcher's Hovel—a ten-minute walk with empty buckets, much longer with full ones! Our next-door neighbours were Mr. and Mrs. Tom Harwood.

Fig. 7   Mrs. Dunford with her fiancé, George Dunford,
outside her former home, 'The Old Parsonage'

There was a store next to the Labouring Man, run by a Mr. and Mrs. Cole. She had eyes like boot buttons. The Post Office was run in the Old Post House by a Mrs. Roberts. We used to ring the bell and wait for ages till she came. She sold the pears from her pear tree, and when we went for some, she gave us children extra pears to eat on the way home.

The Post Office moved to Church Hill, and was run by Mr. 'Ducksie' Besant—old Bezzie. He was a real old muddler, but nice!

On Sunday mornings, sometimes a winkle man came round, and watercress was also sold at the door. During the week, Mr. Fielder and, later, Mr. Payne, came out from Pulborough regularly, selling herring and other fish.

I went to Coldwaltham School. Miss Ford was the infant teacher, and Miss Walley, the headmistress, wore red flannel bloomers. After we had done various jobs at home, we went to school at about 8.50 a.m. We got home about four, and helped some more. I helped a lot at home, because I was the eldest. I did cleaning, breaking sticks, washing up, and things like that.

Fig. 8 The old Coldwaltham School

Along the Greatham road, charabancs came, and we opened the gates across the road for them, and they threw out money — even a sixpence, sometimes. One July, my brother had Scarlet Fever, and we all had to stay off school, so we went down to the gates for a whole month, and made quite a lot of money—enough to go on an outing to the sea.

When I was nearly fourteen, I went into service, first at the house at the top of Lodge Hill called 'Wildbrooks', then I went to Brighton. I met my husband, George, in Lewes, and we lived there until the war came. My husband came out of the Forces, and we lived in one of the little tin huts in Church Lane, until we came here to Brookview.

The woods opposite the school were a popular place for children and grown-ups, and they were called the Pines. You could wander about anywhere there, and it was a sad day when it became private property.

Miss Doris Cooper

"Coldwaltham and Watersfield during World War II, and for some years after, as seen by a newcomer"

Coming from the outskirts of London in September 1940, we found Coldwaltham surprisingly casual about black-out regulations and more concerned about what to do with evacuees. The very few houses were all well filled, Cockney voices contrasting with the then prevailing Sussex accent—the BBC reached every home but had not yet affected speech!

The little school, where normally the headmistress, Mrs. Colwell, and the formidable Infant Teacher, Miss Ford, taught the five- to fourteen-year-olds between them in two class-rooms, would have been overwhelmed by the influx, except that two teachers had come with their pupils, and helped out. The children had some of their lessons in the Sandham Hall. There was school milk for all then, but no canteen: heating was by one open fireplace in each classroom and the same in Sandham Hall: toilet facilities were outdoor earth closets— and a cold tap. There was no radio in the school, and the curriculum basically was 'the three Rs' and Scripture, English History and Geography, drawing and 'drill'. The boys went to the Recreation Ground at Watersfield for football and cricket —at least, they were doing so by the end of the war, for my father (Alexander Charles Cooper) took it upon himself, with Mrs. Colwell's blessing, to take them there and teach them.

Naturally, there were few 'big boys' to be seen, for all those not needed for farm work were called up. It was girls who cycled to Pulborough Station for the newspapers, and cycled back to deliver them, unfailingly, every morning, in all weathers. Older men of course were in the Home Guard, and some were in the Observer Corps. Heavy military vehicles made up the bulk of the traffic; an anti-aircraft gun was stationed for some time in our garden. There was a searchlight at Watersfield, manned by the Royal Engineers.

*Fig. 9   The searchlight, near the old Swallow Inn, Watersfield,
(now 'White Swallow') manned by the Royal Engineers,
with Sergt. Philip Marriage in charge*

Hardham Mill had been bombed shortly before we came, and in another raid the Rector of Stopham had been killed— the only air-raid casualties in the neighbourhood till some three years later, when, in one disastrous afternoon, a bomb was dropped on Petworth Boys' School, killing all the staff and all the boys present except one.

Fig. 10   Royal Engineers who manned the searchlight

Coldwaltham was much smaller in those days. There were no private housing estates then, and only thirty council houses. Watersfield has changed less, but there used to be only small cottages there. Main water had only recently been laid on, and electricity supplied lighting alone. There was no main drainage.

During a lull in the raids, the evacuees drifted home, but when, later, raids became heavy again, with Brighton and Portsmouth suffering badly, there was a fresh wave of evacuation. Coldwaltham and Watersfield did not receive any this time; in fact, we were forbidden *any* extra inhabitants when invasion was expected. (Fittleworth was outside the 'forbidden zone', and, instead of having a holiday with us, some friends stayed at a guest house on Tripp Hill, and walked over to see us.)

The Post Office was in Coldwaltham, in the house opposite Barn Owls Restaurant (now 'Church Cottage'). It was run very differently from the one now in Watersfield. It was in a dark little room, and one could also buy there a few tinned goods—I forget what else. It took ages for 'Old Bezzie' (Mr. Besant) to look for anything! Watersfield had a real village shop—everything from bootlaces to bacon—where we also registered and changed our coupons, and the butcher's shop then was run by Mr. and Mrs. 'Beau' Rowland, the grandparents of the present butcher, John Rowland.

After the war, when rationing was still stringent, a weekly issue was made of meat pies, commercially produced. I fancy this was under the auspices of the W.V.S. (Women's Voluntary Service). A selling point for these was our garage; Mrs. Dorothy Secomb, from Coldwaltham Farm, was in charge.

The Coldwaltham and Watersfield Women's Institute, fairly new but very active, under the chairmanship of its founder, Mrs. Doris Page, and with Mrs. Dorothy Secomb as Honorary Secretary, was the pride and joy of the women in the village; nearly all those who had no small children must have belonged. Monthly meetings were held in the Sandham Hall. During the summer, all available fruit was collected and canned in Sandham Hall. (Probably the W.V.S. were involved, but the W.I. gave active help.) The kitchen then (not the present one) was a poky affair, almost filled by a shallow sink, a tall cupboard and a big copper.

During those years, and for some time after, the Vicarage was the old Victorian house behind the school. There was no electricity, and no mains water. Good drinking water gushed into a long, dark sink when one worked the heavy pump handle over it, but for washing one turned a light wheel in the 'back corridor', which pumped rain-water into a tank upstairs.

'The Pines'[5] had no mains water either, but a very deep bore-hole. We had to turn a large and very heavy wheel in the 'pumphouse', which, after twenty-five turns, sent the water (soft, and tasting slightly of iron) into a large tank in the loft, which supplied the hot water tank below it. Visitors, if able-bodied, were asked to take their turn at the pump! At least we were never frozen up, and the water was deliciously cold in summer.

---

5 Miss Cooper's house, then and now

Prior to the Second World War, 'The Pines' had a filling station. The tanks, underground, were on the flat space behind the tree, on a little 'island' evidently dug out to accommodate them. The pumps had gone—or, at least, I do not remember seeing them there—before we arrived, and the tanks were bought by Mr. Jim Jupp for storing water. There was a sharp drop from the garden at one point, with no barrier, and my aunt, staying with us, was always anxious that my grandfather, who was nearly blind but loved being outside on his own, might fall down the six feet or so to the concrete. I planted a sucker from a white lilac bush there, and now there is a thicket of lilac and wild plum.

During the evenings of the week before Christmas, Mrs. Page got as many women together as possible, and we went to *every house* in Coldwaltham and Watersfield to sing one or two verses of a carol. We had an excellent singer, Miss Lulu Thompson, to lead us. No attempt to use hymn sheets— remember the black-out! Full moon was a blessing. We relaxed after the war—but only in the matter of the hymn sheets!

A VIEW OF WATERSFIELD

a poem by Mr. Eric S. Binns,
who used to live at 'Chennies', Watersfield

Drifts from even-lit fires, waft,
Plume and idly process this combe valley,
Straggling between hill-copse and meadow:
An amalgam of time and enterprise,
With no known, splendid viewpoint
Or calendar-picture view vantages.

In its amiable juxtaposition,
Everyone has his neighbour-friend,
At his own neat garden-bank:
Much more or less wealthy than he,
A lordly, pied manor, here, secluded
By unpretentious and unclassifiable.

A stone "Post Office" or "Crown House"
Of old, now rambling, creeper-clad:
Boarded cott, bungalow or semi
By rambler-wrapped swallow-porch
Or wisteria-mazed shrubbery opposite:
Each entry would be suffered here, friendly.

Unplanned; each kaleidoscope-view,
Without church, guildhall, pomp
Or ceremony; an ancient highway
Would respect, with hamlet fastness;
While the modern fast descends, snakes
And bisects in restless traverse.

But pause, by the nightingale's rock;
Or by the straw-strewn store-yard;
Or in the cottage lanes, athwart the road,
That seek the meads of brown cattle
And the greensand's high pine-slopes:
Firewoods kindle its life at evening.

23-3-83

Neale: a Sussex Yeoman family

(information gathered by a Neale: Mrs. Valerie Wheeler)

I begin with an excerpt from a letter received in 1973, after my beloved mother's death, and written by my father's cousin, Gordon Neale, uncle of Pamela Sutton, wife of Peter Bishop of Nelson, New Zealand, whose grandparents, Rosa and Francis John Neale, are buried in the granite curbed grave in the extreme right-hand (north-west) corner of the new grave-yard (at Coldwaltham Church):

"I expect you know the history of the Neales—three brothers expelled from Ireland by Queen Elizabeth I: Hugh, who was put to death in the Tower, and Percy and Philip—they were given land in Sussex and Wiltshire, and were not allowed to take the name O'Neill. The Wiltshire portion of the family lived at Wooton Rivers—they had the full family history.

"Unfortunately, your grandmother, Kate, clearing up after your grandfather's death, burnt all the papers by accident . . . and also we had a crest of the Kings of Ireland: 'The Blood Red Land of Ireland'."

Now the Neales have left Wooton Rivers, which is near Marlborough, where they are all buried. . . They were ordered, as we were, not to use the name O'Neill, but one of them has O'Neale shown on his tombstone.

One interesting fact in my research is that Arthur Hobden (?) married his second cousin, Fanny, sister of my grandfather, Percy. Both of them are buried in the family vault north-east of Coldwaltham Church. It was Arthur who gave £2,000 for the first Test (Cricket) team to go out to Australia, on 21st September, 1876. He played for Sussex, and thought he would like to take out a team, so began making arrangements, but when his mother, Ann (née Neale) worried, thinking of her son travelling all those thousands of miles, the time he would be gone and the possibility she might never see him again, she became quite ill. He therefore decided to finance the team, and Jim Lillywhite was put in charge. The trip was enjoyable and successful. A few days after their return, Arthur met Lillywhite in Chichester. They arranged a dinner party, at which funds could be handed over. Lillywhite had paid all expenses and handed a sum in excess of £4,000, in gold and notes, to Arthur, and so ended the first of the Test Series in Australia. Sadly, poor, generous Arthur and his wife both died at the age of 38, leaving two orphan sons, who inherited much land, including gravel pits, now the site of Chichester Crematorium.

Arthur's brother Allen married Constance Tribe, and his second cousin, Hugh Penfold, married Blanche Harwood Tribe, of Earnley Grange. Both Tribe ladies were first cousins of Mary Du Caurroy (?) Tribe, later known as 'The Flying Duchess of Bedford', and daughter of the Archdeacon of Lahore, Walter Tribe.

Research on land owned by the Neale family has been done by Mr. Thorpe, and a tithe map of Coldwaltham and Watersfield shows land in 1841 owned and occupied by my grandfather, John, some let out to tenants, and some let out to him; also the same for his brother William. Many historical manor houses and a priory have been owned and inhabited by them through the ages, back to c.1500. The family motto is "By my sword I have won these lands, and by my sword shall I keep them!"

In Coldwaltham Church, the brass tablets below Francis and Elizabeth commemorate my grandfather, John, his son, Percy, and his sons, Percy John and Philip, below. The first-mentioned was originally placed on the right-hand side, but re-sited (without my knowledge) during restoration of the Chancel in 1957, when an ancient doorway was found in the church. The second remaining vault, east of the church, contains my first great-grandparents, John and Mary West Neale, and also has inscriptions, Francis (Jun.), b.1739, d.1811, his wife Ann and their families, Francis (Senr.), b.1688, d.1761 and his wife Mary, who, I believe, is buried inside the church, now covered by the Victorian tiles, with earlier members of the family, whose names appear in the County Records Office.

Mrs. Grace Adsett[6]

(from *Cottage Pie* by Marjorie Hessell Tiltman)

"Don't they trees look pretty-like with the moon just climbin' out of 'em? Have you heerd they ole brown owls a-crowin' to each other in the dell there? They do keep at it and no mistakin'. . . . They must have had some nestes round-abouts here."

"Mum talks old-fashioned," says my Lucy to me.

But how old-fashioned, not even Lucy quite realises.

---

6 Mrs. Grace Adsett, who lives at Brookview, is the "My Lucy" referred to by Mrs. Tiltman, in her three country books featuring Cold-waltham: *Cottage Pie, A Little Place in the Country,* and *The Birds Began to Sing.*

When Mrs. Tiltman had admitted putting "Lucy" in her books, Mrs. Adsett asked why she had not told her beforehand. "If I had," replied Mrs. Tiltman, "you might have stopped talking to me!"

Mum talks Anglo-Saxon; the soft old plurals linger among her speech, giving its Sussex burr a poetic rhythm which the clipped modern grammar has long since decapitated. In Dad's spicy conversation, too, the Anglo-Saxon derivatives and Norman inflections persist, evidence of the days when England and France played sort of Prisoner's Base across the Tom Tiddler's ground of the Channel, and married here and there, where they found the prettiest or the bravest, as Mum's maiden name of Jacques is but one of many witnesses. Mum and Dad, also, are some of the last of their kind. The wireless and the films, elementary schools and freer communications, between them have flattened out all the peculiar chaos of local speech.

*   *   *   *   *

The following extracts from *Cottage Pie* by Marjorie Hessell Tiltman reflect an appeal and timelessness still to be felt and found in the parish of Coldwaltham, and, fortunately, in many other small, rural nooks and crannies in England.

We live on such a small canvas in the country. We are easily pleased . . .

November

Now that most of the trees are bare, the berries stand out with greater brilliance than ever. Nothing more scarlet than the holly berry can be imagined; brighter than any jewel, it shines against the glossy, dark prickly leaves, the very symbol of a jolly and traditional winter. Beside it, the dull crimson of the haws in the hedges is a poor thing, and yet this very dullness is part of Nature's incomparable scheme. The beautifully shaped hips left on the briars are at their best, so much more precious than the roses which preceded them that the idea of gathering them for jam seems a veritable crime . . .

February

There are, however, the floods.

To our distant friends and relations the floods are a menace, threatening to engulf not only our cottage, but Us.

On a morning when the wind has softened and waters lie round us peaceful and translucent, reflecting the sunlight, we are almost sure to receive a letter from an aunt... "Dear child—I am most alarmed by the news in the papers. There was a photograph of your district, apparently totally submerged, and it said underneath that people are being taken away from the upper storeys of their houses by boat ... " [7]

Fig. 11   Mr. 'Alf' Puttick

7   This procedure used to be frequent at Hardham Lock Cottage, where lived the Putticks, including Mr. 'Alf' Puttick, who worked for the Colwells at Ashurst Farm.

... Dad spat in contempt. "Faugh," he growled. "They papers allus has to tark big, else no 'un 'd read 'em. That mus' be them folk in that old cottage by the [Hardham] Mill there. That be the only one I ever heerd tark of getting wetted, although old Charlie, now I minds it—nigh the Green, marm, he lives—told me onct of his bits o' carpet gettin' up and floatin' round him, one flood-time."

And indeed, it is true, strange or not as it may seem, that all the centuries-old cottages in the valley are built on little plateaux of land that remain above high-water mark, if only by a foot or a few inches. There was one, however, at a bend of the Roman Causeway, which was condemned and abolished a year or so ago on account of its being constantly flooded, uncomfortably if not dangerously.

"Terrible, it was," said the woman who lived in it to me. "We had to put duckboards along all the passages downstairs and walk along to our bedrooms in wellingtons."

May

The newly-warm air of May brought all the scents out of the earth and plants, and its dampness held them, infusing them into a compound in which we could occasionally distinguish the echo of the newly-springing bracken, the sticky scent of the bluebells, the pungent ivy and—as suddenly and as strongly as if we had been hounds—the musky trail of a fox, which could only have crossed our path but a few seconds previously. But we remember that particular May day chiefly because, plodding home, both wet and weary, along a dull stretch of main road for the sake of a short cut, a flood of melody suddenly burst forth from under our very feet.

There were three of us. We stopped short and looked at each other. The song continued unceasingly, in spite of our nearness. Soon, as our eyes sorted out the thick tangle of boughs, the gnarled stems and twisted twigs of the hedge, glistening and dripping with rain, we were able to discern on the far side a bush of dogwood and presently, slipping from branch to branch of it, a little grey-brown bird, as slim as a leaf.

It was the nightingale. The rain dripped on us while we stood still, listening to it, forgetting all else, until she took it into her head to make a little hopping flight to the high branches of a pine tree and thus broke the spell she had laid upon us, so that one of us was able to declare himself soaked to the skin, another to look at a watch and remind the party that the dinner must be burning in the oven.

August

The heat has come. The sun is the powerful, scorching sun of late summer. The air is heavy with humidity. Early morning and late evening, a white mist lies over the wild brooks, so dense that it blocks out the whole world behind it. At last the sun rises above it, drawing up the alien moisture as it grows in power, until one by one the familiar landmarks have thrown off their strange cloak of invisibility, and made themselves known to us. And as the day begins, so it is like watching a new world come into being—a world all the more dear for being so familiar to us—distant farms with red roofs, vague clusters of barns and haystacks, warm fields of ripe corn, the everlasting stretches of the water meadows, lush and green in a parched landscape, the white chalk pits and the soft folds of the Downs.

Appendix A
FIGHTING FOR TREES[1]

Hearts pound, hackles rise and money is hard to come by when old trees are fought for. A case in point was the West Sussex yew standing in leafy majesty in Coldwaltham church-yard, and reputed to be one of the twelve oldest in the land. In 1964, a local resident informed West Sussex County Council that the vicar and parochial church council were fearful that parts of the yew might be cut down "to avoid interference" with two new buildings just given planning consent to go up in adjacent plots. Horsham District Council enforced a Tree Preservation Order to prevent the "topping, lopping or wilful destruction" of the yew.

Before the Order comes into force, a careful examination of the tree is made. Assessing age can present problems, although one method is simply to put a tape measure round the tree's girth and multiply the inches by a certain figure to get the total of years. However, this method doesn't work with yews, which grow very slowly. Taking a core sample from the Coldwaltham yew was impossible, too, because most of its core had gone.

Coldwaltham parishioners were displeased when a local newspaper reported that the tree was only 280-plus years old. This contradicted local knowledge, which placed the yew's age at nearer 1000 years. There is no way, however, of proving such a grand old age. The first county maps only date back to 1575, and these are very small-scale, with few features such as specific trees distinguishable. Large-scale (tithe) maps only began to be made in the middle of the nineteenth century.

However, one piece of 'evidence' for there having been a chapel 1000 years ago on the site of the present Coldwaltham church was, in fact, the ancient yew. Even if the yew were not planted until the yard of St. Giles' Church (built in 1120) was enclosed, it could still be around 500 years old, if not

---

1 an article by Sandra MacGregor Hastie (Sandra Saer), published in *The Antique Collector*, February 1985

more. The latter is the theory of Mr. Derry Watkins, the tree
surgeon responsible for its repair.

The age of the tree was stated as 280-plus years by
Horsham District Council's report in November 1982 on the
work which needed doing. This, in the council's opinion,
was sufficient age to merit the importance of continued
preservation; plus the fact that the Tree Preservation Order
demanded it.

There is something reassuring about having a 'Tree
Preservation Order' and certainly an order gives a measure of
protection, by its very existence. Penalties are inflicted for
the violation of Orders, via the courts, by the local authority
concerned. Such penalties vary in severity, according to a
tree's importance. In Kent recently, a man felled a whole
avenue of preserved trees and was sent to prison for six
months, and fined heavily. In Sussex, a developer who cut
down preserved trees was fined £300 per tree—£1500 in total.

The Tree Preservation Order's main weakness is that a
piece of paper, however official, cannot alone suffice. The
Council for the Protection of Rural England discovered in
a survey that TPO legislation is at fault, in failing to ensure
positive management of protected trees. Yet without the
brief, or the resources, those making the Orders cannot stand
guard over the trees. It is usually left to those living nearby to
enforce the Orders by 'keeping an eye open'. That is rather
haphazard, to say the least.

Ironically, these same voluntary guardians raise another
weakness in the system. When it became apparent that
the Coldwaltham yew needed attention, Horsham District
Council, as the councils do, suggested to the churchwardens
the names of several reputable tree surgeons, including that
of Mr. Watkins. But often people, wanting to save money and
ignorant of the complications involved, use their own labour,
or that of people not good at that kind of work, to do
repairs. They end up by inflicting worse damage, and some of
the "jobs done", according to Mr. I. C. Richardson, the Tree
Officer for Horsham District Council, are "appalling".

Anyway, back in Coldwaltham, Mr. Watkins set to work,

bracing and stapling. The yew was repaired, and the bill for
£299 was sent to the churchwardens for the Parochial Church
Council to pay. The Diocese of Chichester had no money to
spend on a tree. The Historic Churches Preservation Trust
only give grants towards essential church-fabric repairs. The
District Council, also approached, had no money to spare. The
County Council, much involved in its share of the national
forward-looking tree-planting campaign, had no grant aid
available for 'private' trees, however old.

So it fell to the caring parishioners of Coldwaltham, plus
lovers of the village from all over the district who saw the
tree as part of their heritage, to foot the bill. Various fund-
raising events brought in two-thirds of the cost. There is no
resentment. Pride has won the day.

It seems hard, though, that they should have to pay that
bill, in addition to the many other charities and works they,
and their counterparts all over the country, unfailingly support.

There are very few national bodies who can help. The
Men of the Trees Society has long been aware of the need to
help not only churches with their trees, but individuals who
might buy a house and find that thrown in with it was a
'protected' tree, the maintenance of which they would be
forced to take on. The Men of the Trees do give financial
help for individual trees, on the advice submitted to headquarters by all the county bodies.

The Royal Society for Nature Conservation, to which are
affiliated organisations in 44 British counties—called county
naturalist trusts, conservation trusts or nature conservation
trusts — does provide money for important tree-preservation
projects, either through governmental bodies or special
charitable trusts.

Equally prepared to help, if the tree merits it, are the
Countryside Commission, to which the county councils
are affiliated, giving grant aid to protect and repair existing
trees, if they are an important feature of the landscape. In
the summer of 1983, for example, they offered a grant, via
East Sussex County Council, to repair the Crowhurst churchyard yew similar to that at Coldwaltham.

220

Appendix B

BIRDS OF WILDBROOKS   [Waltham Brooks]

observed over fifteen years of watching
by Eric J. Binns, a former resident of Watersfield

Resident

Lapwing	Willow Tit	Green Woodpecker
Goldfinch	Long-Tailed Tit	Pied Wagtail
Mute Swan	Coal Tit	Tree Creeper
Carrion Crow	Heron	Barn Owl
Rook	Mallard	Little Owl
Jay	Kestrel	Tawny Owl
Jackdaw	Sparrow-Hawk	Grey Partridge
Magpie	Moorhen	Tree Sparrow
Snipe	Nuthatch	Goldcrest
Stock Dove	Lesser Spotted	Woodcock
Blue Tit	Woodpecker	Wood Pigeon
Great Tit	Great Spotted	Wren
Marsh Tit	Woodpecker	Collared Dove

Winter

		Summer
Fieldfare	Hen Harrier	Swallow
Redwing	White-Fronted	Sand Martin
Bewick's Swan	Goose	House Martin
Canada Goose	Dunlin	Swift
Cormorant		Reed Bunting
Teal		Cuckoo
Gadwall	*Passage*	Yellow Wagtail
Wigeon	Whinchat	Redshank
Shoveler	Stonechat	Sedge Warbler
Pintail	Common	Reed Warbler
Shelduck	Sandpiper	Grasshopper
Kingfisher	Curlew	Warbler
Siskin	Spotted Crake	Blackcap
Redpoll	Coot	
Water Rail	Green Sandpiper	

Appendix C

Articles published in the *West Sussex Gazette* 1983-1984 by Sandra Saer, when she was Coldwaltham correspondent and wrote features for that newspaper

The Village Scene Remembered

"I remember a great lump of butter on a marble slab covered with muslin, chopped off and weighed on a marble scale and then slapped into shape with two wooden butter pats, then plonked on to a suitable wrapping paper."

This was just one of many memories of the small village of Watersfield recalled recently by a retired teacher who used to spend holidays there as a girl.

Staying with a friend in Coldwaltham, the former teacher, Miss Margaret Simmonds, who lives in Hainault, Essex, happily retraced her steps . . .

It was throughout the 1920s that, following a week spent with her grandparents in Southwick, Margaret Simmonds and her parents would come for one week each August to stay with her great uncle and aunt, Edward and Isabel Unsted.

Mr. Unsted will be remembered by older residents as the proprietor of Watersfield's old shop. Then it stood on the other side of the road, opposite the village pond (now, alas, filled in and almost forgotten).

Great Uncle 'Ted' bought Cherry Tree Cottage, however, and next to it he built, in the early 1920s, what in those days was considered a very grand little shop indeed.

At that time, there was no sewerage and no electricity. Edward Unsted regularly supplied the whole village with oil for their lamps.

Margaret remembers playing stoolball (now undergoing a revival in Sussex) when she was 14 ("I was caught out, first ball!") on the recreation ground, which looks little different now, in its beautiful, unspoilt setting of pinewoods and hilly fields.

The old pub was next to Cherry Tree Cottage and across the lane from the pub was the old Post Office. This was run by the Pennicotts, who also roasted villagers' chickens on Sundays in their large ovens—for they were the local bakers as well.

Margaret would often sit on the wall of Cherry Tree Cottage watching the cars and carts go by, with regular buses roaring along between Pulborough and Arundel (a thing of the past indeed!).

The wife of the tenant of Watersfield Farm, Ivy Ruff, would daily walk round the village with a pail of milk, taking it to every house.

In those days, the family did much walking. Margaret recalls walking over to Fittleworth, two miles away, and to Bignor and Coates Common. There were hikes over the Downs too, and round Arundel Park.

Once, in the park, the young girl had a frightening experience. "I eyed this fallen log, which suddenly got up and walked away. It was a deer!"

The Unsteds retired to Southwick in the 1930s and young Margaret's visits to Watersfield ceased. But although it happened so long ago, she remembers those short, peaceful holidays as though they were yesterday.

COLDWALTHAM: Work Rewarded   27/10/83

The Wildbrooks Society garden plant and produce sale, held at the Sandham Hall, Coldwaltham, on Saturday, provided the last amount necessary to pay for repairs to the ancient yew tree.

Over the past few months, the parishioners of Coldwaltham and other well-wishers have worked hard and given donations to foot the bill for this monument, which is of national as well as local importance.

Now established as a popular annual event, the garden sale, which disposed of items ranging in size—and usefulness— from a minute spider plant to a lawnmower, raised a total of £146. Surplus proceeds will be put towards churchyard maintenance.

COLDWALTHAM: *Special Remembrance* 10/11/83

A special ceremony, at 10 a.m., will immediately precede the Service of Remembrance at St. Giles' Church, Coldwaltham, on Sunday.

Former vicar of Coldwaltham, the Rev. Ronald Chatwin, who is now vicar of Saltdean, will dedicate a memorial in the church to Mr. Charles (Charlie) Cousens.

Mr. Cousens, who was verger at St. Giles' until shortly before his death, aged 83, two years ago, had served a total of 30 years as a church verger. On his 80th birthday, he received a letter of congratulations from the former Archbishop of Canterbury, Dr. Geoffrey Fisher, and was very proud of it.

COLDWALTHAM: *Sale Proceeds* 1/12/84

Special guest at the Christmas fayre on Saturday, run by the Parent-Teacher Association at St. James's C. of E. Primary School, Coldwaltham, was the former headmistress, Mrs. Monica Pateman, who retired in July.

Proceeds of the sale topped £600, a satisfactory reflection of hard work over the months by the organizers.

Half the money raised will be spent on buying a new liner for the school swimming pool, and the other half will go into the school fund, much depleted by the recent purchase of a BBC computer for the pupils.

COLDWALTHAM: *Dreamy Evening* 8/12/83

More than 60 over-sixties sat down to a succulent supper at the Christmas party organized for them in Coldwaltham Youth Centre, by neighbours and friends.

A four-course meal was served, including vol-au-vents and pâtés, cold turkey and other meats, a choice of four desserts, and cheese with biscuits.

Star guest was Mrs. Ivy Ruff, who appropriately enough celebrated her 91st birthday on Christmas Eve. Mrs. Ruff was specially driven from St. Richard's Hospital, Chichester, for the occasion, by her grandson, Mr. Charlie Ruff.

When he arrived to pick her up, the invitation had been forgotten, and Mrs. Ruff was asleep in bed. She was soon dressed, and speeding towards Coldwaltham, but it is not surprising that the whole happy evening was a "dreamy" one for her.

The guests were entertained by Novio Magus, part of St. Richard's Folk Group, who played and sang carols and folk music.

Much credit must go to Mr. and Mrs. Joe Street, who, through running weekly crib and whist drives at the Sandham Hall, were able to contribute £85 to the cost of the party.

One of its highlights came when, the room darkened, guests looked out the windows to see Santa with his illuminated sledge, full of presents for them, arriving through the trees which surround the youth club. Santa came by courtesy of Storrington Round Table.

COLDWALTHAM: Christingle Service   *8/12/83*

When St. Giles' Church at Coldwaltham holds a Christingle service on Sunday, December 18th, ancient traditions will be observed.

'Christingle' means Christ Child. The Romans recognised a form of Christingle, by a different name, and the ancient Welsh had a similar one, which they called Calenig.

But it was the Moravian church that adopted the theme, and on Christmas Eve their families would gather together in church, where each child would be given a 'Christingle'. By the light of these candles, carols would be sung.

Children attending the Coldwaltham service will each receive an orange (representing the world), with a candle (signifying the light of the world).

A collection will be held for the Children's Society.

COLDWALTHAM: Tractor Lights   *5/1/84*

A total of £42, raised by carol singers in the parish, has gone to the Save the Children Fund.

This was the satisfactory sequel to a cheery evening touring Coldwaltham and Watersfield, which was rounded off when the companionable band called, by invitation, at the Barn Owls Restaurant. There they sang request carols to dinner guests and their hosts before blazing fires, and were amply rewarded with hot mince pies and coffee.

Transporting the carollers was Mr. Charlie Ruff, of Watersfield, who decked his tractor-driven trailer for the occasion with fairy lights.

His neighbours enjoyed the bright sight of Charlie's tractor right through the Christmas period, as he left the lights on while he worked.

COLDWALTHAM: Transport Needs 2/2/84

After further consideration of West Sussex County Council's Transport Plan, Coldwaltham Parish Council has decided to form a sub-committee to look into the transport needs in and around the village.

The sub-committee—Mr. J. Rhodes (chairman of Coldwaltham Parish Council), Mrs. W. Morum, Mr. P. Sherratt, and Mr. B. Mount—will be meeting shortly to discuss the matter.

Its major aim will be to convince the Minibus Association, based in Pulborough, that Coldwaltham and Watersfield have a greater need than that already satisfied by the association's services.

There are many old people in the area who have little, if any, means of getting about, and getting out to shop.

At present, the parish has the use of only one bus a week for half a day.

COLDWALTHAM: Prize Tree 9/2/84

Following the award to Coldwaltham by West Sussex County Council of a prize of £250 for the best new entrant in the Best Kept Villages Competition, with part of the money Coldwaltham Parish Council bought a printer to complement the computer at St. James's C. of E. Primary School.

After much deliberation, it was decided that the remainder of the prize should be invested in planting trees in the parish "to benefit as many residents as possible".

The sites on which the trees will be planted—to provide "a permanent and visible memento" of the parish's success—have now been determined.

Parishioners were invited to put forward ideas as to where
the trees should go. As no suggestions were forthcoming, the
parish council took it upon itself to choose three sites in the
area: in front of the old people's bungalows, at the Brookview
estate; beside the entrance to Arun Vale estate, near the
noticeboard; and on the A29, opposite Cooper's Farm by the
public footpath. It is hoped that planting will take place soon.

WATERSFIELD: Local Plan   *1/3/84*

The parts of the West Chanctonbury Local Plan which
relate to Watersfield and Coldwaltham have been posted up,
with explanatory maps, on the villages' noticeboards.

Watersfield is the subject of special consideration, because
part of it is within the Sussex Downs Area of Outstanding
Natural Beauty, containing the Wildbrooks beauty spot, a
haven for bird-watchers.

There could well be local concern over the clause about
"a site to the north of the A29 allocated for residential
development". The area has already been the subject of a
controversial planning application, which was almost refused
two years ago.

In the Coldwaltham section, the plan promises that spaces
between buildings which provide views across the flat Wildbrooks will be protected wherever possible from development.

Horsham District Council has invited the parish council to
submit its comments by March 30th. Parishioners should make
their views known to the parish council as soon as possible.

The next meeting of the council is on March 1st, and the
general parish meeting will be on March 22nd in St. James's
C. of E. School, Coldwaltham, at 7.30 p.m.

A Shackleton Connection   *16/6/83*

The recent BBC2 series on Shackleton, the explorer,
reminded many in Coldwaltham of his family connections
with the parish. For tucked away in a quiet, leafy corner of
the cemetery of the village's St. Giles' Church, is the simple
grave which Emily Mary Shackleton, his wife, shares with
their daughter Cecily.

W.S.G. reader Madeline Harding has uncovered the interesting story behind this fact. She writes:—

At the time of Sir Ernest Shackleton's departure from Plymouth in 1921, Emily and their three children—Raymond, Cecily and Edward—were living in the family home at Eastbourne.

There it was that, in January 1922, news reached Lady Shackleton of her husband's tragic death at 48 from a heart attack on South Georgia Island. She was, of course, a wife and mother used to managing on her own. With a husband so often absent from home, she had assumed on his behalf the role of 'head of the household'.

So Lady Shackleton continued to devote herself to the needs of her young family, with surely enough duties and responsibilities to occupy her days. Yet, in addition, this remarkable lady of her time continued an active commitment, begun in 1917, to the Guide movement. She was District Commissioner for Eastbourne until 1927, and was also deeply interested in the many Scout Groups named after her husband. For recreation, it is said that Lady Shackleton used to enjoy walking, and particularly liked the Downs towards Beachy Head.

In 1930, she moved into a grace-and-favour apartment at Hampton Court Palace, a privilege granted by Royal Warrant. Here she resided until her death in 1936. Her body was cremated at St. John's Crematorium at Woking, Surrey.

Meanwhile, as the years passed, Cecily Shackleton's own health was deteriorating and giving cause for concern. In 1953 she bought Bardsley Cottage in Watersfield, in the parish of St. Giles, and made this her home.

. . . On June 12th, 1957, Lady Shackleton's ashes were interred in St. Giles' Church cemetery, with a brief service conducted by the then vicar, the Rev. R. T. Newcombe. In October of that year Cecily herself died, aged 51, and her ashes were placed next to those of her mother.

A magnificent gold altar frontal was given to St. Giles' in 1959 by Mrs. Norley Dodds, a niece of Lady Shackleton, and this beautiful frontal is used on festive occasions.

BIBLIOGRAPHY

Waters of Arun Arthur H. Allcroft (Methuen, 1930)
Victoria County History of Sussex (Oxford University Press)
With a Spade on Stane Street Samuel E. Winbolt (Methuen, 1936)
The Place Names of Sussex Part I (Cambridge University Press, 1929)
The Archaeology of Sussex Eliot C. Curwen (Methuen, 1954)
Roman Roads in Britain Vol. I Ivan D. Margany (John Baker, 1973)
A Description of the High Stream of Arundel ed. Fowler
Notes on Sussex Churches Frederick Harrison (Hove, Combridges, 1920)
Sussex Archaeological Collections Vols. 51-75 (Sussex Archaeological
   Society)
The Weald Sidney W. Wooldridge & Frederick Goldring (Collins, 1953)
The History, Antiquities and Topography of the County of Sussex Vol. II
   Thomas W. Horsfield (Lewes, Baxter, 1835)
Sequestered Vales of Sussex John B. Paddon
A Study of the Parish of Coldwaltham, 1958-1959 D. R. Holt (un-
   published)
A Short History of the Parish and Church of St. Giles, Coldwaltham
   (church booklet, compiled by Marjorie Hessell Tiltman, 1965)
A Short History of St. Giles, Coldwaltham (revised, updated, but
   shortened version of the above, by Rev. Roger Hodgson, 1984)
Sussex Bells and Belfries George P. Elphick (Phillimore, 1970)
Hardham: Its History and its Church (church booklet)
Cottage Pie Marjorie Hessell Tiltman (Hodder & Stoughton, 1940)
The Birds Began to Sing Marjorie Hessell Tiltman (Hodder & Stoughton,
   1952)
*History of the Western Division of the County of Sussex, including
   the Rapes of Chichester, Arundel and Bramber, with the City and
   Diocese of Chichester Vol. I* James Dallaway (Bensley, 1815)
Branch Lines to Midhurst Keith Smith & Vic Mitchell (Middleton
   Press, 1981)
Old Farms: An Illustrated Guide John Vince (John Murray, 1982)
Farm Tools Through the Ages Michael Partridge (Osprey, 1973)
London's Lost Route to the Sea Paul A. L. Vine (David & Charles, 1973)
Sussex Church Music in the Past K. H. MacDermott (Moore & Wingham,
   1922)
A Short History of Coldwaltham and Watersfield W.I., 1933-1950
   D. M. Page & D. F. Secomb (unpublished paper)
The Story of Fittleworth Lady Mary Maxse (The National Review,
   1935)
Petworth in Ancient Times Lady Mary Maxse (articles reprinted from
   Petworth Parish Magazine, Petworth Parochial Church Council,
   revised edition 1972)
Pulborough Village in Living Memory (Women's Institute, 1958)
Pulborough Scrapbook (W. I., 1947)
Pulborough 1965 (W.I.)
   (the above three are all unpublished scrapbooks)